T0247786

DRIVE

ALSO BY BOB HARIG:

Tiger & Phil: Golf's Most Fascinating Rivalry

DRIVE

THE LASTING LEGACY OF TIGER WOODS

BOB HARIG

ST. MARTIN'S PRESS
NEW YORK

First published in the United States by St. Martin's Press, an imprint of
St. Martin's Publishing Group

DRIVE. Copyright © 2024 by Robert Harig. All rights reserved.
Printed in the United States of America. For information, address
St. Martin's Publishing Group, 120 Broadway, New York, NY 10271.

www.stmartins.com

Library of Congress Cataloging-in-Publication Data

Names: Harig, Bob, author.
Title: Drive : the lasting legacy of Tiger Woods / Bob Harig.
Description: First edition. | New York, N.Y. : St. Martin's Press, 2024. |
Includes index.
Identifiers: LCCN 2023045825 | ISBN 9781250288752 (hardcover) |
ISBN 9781250288769 (ebook)
Subjects: LCSH: Woods, Tiger. | Golfers—United States—Biography.
Classification: LCC GV964.W66 H367 2024 | DDC 796.352092 [B]—dc23
LC record available at https://lccn.loc.gov/2023045825

Our books may be purchased in bulk for promotional, educational, or business use.
Please contact your local bookseller or the Macmillan Corporate and Premium
Sales Department at 1-800-221-7945, extension 5442, or by email at
MacmillanSpecialMarkets@macmillan.com.

First Edition: 2024

10 9 8 7 6 5 4 3 2 1

For Jackie and Jack, who never wavered in their support, encouragement, and love

CONTENTS

1. The Legacy 1
2. The 40 16
3. The Cut Streak 26
4. The Stress Fractures 38
5. The Scandal 53
6. The 85 73
7. The Bahamas 84
8. The Doctor 95
9. The Comeback 110
10. The Coronation 126
11. The Admirers 133
12. The Speech 144
13. The 12th 152
14. The Victory 162
15. The ZOZO 183
16. The Septuple 200
17. The Crash 212
18. The Masters (Again) 229
19. The Golden Bear 243
20. The Swilcan Bridge 257

Ranking Tiger Woods' Major Victories *285*

Acknowledgments *293*

Index *299*

DRIVE

1

The Legacy

Tiger Woods didn't want to hear it the first time. And when he heard it again, he made it clear—forcefully—that perhaps the conversation ought to move on to something else.

The golf world knew he was in pain and that he was trying to play for the first time since a relatively minor knee procedure several weeks earlier. But nobody knew what was really going on, save for a few souls close to Woods.

One of them was his caddie, Steve Williams, who upon seeing Woods was shocked to witness such poor form. He had not been with Woods since the Masters Tournament, and now he was trying to get ready for the U.S. Open two months after the procedure, which was meant to take care of some issues with his knee and which Woods figured would be routine.

A practice round days prior to the start of the 2008 U.S. Open at Torrey Pines in San Diego was horrifically poor.

Worse, Woods could barely walk. He learned as part of that "benign" knee procedure that his ACL (anterior cruciate ligament) was completely shot and would need surgery to be reconstructed. And to make the situation worse, he had suffered two stress fractures in the tibia of his left leg while trying to rehabilitate the knee.

The damaged knee was bad enough, but those stress fractures caused immense pain every time he swung the club and struck the ball, not to mention with every step he took over the Southern California course.

The opening round saw Woods walk eighteen holes for the first time in months, and discomfort and pain were evident throughout. Williams, who had been working with Woods since 1999 and as his caddie for twelve major championships, wondered—aloud—if this was a good idea.

"I think I said to him on three separate occasions, asked him if it was the right thing to carry on," Williams says. "And I got the same reply each time: 'Fuck you, Stevie, I'm winning this tournament.'"

Woods didn't want to hear it.

"I wasn't going to say it to him again," Williams says.

It is the sort of drive that has marked Woods' career, the trait beneath all the talent, sometimes to his own detriment.

Woods could bomb it farther, strike his irons crisper, hit his chip shots closer, make putts with his eyes closed. His skills undoubtedly would have carried him to numerous victories. But without that uncanny determination, a resiliency that saw him return from all manner of maladies or obstacles, the record unarguably would not be as great.

There's no way he wins that U.S. Open at Torrey Pines without such guile. Or makes 142 consecutive cuts on the PGA Tour without immense pride. Or wins the Masters after shooting a first-nine 40, the gaze of the golf world upon a 21-year-old who had already taken the game by storm. Or all manner of feats going back some thirty years.

Perhaps his biggest win was his epic 2019 Masters victory, one that saw him return from a career-threatening back procedure to beat players a decade or more younger on golf's grandest stage, the crowning achievement of his Hall of Fame career. Five years on from his fifteenth major championship title, you cannot help but consider all that went into that victory.

The win required great fortitude, given what he was up against physically, not to mention a slew of young stars who may have idolized Tiger but were not afraid of him. Why would they be? He was undoubtedly physically diminished. He could not practice and prepare as often as they did. The last time he won a major championship, many of them were in grade school.

And while his results leading up to that Masters were solid—he had won the Tour Championship seven months earlier—victory at a course where he had not won in fourteen years was something to talk about, dream about. It was far from something to expect.

Less celebrated but in many ways just as impressive was his return from a horrific car crash in February of 2021 that severely damaged his right foot, ankle, and leg.

Woods had numerous surgeries, couldn't walk for months, and somehow managed to play the 2022 Masters, opening the tournament with a 71 and making the 36-hole cut while traversing the undulating course with a noticeable limp.

Woods probably summed it up best at the 2023 Masters, where he was playing just his fifth official event since the crash, and what would be his last for some time.

"Stubbornness," he said. "I'm a little on the stubborn side. I believe in hard work, and I believe in getting out of it what you put into it. I've worked very hard throughout my career and in my craft; I've always loved it.

"I've certainly had my share of adversity physically and had multiple surgeries and I've had to come back and work through that. Those were tough. They were never easy. But it's just that the overall desire to win has always been there, and I've always worked at it and believed in what I could do.

"I've been stubborn and driven to come back and play at a high level. I think that has been shown throughout my career. And it's one of the reasons why I was able to make how many cuts I've been able to make in a row and how many tournaments I've been able to win over the course of my career.

"And that's just hanging in there and fighting on each and every shot. It means something. Each and every shot means something."

THOSE WORDS WERE UTTERED SIX YEARS TO THE DAY THAT everything changed for Woods: April 4, 2017. The date is not historically significant, other than the fact that what seemed like the end was actually the beginning. He hardly knew it at the time—heck, the man could barely walk—but it was noteworthy in ways that took years to recognize.

For the second straight time and third time in four years, Woods was not playing in the Masters due to back troubles that had plagued him going back to 2013—and perhaps longer. A return to competition earlier in 2017 was aborted after just three full rounds, halfway around the world in Dubai, where Woods had to withdraw from a European Tour event at which he was being paid handsomely simply to show up.

For one of the rare times with Woods, it was money poorly spent. Tiger looked old and hobbled, and despite saying otherwise, was in considerable pain. An opening round without a birdie at Dubai in early February was but one clue. The way he walked, the way he carefully navigated mounds and bunkers and tees—everything—suggested something was amiss. He withdrew after just eighteen holes, with hopes he might be back in a couple of weeks, which turned into months, which turned into . . . the entire year.

Woods had good reason for the prolonged absence: He had a herniated disk in his lumbar spine.

At first, Woods' agent, Mark Steinberg, reported that the golfer had back spasms but they were not specifically related to the three microdiscectomy procedures he had done in 2014–15. However, it later turned out to be exactly related to those issues. The fact that he had this procedure not once but three times—including twice within six weeks in 2015—was not a good sign.

And sitting out all of 2016 before his brief return apparently did not alleviate the problems, and certainly not the pain.

But Woods summoned the strength to get to Augusta National for the annual Champions Dinner on that Tuesday in April. Dustin Johnson, the No. 1–ranked player in the world coming off a victory at the Match Play Championship and a torrid stretch of golf, was the main source of conversation that day.

The groupings and starting times were announced, and Johnson was scheduled to tee off in the last threesome with reigning PGA Championship winner Jimmy Walker and two-time Masters champion Bubba Watson.

As late as a week earlier, Woods was on the pre-tournament interview schedule for that day, his inability to play not disclosed until just a few days prior to Augusta National opening to the masses. Normally the big story of any Tuesday, Woods was absent.

So it fell to Johnson (who would withdraw minutes before his tee time due to a back injury suffered during a fall at his rental home), defending champion Danny Willett, fellow green jacket winners Adam Scott, Phil Mickelson, and Jordan Spieth, plus Rory McIlroy, Henrik Stenson, Jason Day, and Justin Rose to fill notepads and interview rolls.

"His lack of presence is felt here, because he would bring so much to the tournament," said Mickelson, echoing the comments of others who were asked.

While it was once again a blow to have Woods miss the tournament, golf fans and those who competed against him were getting used to the idea. Going back to the fall of 2015, Woods had played just three worldwide tournaments. He would end up missing eight consecutive major championships throughout 2016 and 2017.

The very venues where his greatness shone brightest came and went without him. And at the 2017 Masters, Woods was missed, but the tournament would go on without him—again.

Very few knew that during the afternoon, while all those pre-tournament media sessions were taking place, Woods arrived early to be interviewed by Jim Nantz, the longtime CBS Sports broadcaster who had been working the Masters since 1986.

Nantz was to conduct an interview with Woods that would not be for public consumption. The then-four-time Masters champion had agreed to the conversation, which was being produced for Augusta National, never to be aired, meant for the club's archives.

What Nantz heard that day shook him. Woods sounded almost despondent, resigned to a fate without competitive golf. And it led Nantz to believe we very likely would never see Woods competing at a high level again, let alone winning another Masters.

"I thought he was uncomfortable," Nantz says. "His every movement I thought brought pain. We sat down and I can't tell you how long it went. He just did a good job on that interview. He was so openhearted.

"There was a sense of resignation in his voice. He was talking in the past tense; he wasn't looking forward. He was reviewing his career at Augusta as if it had been completed. That's what struck me most of all. He wasn't talking like he was still in the game at Augusta. He was reviewing what he had done there without leaving any sliver of any indication of hope that he was going to be coming back there. He didn't say he was done, but he talked like someone who was reviewing his playing days as if they were final.

"With all the highs and lows he had to live with and being very public in his life, I think the lowest of the lows for him was probably that very night. Coming to the Champions Dinner and having to turn around and leave. From a golf perspective, it had to be the lowest of lows. He felt a sense of being done."

Woods later acknowledged, "I was done." At least that is what he believed in those dark, painful moments.

And why would he have thought anything else?

Woods needed help to navigate the stairs in the Augusta National clubhouse. He had taken a nerve block prior to attending in order to alleviate pain. Past champions Jack Nicklaus and Gary Player would later disclose that Woods had suggested his career was over, that he was simply looking for quality-of-life relief. But it was another former champion who was the first to lift the lid publicly.

Only sixteen months later, after Woods would remarkably contend in two major championships in 2018, three-time Masters winner Nick Faldo went on the Dan Patrick radio show and told a tale that had never been expressed openly: that Woods said at that Champions Dinner his career was finished.

The details were fuzzy, and who told whom what and exactly where was something that Woods was not going to delve into after the Faldo story came out. I carefully broached the subject with Woods while he prepared for the Northern Trust tournament, his next event following that PGA Championship, at Ridgewood Country Club in New Jersey.

It was territory that Woods did not want to travel. He was annoyed the story had come out, and it felt possible he might shut this conversation down, and quickly. Knowing how Woods was about these matters, getting him to say anything of consequence seemed hardly a positive proposition.

"I didn't know what I was going to be doing," he said while in between shots of the tournament pro-am. "I had no golf in my future at that time. I couldn't walk. I couldn't sit. I left from there to go see a specialist about what my options were."

Even that story has a backstory.

Woods has always kept a small, tight team around him and was never one to offer many details. But one of those helping him was a Fort Lauderdale physical therapist named Dan Hellman.

Hellman, an avid golfer, practiced physical therapy on young and old, athletic and non-athletic, taking an interest in helping those with various injuries associated with the game.

Hellman studied extensively under a pioneering French osteopath whose training and therapy method Hellman advocated. The program focuses on training for high-level athletes, along with treatments. Hellman developed a program for golfers with something he undoubtedly tailored for Woods specifically when he began working with him sometime in 2016. He attended his first tournament with Woods later that year at the Hero World Challenge, where Woods showed promise before his season was shut down just a short time later.

"We worked for six to eight months to try and get him to be able to play without surgery," Hellman says. "He was at the point where we needed to seriously look at this. 'Forget being a golfer, but we need to get you healthy for life. If you can play golf again, that's a bonus.' At that point, beers on the golf course was the goal."

It was Hellman who convinced Woods that he needed to consult with a team that would recommend a best course of action. "I knew that any surgeon in their right mind would want to operate on him," Hellman says. "But I didn't want to start calling around to surgeons."

So Hellman reached out to a colleague he knew in London, Jon Bowskill, who specialized in finding the right doctors for patients. After that arduous day at Augusta National, Woods headed to the Augusta Regional Airport and left for London, enduring a most uncomfortable flight before meeting with a team of people who not only ran a bunch of tests but were the vetters for a U.S.-based doctor to handle Woods' surgery.

"He came back with Dr. Guyer," Hellman says.

That would be Dr. Richard Guyer, who cofounded the Center for Disc Replacement at the Texas Back Institute near Dallas. A spinal fusion, something Guyer had performed thousands of times in his career, was prescribed.

"I wasn't confident; I was having a fusion," Woods says. "At that time, I needed to try and get rid of the pain. It wasn't so much about golf. I tried everything. I tried stem cell; I tried lidocaine; I tried Marcaine—nerve block. Nothing took the pain away."

Little time was wasted. The surgery was scheduled for April 19, 2017.

TIGER WOODS HAS PROVEN TO BE A COMPLICATED FIGURE throughout his decades in the spotlight. Child prodigy. Guided by a nurturing, some say overbearing, father. An accomplished junior player who turned into a record-setting amateur player and then a pro without peer. Woods transformed the game, turning golf geeks into keen observers, casual golf fans into ardent followers, and even indifferent sports fans into curiosity mavens.

He will undoubtedly be known for the raw numbers: eighty-two PGA Tour titles, tied for the most all time with Sam Snead; fifteen major championships, three behind Jack Nicklaus; a billionaire, according to Forbes, who amassed more than $110 million in official PGA Tour earnings. He was vastly underpaid, if you think about it.

But even before his historic Masters title at Augusta National in 2019, Woods had emerged with a different outlook and was received with warmth and adulation. Sure, there are still the haters, those who wonder why he continues to play, almost jealous of his accomplishments. But there's undoubtedly been a transformation, due in part to maturity, having two kids, and the perspective that he's lucky to be alive following his February 2021 car crash. And certainly, fortunate to be competing.

It is a long time removed from "Hello, World," the words he uttered as part of a marketing slogan for Nike upon turning pro in 1996. And from that 12-shot Masters win in 1997. Or the "Tiger Slam" of 2000–01. The amazing consistency from 2005 through 2009. The scandal of 2010. The return to No. 1 in 2013. And the subsequent back problems that somehow did not keep him from winning a fifteenth major title and tying Sam Snead's PGA Tour record for victories.

Not so long ago was the horrific one-car crash that Woods somehow survived on February 23, 2021. According to the Los Angeles County Sheriff's Department, "The primary causal factor for this traffic collision was driving at a speed unsafe for the road conditions and the inability to negotiate the curve of the roadway." He was traveling at more than 82 miles an hour in a 45-mile-per-hour zone, and it was unclear whether Woods attempted to negotiate the curve in the road.

His Genesis SUV went into a median, struck a curb, knocked down a wooden sign, and drove into opposite lanes before hitting a tree and rolling over.

He suffered broken bones in his right leg and injuries to his right foot and ankle.

That is the straightforward explanation. Woods needed several surgeries to fix the broken bones in his leg. He has never fully disclosed what occurred to his right foot and ankle, other than to suggest he needed "pins and screws" to put them back together. It's fair to say that Woods had multiple tiny broken bones in his foot.

And yet somehow, barely a year later, he returned to play in the Masters, where he broke par in the first round and made the 36-hole cut. He also played in the PGA Championship, again making the cut but suffering through the third round, then withdrawing—with something amiss, causing him to fly to California afterward to meet with doctors. Woods later disclosed that he had two procedures in 2022 related to his right leg, but didn't say what they were for or when they occurred.

It's reasonable to believe one of the procedures took place following that withdrawal at the PGA Championship. Later, it was learned that one of the screws in his foot was protruding through the skin. Woods then skipped the U.S. Open.

But he returned for The Open at St. Andrews, the one goal he had all year. Woods desperately wanted to be part of the 150th playing of the game's oldest championship at the Old Course, the home of golf. It is where he played as an amateur in 1995, where he won in 2000 and 2005, where he competed six times but might never again as a competitive golfer.

That he managed to get around despite what appeared to be serious limitations was one of the stories of the golf year, despite a score well over par and nowhere near making the cut.

"It's pretty insane, actually," says Justin Thomas, who despite an age difference of eighteen years became close to Woods. "To make the cut at Augusta for how he felt early in the year, it's mind-blowing, honestly. I can't put it into words how much his mind just works in his favor compared to everybody else and how much better it is than everybody else's.

"He's a different person when he gets out there, and especially at Augusta, all the good vibes and memories and everything he has. When that focus clicks on, it's a different person."

The latter years of Woods' career help form a different picture. Sure, all the records remain framed for history, and his overall résumé of greatness will be how he is remembered most. But all along, there was an inner drive, a never-say-quit attitude that served him extremely well when he made the game look easy—and that was all the more apparent when the game suddenly was not easy.

Woods' true legacy is one of resolve and redemption, of desire and determination. Of drive. Immense drive. His return from a near-death accident highlighted these traits in a different way, as if to remind us that they were there all along. And they served to further highlight the ultimate comeback story that resulted in his compelling 2019 Masters victory.

"I think it shows why he did all that stuff back in his prime," says Adam Scott, who played throughout Woods' tenure. "The no-quit, the no-give-in attitude. He was so limited in what he could probably do in the lead-up to winning that Masters, but he knew he could do it if he put his mind to it. He'd done so many things that he put his mind to it was incredible. Even the comeback [in 2022] again, which seems almost crazy.

"He nurtured this attitude of being able to push himself to the extreme levels. And that's what from my vantage point the greatest in all their respective sports do—they do something different than the rest. That's why they're not the rest."

Nobody saw that Masters victory coming in the dark days of 2016 and 2017. It didn't even seem possible in 2018, the year when Woods' remarkable comeback truly took shape.

While his 1997 win at Augusta National was the most culturally significant win, and his 15-shot U.S. Open victory at Pebble Beach was history-making, his win at the 2019 Masters brought together all the qualities that ultimately make up a man who has been an enduring figure for thirty years.

Along the way there were numerous signs of resolve, some of them taken for granted. Who makes 50 consecutive cuts in a row these days, let alone 142? Who wins a U.S. Open with stress fractures in his leg and a knee so savaged it would require a complete reconstruction just a few days later? Who bounces back from the humiliation of a personal scandal to play his first tournament in months—at the Masters, of all places—and contends? Who shoots

85, his worst professional score ever, then returns the next day to play by himself, exhibiting pride and perseverance? Who shoots 40 for his first nine holes and wins the Masters?

And who returns following four back surgeries—including a spinal fusion—to win another Masters?

Through the 2023 Masters, Woods played in eighty-five major championships as a pro, starting with the first at the 1997 Masters. I was fortunate to be there for all fifteen of his major victories, as well as 40 of his 41 top-10 finishes. The closest I came to missing a Tiger major win was at the 1998 Open at Royal Birkdale, where he missed a playoff by a stroke and finished third behind his friend Mark O'Meara.

The difference in 2019 was that Tiger was no longer Tiger. Certainly not the Tiger of his youth, of his prime. He was different not only as a player, but as a person, as a public figure, as someone comfortable in his own skin. If he was not ready to take on the mantle of "elder statesman"—although he was certainly on his way—he was comfortable embracing a leading role, offering an opinion.

Unlike years gone by, when he might have been portrayed as a cold-blooded killer with blinders on who left spike marks on the back of those in his way, Woods, then 43, was a more modest, appreciative player who had come to embrace the younger generation of golfers who idolized him when they were growing up. Not only did Woods take them under his wing, but they served as motivation for a player who relentlessly pursued greatness, even amid great pain.

What was left to prove? Nothing, really. Woods had had a remarkable career to that point, and another victory or two was not going to change that, right? Well, look what three more wins, including a Masters, has done. Woods was long respected as a great player, but embracing him was more difficult. For years, he was frustrated that Mickelson, a longtime nemesis whose record was better than almost everyone else's but nowhere close to Tiger's, was beloved. Phil was the People's Champion. Tiger was just, well, a champion.

That all changed through 2018 and into 2019 as Woods returned from what even he believed could be career-ending spinal fusion surgery. The cheers, the reception, the aftermath of his win was received with more emotion, more regard, than any of his previous wins. Woods not only won, incredibly, but he did so with the world cheering him on.

And the applause never stopped. The assemblage of people to watch him on a *Monday* of Masters week in 2022 was astounding. Sure, there are always tons of people at a Masters practice round. But this was different. Woods arrived in the afternoon to play with Thomas and Fred Couples, celebrating the 30th anniversary of his 1992 Masters victory. And it was a final-round vibe, with fairways and greens packed, ten spectators deep.

Woods would later quip that "they were there to see Freddie," and while there might have been a scintilla of truth to that, even Couples knew better.

"I guess he played nine [holes] yesterday, but as a friend and the way he looked, he's very impressive," Couples marveled after the practice round. "He's doing all this to play in this, which is impressive in itself, because I'm telling you, you guys walk, you follow players. It's brutal to walk, and to go through what he's gone through, whatever it is, fourteen months ago, to be playing today?"

Yep, Woods not only started—but he finished. It wasn't the same walk up the 18th fairway as the one in 2019 as he was about to wrap up an improbable victory. But this was improbable in its own way, with Woods adding another unlikely segment to his legacy.

"We know that Tiger loved the whole mentality behind the Green Berets and the SEALs," says Sean Foley, who coached Woods from 2010 through 2014. "He would kind of say that greatness comes after. Once you've had a massive issue, how you come back from it is really a sign of greatness as well. It never ceases to amaze us.

"Years ago, if you asked me if he wins another major, I would have said of course. And he still might. His brain and his nervous system are full of so many good shots and so many majors. We can't be surprised if he's 56 and has a lead through three rounds of a major. It's Tiger Woods, right? Who knows if this time with his right leg he can do it. But it doesn't seem to be the roadblock physically as far as golf at all. He hits it more than good enough. He's still a top 10-iron player. It's the function of walking around the golf course."

We came to learn how difficult that is, how taken for granted walking 18 holes, 72 holes, all the practice and preparation is for a professional golfer.

But Tiger grimaced through the pain and found a way. Just as he did all those other times in his career when he accomplished things that required more than just great skill. There was and still is an inner drive that is at the basis of his legacy.

Eerily, Woods might have said it best the day before the car crash near Los Angeles, when he was shooting a series of playing lessons with celebrities at Rolling Hills Country Club in Rancho Palos Verdes. He was on his way to a second day of filming when the crash occurred.

In the series, which was released later that year as part of a *Golf Digest/GolfTV* collaboration, Woods is giving a lesson to actress Jada Pinkett Smith during which he tells her: "I'm always fighting. It's all I know."

2

THE 40

Throughout his career, Tiger Woods faced plenty of adversity. It might not have seemed that way at various times, given his preponderance of success. There were victories by wide margins, victories at the majors, victories at regular PGA Tour events.

He took appearance fees and won overseas. He won Skins Games and exhibitions. He never missed cuts. He performed well after long layoffs.

But the numbers always belied another truth: The guy just never gave up.

So as the 2019 Masters approached, it had been nearly eleven years since Woods last won a major championship. A length of that sort between major victories is incredibly rare. Most of the game's greats won their entire haul of majors in a short period of time.

Arnold Palmer, for example, won his seven majors from 1958 to 1964. Tom Watson won his eight from 1975 to 1983. Ben Hogan won nine from 1946 to 1953.

Gary Player's nine from 1959 to 1978 is an outlier. And so, of course, is Jack Nicklaus' eighteen majors from 1962 to 1986.

Woods notably won his first major championship at the 1997

Masters. The last of his fifteen came at the 2019 Masters, a span of twenty-two years. His first fourteen were across eleven years.

The 1997 Masters was Woods' first major as a pro. It was just his fourth career victory on the PGA Tour and it was just his third Masters start. The year prior, as an amateur, Woods missed the cut.

It was following a practice round in 1996 that Nicklaus proclaimed Woods should "win as many Masters as Arnold and I combined." That would be ten, and while Nicklaus was being hyperbolic, the message was clear: Tiger had transcendent talent, and Augusta National suited him perfectly.

That didn't mean he *should* win in his very first try as a pro. Despite considerable hype going into that Masters and unbridled optimism that he would win, those close to the game didn't necessarily expect it.

For all of his incredible potential and accolades, Woods never sniffed a victory in a pro event as an amateur. In addition to missing the cut at the Masters in 1996, he tied for 41st in 1995 when he was the low amateur. His best finish in a major was a tie for 22nd at The Open in 1996, a tournament that he later said helped him finalize the decision to turn pro later that year.

Then there's Augusta National itself. Rare is the player who understands it quickly. Fuzzy Zoeller remains the only one who won the Masters in his first attempt (1979), aside from the first two tournaments in 1934 and 1935. Getting to know the intricacies of Augusta National can take time, and you are playing against those with vastly more experience.

Woods worked to learn Augusta National. In his amateur starts, he sought practice rounds with the likes of Raymond Floyd, Fred Couples, Greg Norman, and Seve Ballesteros. He played with Nicklaus and Palmer. He studied old video of the place. And he swallowed in all the knowledge.

It didn't show on the scorecard in his first two attempts as an amateur, but nobody expected much different. Woods was a student at Stanford and playing a college schedule. He wasn't competing against pros.

When Woods showed up for the 1997 Masters, he had just six competitive rounds at Augusta National. Still, the way he had won his third consecutive U.S. Amateur the year prior, turned pro with considerable fanfare, won twice in his first seven PGA Tour starts, and added another victory at the start of 1997 had the place buzzing.

That last victory was at the Mercedes Championship, known as the season-opening Tournament of Champions. Woods was in the field at La Costa Resort & Spa in Southern California by virtue of his victory in Las Vegas a few months prior.

Woods and Tom Lehman, who'd won The Open at Royal Lytham the previous summer, ended up tied through 54 holes, setting up a juicy final-round pairing between reigning major champion and young upstart.

But it never happened. Heavy rains and a forecast for poor conditions wiped out regular play, and tournament organizers decided to shorten the event and find one hole where the two leaders could stage a sudden-death playoff.

They went to the seventh tee, where Woods added to his already growing legacy, launching a 6-iron from 186 yards as rain-soaked, lighter-holding fans cheered the ball through the air. The ball landed 2 feet behind the hole, then rolled back to 8 inches for an easy victory and the third win of his PGA Tour career.

It had been made easier by Lehman, who went first and promptly hit his tee shot into the water, meaning Woods basically had to just get his ball on the green.

"Tiger hit a great shot," an annoyed Lehman said afterward. "Of course, he had no pressure on him. I hit it a little high on the clubface, the wind caught it, and it went in the water."

They were five shots ahead of third-place finisher Guy Boros.

In an amazingly prophetic observation, Lehman said: "I may be the player of the year. But he's the player of the next two decades. It's like bailing water out of a sinking boat trying to hold off the inevitable."

It was a great start to his first full year as a professional golfer, but Woods added no more victories before his first major championship as a pro.

Still, all of the talk was about Tiger, and he was even among the pre-tournament favorites, along with defending champion Nick Faldo and Norman, who at the time was the No. 1–ranked player in the world. Woods had all of sixteen worldwide events as a pro on his résumé.

There were clues, naturally. A few days prior to Masters week, Woods shot 59 at his home course, Isleworth, in Orlando. His friend Mark O'Meara has told the story so many times that he deserves residuals.

Woods had become friends with O'Meara, who was twenty years older, as they lived in the same neighborhood. The association proved beneficial to both—O'Meara showed Woods the ways of tour life, and Tiger's game provided an inspiration that saw O'Meara win two major championships in 1998 at age 42.

Shooting the course record of 59 (32–27) from the back tees and at 7,179 yards was impressive enough. But what O'Meara loves telling is what happened the next day when they played again at Isleworth. A ten-dollar bet consisting of automatic "one-downs" (whenever you are down a hole, another bet for the same amount commences for the rest of the nine holes).

Starting at the 10th hole, Woods made a birdie to go 1-up and trigger another bet. At the 11th, a par-3, Woods went first and one-hopped his approach into the hole for an ace.

O'Meara quit on the spot.

"I put a hundred dollars on his cart and said I'll see you on the range." O'Meara chuckled. "You're sixteen under par for twenty holes. I quit. I'm outta here."

YOU CAN LIKELY CITE NUMEROUS POINTS IN HIS CAREER, BUT the first round of the 1997 Masters is a good place to start in building Woods' legendary status. Sure, he had all those amateur wins, and three victories as a pro, and a multimillion-dollar endorsement deal. But he was about to shock the world at just 21 with some incredible resiliency.

Paired with Faldo for the first round, Woods was playing with a six-time major championship winner who had won in his previous start at Riviera in Los Angeles.

With a 1:34 p.m. tee time and the eyes of the world upon him, Woods hardly got off to the start that was expected. He was nervous on the first tee, missing the fairway. He then putted his ball off the first green and made a bogey.

He failed to birdie the par-5 second, and he added another bogey at the par-3 fourth when he blew his tee shot so far right that it nearly came to rest amid the bamboo trees. And then at the par-5 eighth, another poor drive and a chip out and approach over the green meant a third bogey. And another at the ninth. No birdies, four bogeys.

Forty strokes.

He was 4 over par through nine holes and, all things considered, this was a borderline disaster, something that could have derailed his chances. He needed to make a nice bogey putt on the ninth green to keep things from getting worse. This was not the way a phenom with such high expectations should be playing. It had to jolt his confidence, and at Augusta National, with thousands on-site and millions more watching on television trained on his every move, there was no place to hide.

Woods had other times in his brief career to draw upon, such as his first U.S. Amateur victory three years earlier, when he was 6-down through 13 holes of the 36-hole final and came back to win against Trip Kuehne.

A year earlier, Woods had trailed by five holes through the morning round of the 1996 U.S. Amateur final against Steve Scott, rallied to tie by the 17th hole, then won on the second extra hole.

That capped a remarkable streak of six consecutive USGA titles, starting with the U.S. Junior in 1991 and concluding with a third straight U.S. Amateur just days before he turned pro.

Still . . . that was the U.S. Amateur.

This was *the* Masters.

Woods made the trek from the ninth green to the tenth tee, a distance of some 100 yards, the gallery ropes lined with spectators on each side, surrounded by a bevy of security guards. "I could now feel everybody's eyes on me," he wrote in his book *The 1997 Masters: My Story*. "I was dimly aware that some were saying the tournament was already over for me."

But Woods would later say that he tried to return to the feelings he had a week earlier, when he'd shot a 59 in Florida. He used that brief interval between the ninth green and the tenth tee to regroup and figure out a few things. Woods said he tried to draw on his memories of all the times he was behind in various matches on his way to winning amateur titles.

"Going in it was, 'What do you think of Tiger?' Didn't ask you anything [about yourself]. It was so total Tiger," Faldo says. "It was unbelievable. It was so total Tiger it was annoying. He came in with such major attention. And he used it in his favor. No player before walked to the first tee with eight policemen around him. Suddenly Tiger decided he needed security. He had a whole different aura, an aura around him where everybody watched him and listened. And everybody wanted a piece of it. Yes, it was amazing."

What came next was an early sign of Woods' inner fortitude. Yes, there was the incredible talent. The ability to hit jaw-dropping shots that fell softly out of the sky. The driving ability, the crisp irons, the putting. Woods put that all to good use over those closing nine holes.

But what happens when things don't go according to plan? How do you respond to adversity? Sure, Woods had battled back many times. But how would he do it under the gaze of what was likely the most pressure he'd ever felt?

He said he was "bewildered and furious" over the start to his first round in a major as a professional.

Woods hit a 2-iron down the 10th fairway and said later he felt as if he had found something. His backswing had gotten too long as he played the first nine holes, and he sought to figure out a technical solution. "I had to get back on the right path to the ball by using my arms alone, rather than allowing my lower body to carry them through," he said in his book. "Swinging that way meant I had to depend on my timing, which wasn't reliable."

Fixing a swing flaw on the fly is a rare ability. There's enough going on in golf, especially under pressure, to make it extremely difficult to work things out in the middle of a round. But Woods was famous for correcting himself, and this was a great example. He sought to return to the ease with which he was striking the ball a week prior when playing at home with O'Meara.

The anger he felt as he came off the ninth green waned. He reminded himself that 63 holes remained. That 2-iron shot convinced him he would be okay. "Right there, that was it," he said.

The goal was to see if he could get back to even par. Handle both of the par-5s by making birdies. Make a couple more birdies somewhere else. Lofty goals, but attainable.

He birdied the 10th having hit an 8-iron second shot to 15 feet, and then chipped in for a birdie from behind the green at the par-3 12th. "That shot was basically the beginning of the rest of his career," Faldo says.

Woods then found the thirteenth green in two shots with a 6-iron, making a birdie to get back to 1 over par. At the par-5 15th, he had just 150 yards left after his drive, and hit a pitching wedge to 4 feet for an eagle. Now he was under par for the first time. He added another birdie at the 17th hole leading to a back-nine 30. From 40 to 30 and a total of 70 shots, Woods was right back in the tournament. Of those 30 shots, you could argue he missed one—the tee shot that went over the green on the par-3 12th. That's it.

He was one of only seven golfers in the field of eighty-six to break par that day, and Woods celebrated—after first practicing on the driving range—by heading to the Arby's on Washington Road, just outside the front gate, along with two of his friends from Stanford.

It was an amazing turnaround, and it set the tone for the rest of the weekend.

"He went out in 40 and back in 30 and then we didn't see him for the next fourteen years," Faldo says. "He left us in the dust. It was a special day. It was the way he went out in 40 and then to win by twelve. That's something pretty unique. [It's like] you miss the first corner and then don't see him for dust. That's really what that week was."

Woods' back-nine charge on Thursday turned his status from first-round disappointment into contender. He trailed the leader, John Huston, by just three shots and was in the second-to-last pairing with Paul Azinger, who had won his only major title in 1993.

This time, the round got off to a much better start. His 66 included an eagle-birdie-birdie run from the 13th through 15th holes as he surged into the lead by three strokes over Colin Montgomerie.

He led the tournament for the first time when he eagled the 13th, with Jim Nantz noting on CBS: "Let the record show that just past five-thirty on this Friday, Tiger Woods has taken the lead at the Masters."

And he never looked back, waxing Montgomerie with a 65 in the third round to take a commanding lead into what amounted to a final-round stroll amid the pines, turning the entire four-day occurrence into something to be remembered for a lifetime.

"I'll never forget what I saw close at hand," Montgomerie says. "I was the closest to it all day. That was very special playing with someone we'd never seen at the level. He shot 65, and it was the easiest 65 I ever saw. Just something different about it. Never witnessed anything like that. I didn't really know what he was capable of. I felt I had experience over him. We could do something. I was sorely misjudged. And we all were. Nobody could have said what was going to happen and what was the writing on the wall over the next twenty years. Very lucky to have lived in the era of Tiger Woods."

Woods became the first non-white player to win the game's most tradition-filled event, one that had not invited its first Black player—Lee Elder—until 1975. It was but another step in a journey that saw Woods become one of the world's most recognizable people.

Elder was among those to witness the historic final round. He had decided to get to Augusta National from his home in Florida, and in his haste got a speeding ticket while driving from Atlanta to Augusta on I-20. An honorary starter at the 2021 Masters just seven months before his death, Elder said at the 1997 Masters: "Nothing was going to stop me from getting here, and I came here today to see more history made. After that day, no one will turn their head when a Black man walks to the first tee."

For Woods, it was but one more memory to draw upon. He

had a slew of them, but to be able to put all the distractions aside, rebound from a horrible front nine, and surge past some of the greats of the game was something he'd always have stored away for when times were tough.

All of it was there to be called upon if needed. For all of his incredible victories, it was twenty-two years later that he embarked on what many believe is his most remarkable feat of all.

3

The Cut Streak

Tiger Woods could summon dozens if not hundreds of moments from his career if he were looking to soothe his scrambled psyche and dull the pain and uncertainty of what lay ahead.

His time as a professional golfer was filled with gallant victories, boisterous comebacks, huge putts, remarkable drives, incredible long-iron shots, chip-ins, hole-outs, aces . . . you name it.

The 1997 Masters win made him famous around the world.

But a year later he embarked on a less-celebrated accomplishment, one that played out over seven years. It is among the examples of his resiliency but is often glossed over, sometimes forgotten, and certainly underrated.

His cut streak.

Woods made 142 consecutive cuts on the PGA Tour, a streak that began in 1998 and ended in 2005. During that time, Woods never failed to advance to the final two rounds of any PGA Tour event.

For events with a hundred players or more, the size of the field is typically cut after 36 holes to better manage play on the weekends. For the majority of Woods' career, you had to be among the top 70, and anyone who is tied for 70th place, to make the cut.

(The PGA Tour has since changed this to the top 65 and ties.) The Masters, as a smaller-field major championship, has been 50 and ties. The U.S. Open is 60 and ties.

While making a cut seems like a simple enough goal, the fact that nobody has even come within half of Woods' number over the length of his career is testament to how difficult it is to do.

And, yes, there were times during that stretch of events when Woods was credited with making a cut in a tournament that didn't have one. None of the World Golf Championship events, of which Woods won eighteen, had a 36-hole cut. The Tournament of Champions didn't either. Nor did the final two FedEx Cup playoff events, including the thirty-player Tour Championship. Of his 142 in a row, 31 came in those "no cut" events.

That, however, is hardly reason to diminish the feat. All of the players Woods competed against had those same opportunities to run up such numbers and never did.

Many times, Woods was simply playing so well that the 36-hole cut was never even a bother. But there were inevitably times when his game was not quite there. A poor driving week. The inability to get putts to drop. A sore back or wrist or shoulder. There are dozens of reasons why a player might have every reason to miss a cut, without a moment's thought given to it.

In 2022, Woods showed some of the mindset associated with the quest to make it past 36 holes. He was hobbling on that right foot, injured in the car crash, through difficult conditions at the PGA Championship played at Southern Hills Country Club in Tulsa, Oklahoma. It was his second tournament of the year after having remarkably made the cut at the Masters.

But Woods was finding the going difficult during the second round and it appeared he would not qualify for the weekend.

That he somehow made the cut for the second time since his return five weeks earlier could not be overstated. His 1-under-par

69 followed an opening-round 74 to put him at 143, 3 over par, and in a tie for 53rd place.

He did it by birdieing two of his last six holes and overcoming what appeared to be a tournament-ending double bogey on the 11th hole. Birdies at the 13th and at the 16th—a 521-yard par-4 where he hit his second shot with a 5-iron to 4 feet from 209 yards—were scores a majority of the field would have coveted.

It was impressive stuff and meant Woods would be around for the weekend—although he ended up withdrawing following the third round.

"Just unbelievable making the cut at Augusta and making the cut here," said Rory McIlroy, who played with Woods during the first two rounds. "I was joking with Joey [LaCava, Woods' caddie] and saying he could have come back and played like Honda and Valspar [both in Florida], two of the flattest courses on Tour. It might have been a bit easier for him, but he comes to two of the toughest walks that we have.

"Just incredibly resilient and mentally tough. To get a front-row seat—he's feeling it, and he's feeling it on every swing, but to see what he did on that back nine—he missed a few iron shots, but he got it up-and-down when he needed to make an incredible birdie on 16 to sort of get him inside the cut number a little bit more.

"Look, he's the ultimate pro. Looking at him yesterday . . . If that would have been me, I would have been considering pulling out and just going home, but Tiger is different, and he's proved he's different. It was a monumental effort."

At that point, was it worth it for Woods to endure what he must to grind his way to making cuts? While the details are scarce, Woods has said that ice baths are part of his repertoire, to reduce swelling. He has physical trainers who then help him get ready in some form or fashion. Certain swings hurt more than others. During the opening round, Woods said he had difficulty pushing off on his right leg, and that there is pain when he twists and when he walks.

And yet there he was again, having made the cut for the second straight major championship, the gain apparently worth the pain.

"Just the fact that I'm able to play golf again and play in our biggest championships," Woods said afterward. "As I alluded to earlier, you guys all know, I'm not going to be playing a lot of tournaments going forward. They're going to be the biggest tournaments. I want to be able to play the major championships. I've always loved playing them.

"Coming back here to a place that I've had success on [he won the 2007 PGA Championship for his thirteenth major title], to play against the best players in the world, that's what we all want to be able to do. Fortunately enough, I'm able to somehow do it. I've had a great PT staff that have put Humpty Dumpty back together, and we'll go out there tomorrow, and hopefully tomorrow I can do something like what Bubba did today."

Woods was referring to Bubba Watson, who shot 63 to get into contention. That was Woods' mindset, even if it might appear unrealistic. It's why when asked about grinding to make a cut instead of what he had become so used to in his career—grinding to be atop the leaderboard—Woods said there was not much in the way of an adjustment to be made.

"Well, you can't win the tournament if you miss the cut," Woods said. "I've won tournaments—not major championships, but I've won tournaments on the cut number. There's a reason why you fight hard and you're able to give yourself a chance on the weekend. You just never know when you might get hot."

WOODS DIDN'T WIN THAT TOURNAMENT AT SOUTHERN HILLS. The weather turned unseasonably cool and rainy and when Woods teed off on Saturday morning, it was clear it would be a difficult day for him.

The result was his worst score ever at the PGA Championship, a 9-over-par 79 that included five straight bogeys—a first for him in a major championship as a pro—as well as a triple-bogey.

Later that night, Woods withdrew from the tournament, and the next day he headed to Los Angeles on his private jet, where he likely visited the medical team that treated him in the aftermath of the crash.

Later in 2022, Woods acknowledged he had two additional surgeries on his right leg, although he did not disclose when and where. Then, at the 2023 Masters, Jason Day disclosed why Woods had a pretty good reason to withdraw from that PGA.

"I was talking to him at the end of last year, and then he was saying the reason why he pulled out of the PGA was that a screw went through the skin on Saturday or whatever it was," said Day after learning Woods had to withdraw. "I don't know how bad it is this time. . . . Once again, it just sucks that he's not here playing."

All of this happened well after Woods' incredible cut streak ended—but during the midst of another one. Before having to withdraw at the 2023 Masters, Woods made the cut in the tournament for the 23rd straight time, matching a record held by Gary Player and Fred Couples. It only serves to highlight the mindset: You can't win if you don't make the cut; and if you make the cut, no matter how painful or difficult things have been, you always have a chance.

Woods, of course, expected to win every time he teed it up.

The streak began in 1998 at the Buick Invitational, a tournament he would win seven times but where he finished third that week. (He might have won had the tournament not been shortened to 54 holes due to weather.) And throughout the next six years and into the seventh, he never missed a cut.

"Just remembering when he was rattling off records left and right, you could find so many things," says Adam Scott, who reached 45 cuts in a row from 2012 to 2015. "But a lot of people always felt like one record that would never be broken is the cut streak. No one's really getting close anymore these days.

"The game is played differently today, to be honest. It's nothing bad about today, it's probably just not going to happen. For example, the way I guess I can explain it, there are cuts on Tour that are 6 and 7 under par for two days. You can play pretty good for two days and not be 6 and 7 under.

"The fact that he managed to spend seven years without missing . . . I know he didn't play as much as everyone, but 142 . . . that's a lot. Guys struggle to get into the thirties now. That's two years of play. The standard is high, and it was before, but that's incredible."

Along the way, Woods passed the players who held the top five spots in PGA Tour history for consecutive cuts made.

Byron Nelson held the previous record at 113 consecutive cuts from 1941 to 1949. But there was an interesting aspect to Nelson's streak that makes it all the more remarkable.

In a 2000 interview, Nelson said: "I saw where it was written that I made 113 straight cuts, but I actually made money in 113 straight tournaments. There's a difference. In those days, sometimes they paid only fifteen to twenty places. You could make a cut and not make any money. So that's a lot better than making a cut. But I was very fortunate."

In modern times, making a cut equated to making money. You only got paid if you made the cut.

Jack Nicklaus had the next best cut streak, 105 in a row from 1970 to 1976. Then it was Hale Irwin with 86, Dow Finsterwald with 72, and Tom Kite with 53.

After that? Steve Stricker had the longest streak of any player,

49 in a row that ended at the 2012 Players Championship. Adam Scott got to 45 straight.

So we're basically talking a level that barely reached one-third of the feat Woods accomplished.

"It's probably always going to be underrated," Scott says. "I generally think the game has changed. Consistency isn't rewarded like it used to be. You can be consistent out here and you're nowhere in the world rankings, you're nowhere in the FedEx Cup rankings. You play pretty good all the time and it doesn't get you much.

"You have to be spectacular to be out here now. I can't speak for Tiger, of course, but certainly at the time when I turned pro, we looked at great players, and Tiger, his consistency was mentioned. Not only everything being brilliant, but Nick Faldo and Greg Norman, these guys who played consistently well all the time and that's how you won big tournaments.

"And Tiger did that. And if you look at the best over the last ten years, there are a couple of exceptions, of course. But the top players are not always the most consistent over the biggest tournaments. They're still the top players. But it's like my era, Tiger, Phil [Mickelson], Ernie [Els], Vijay [Singh], Retief Goosen who were always up there in the biggest events. At least it felt like it to me. It's more spread out now."

Woods tied Nelson's record at the 2003 Funai Classic, a tournament played at Walt Disney World in Florida. The following week, at the Tour Championship, he broke the record.

"It'll never be broken," says longtime broadcaster David Feherty of Woods' record. "It's been overlooked. In some sense it's his most remarkable record. It was 142. If you look at the second best, it's extraordinary, especially in the era he played. The strength and depth were there. People asked me all the time: Who was the greatest player who ever played? Tiger Woods was the greatest player who ever played. Jack Nicklaus would tell you that nobody has ever played golf like Tiger Woods played it. Jack is the greatest champion. But Tiger Woods is the greatest player who ever played the game and that cut streak will never be touched."

And it would continue for another eighteen months, coming to an end at Nelson's tournament, the Byron Nelson Championship in 2005.

As happened several times during the streak, Woods found himself outside of the cut line as he played the second round. These were the times he typically had to summon something from inside to make it. If you're outside the cut line, it typically means you are not playing well, that your game is off. Turning it around is difficult.

But as Woods played the final nine holes at the TPC Los Colinas course outside of Dallas, he put together a mini rally that had him on the cut number with one hole to play. A par on the final hole would assure another made cut.

And yet, after a perfect drive, Woods found a greenside bunker, blasted out to 15 feet . . . and missed. It's the kind of thing that happens every week on the PGA Tour: A player in position to make it hits a poor shot at the wrong time and misses the cut by a shot.

Remarkably, Woods had gone all those years and all those tournaments without doing so.

"It's amazing," says Butch Harmon, Woods' coach for a good bit of the streak. "A hundred forty-two cuts in a row is amazing. I don't know how you can do that. He spoiled us. Tiger Woods spoiled us. He made golf look so easy."

At the time the streak ended, Els had the next-best streak—at 20.

"Even in that one [where the streak ended], he was playing two different courses," says Hank Haney, Woods' instructor from 2004 to 2010, of the Nelson event that used two courses for the first 36 holes. "It's not normal on the PGA Tour. It happens only a few weeks out of the year. It was the Cottonwood course where he didn't make the cut; the last hole is kind of tough, and those circumstances made it a little harder for him to dig it out at the end. And yet, he almost did.

"Most of the time when teams have big streaks going, when it ends, it's barely. He still just barely missed; it's not like he missed by five shots. The cut streak was great. He never gave up and he could always reach in, and sometimes players are better when their back is to the wall to a certain extent. It's almost like an extra challenge. And that extra motivation is always when he was at his best."

Woods noted afterward that the only cuts he had missed to that point in his career came with a bogey on the last hole. "So that's frustrating," he said, even as his pride in what he had accomplished was evident.

"Yeah, I fight all the way in. That's how I am," he said. "I think that's indicative . . . of the streak. You've got to give it everything you've got, got to have some good breaks along the way, and I've definitely had my share, but also I've gutted it out at times. Like today, I didn't quite feel very good, but other times I've gotten it in the clubhouse."

WOODS NOTED THAT HE HAD A BAD WARM-UP SESSION ON THE range and that he could never quite get his swing to feel comfortable. That is very common among professional golfers. To think it wouldn't happen at least a few times a year would be naive.

And yet, Woods managed that throughout the streak. And it's important to point out that he wasn't just making cuts during that period. From the time the streak began in 1998 to its end in 2005, Woods won eight major championships. He won the Masters a month before the streak ended and captured The Open two months later. Despite the missed cut—and there was another late in the season—it was a great year for Woods.

All that success—you'd think—would lead to times when mailing it in would be easy. Some weeks, you just don't have it. A niggling injury. A bad attitude. A balky putter. Maybe you'd rather be home that weekend. Perhaps the hotel food is lousy.

Nicklaus recalled a time in 1968 at the PGA Championship, the only time he let his mind wander to the point that he rationalized that a missed cut would not be the worst occurrence in the world.

"I was on the last green of the day at Pecan Valley [in San Antonio, Texas]," Nicklaus says. "It was hot, I wasn't playing well, and at the last hole I had about an 8-footer. I remember thinking to myself, 'I don't care whether I make it or not.' And I missed. And then I immediately regretted it. I was mad at myself later for thinking that way. And it never happened again."

That came in a year when Nicklaus tied for fifth at the Masters, finished second at the U.S. Open, and tied for second at The Open. He was playing well and still succumbed. It happens.

Sometimes it is due to golfers having a lot of time to ponder all kinds of reasons to justify taking a weekend off.

"I do recall having a conversation I had with Tiger about this once," says five-time PGA Tour winner Tom Lehman, who won the 1996 Open and captained the 2006 U.S. Ryder Cup team. "He played a limited schedule, and his comment was it's the most he could play and give it everything he had. That's one of the things that made him so great. He was so prepared every time he played. He came ready to play every time he played.

"Most of those mistakes you make are because you took two weeks off and went skiing and haven't touched a club. Or you played four in a row and you're so tired you just make dumb mistakes. He never let himself get in that position to make those errors. He came to play every time. And therefore, a focused Tiger Woods . . . it was almost impossible for him to miss a cut. He was that good."

Stewart Cink, who turned pro around the same time Woods did in 1996, marveled at the consistency.

"As competitive as it is, you don't have to be very far off to miss a cut," Cink says. "To me, even more, though—there was some streak where he was nearly a hundred-something consecutive rounds better than the field average. The only reason I know that is I was told at the time I was like third on the list. And I had like nineteen!

"To me that's so impressive to go that many rounds. You don't have to go that many rounds in a row where one day you are a little off your game. A weird bounce where the ball goes out of bounds. And all that is going to happen. So you have to do enough good stuff to overcome all of that for a hundred straight rounds? The field average against the best players in the world. That's amazing."

Cink was referencing a period when Woods went eighty-nine consecutive rounds where his score beat the field average for the day.

The streak began during the third round of the 1999 WGC-NEC Invitational at Firestone and went through the third round of the 2000 WGC-American Express Championship. That's more than a year, and it covered 23 stroke-play tournaments. During that stretch, Woods won thirteen times. His worst finish during that time was a tie for 23rd.

As impressive as beating the field average is, Woods did that at a time when he was absolutely ruling golf. Nobody could touch him. And while it's incredible to do that, it's a streak that would be tough to have front of mind. He couldn't know what everyone else was doing in relation to their scoring average.

Still, it's another example of the amazing fortitude he showed while dominating the game.

"The same mindset that resulted in that big, long cut streak also resulted in him being around at the end of so many tournaments," Cink says. "He would tell you a lot of his wins would come from other people giving up or giving him the win. That's the way golf is. It's not always going out there and sprinting to the finish. We play hard courses. There's bogeys and doubles and disasters out there.

"He'd shoot 76 on Saturday and next thing on Sunday, there's four holes to go and he's in fourth. It's that mentality. He just never believed he was out of it."

That trait has served Tiger well. And it was especially useful when circumstances seemed to suggest that all was lost, that he had no chance. Willing yourself to play better is one thing. To do so when injured is quite another.

4

The Stress Fractures

The scars are both physical and mental. Good luck getting into all the minutiae when it comes to Tiger Woods and all of his surgeries, treatments, rehabilitations, and recoveries.

We know he's had five back procedures. There were also five surgeries or procedures performed on his left knee, the first one all the way back in 1994 when he was in college and had a benign cyst removed.

Woods also had an Achilles issue, neck problems, and an elbow injury, all of which cost him tournament time.

And there were multiple surgeries in the aftermath of his February 2021 car crash, on his right foot and ankle, some of which were performed in 2022 and 2023.

But it was what was then considered a minor knee procedure that was the backdrop to perhaps one of Woods' greatest victories.

Two days after Woods finished second by three strokes to Trevor Immelman at the 2008 Masters, he had arthroscopic surgery on his left knee. There was barely a ripple of concern. Woods had bounced back from plenty of other health issues to that point, and often prospered following the time away.

And he had plenty of time to get ready for the U.S. Open, to be played that year at Torrey Pines in San Diego, perhaps his favorite venue, the one where he first attended a PGA Tour event with his late father, Earl, as a kid.

There was little doubt Woods would be back in time for the Memorial Tournament in late May. The information shared said that Woods had a simple procedure to repair cartilage damage. It was his third operation on the knee and second in five years, but the recovery was expected to last just a month.

Having turned 32 at the end of 2007, Woods was in the midst of another strong run of success. He won seven times that year, including the PGA Championship. In late 2007 and early 2008, he had captured six straight tournaments. A knee procedure was certainly a setback, but nobody could foresee what lay ahead.

"He was incredibly motivated, because this is a mountain nobody could ever climb," says Hank Haney, Woods' coach at the time. "[Tiger said,] 'And I'm going to climb it.' This will be one for the ages, and we'll talk about it forever. And we do."

Haney, who coached Woods from 2004 to 2010, a period that saw 31 PGA Tour victories and six major championships, was unaware the surgery even took place.

That is how Woods rolled. Everything was on a need-to-know basis, and so Haney didn't need to know . . . until he did. "It ended up setting him back," Haney says. "It was meant to clean things out but made it a lot worse. He couldn't practice, and in a few weeks he is going to walk?"

From a simple, no-big-deal procedure to maybe missing the U.S. Open? At Torrey Pines, where he had won numerous times?

Dr. Thomas Rosenberg, an orthopedic surgeon based in Park City, Utah, performed the procedure, and what he found was shocking: Woods' anterior cruciate ligament was fully torn.

This is the kind of injury that keeps football players out for up to a year. For Woods, it would mean something similar—once he had it fixed. He wasn't willing to do that right away, however. He'd more or less been living with it for ten months and figured the "routine" cleanup in April would be the quick fix he needed to get himself through the remaining major championships at the U.S. Open, The Open, and the PGA Championship. Then he would have the surgery and get ready for the 2009 Masters.

As it turned out, Woods needed masking tape, glue, and all manner of treatment 24/7 in order to play the U.S. Open at Torrey Pines.

But as Woods tried to come back, he suffered a setback that was not disclosed until later: while taking part in a photo shoot, Woods said he hit a shot from a downhill lie that caused stress in his left leg.

"I didn't know what was going on so I went to get an X-ray first, and that's when it showed that 'Y' with a lightning bolt at the bottom of it and I had fractured it," Woods says. "From there, they were saying I was pretty much done for the year. I said, 'Ah, I don't know about that.'"

Haney recalled Rosenberg coming to Orlando and showing Woods two stress fractures as well as the torn ACL, with Woods barely paying the doctor any attention.

"He's limping out of a golf cart to go hit forty golf balls," Haney says. "How are we going to go play in a major championship in a few weeks? There was no chance.

"Tiger looks up and says, 'I'm playing the U.S. Open and I'm going to win.' Just like that. Then he says, 'C'mon, Hank, let's go practice.' The determination was absolutely incredible, and clearly I'll never forget it."

WOODS' DESIRE TO PLAY IN THE 2008 U.S. OPEN STEMMED FROM his love of the course, dating from his time attending the tournament with his father in the late 1980s, to his success there throughout his career.

Given his affinity for the place and the state of his game, it was viewed as a cruel blow that he would not be at his best, that he might not even be able to play. But despite all the physical pain he endured with a blown-out knee and the assorted issues that came with that, Woods was playing phenomenal golf.

He started the year with an eight-shot victory at the Farmers Insurance Open, his sixth professional win at Torrey Pines. He went overseas to the Middle East and won in Dubai. He returned to win the WGC Match Play event, defeating Stewart Cink in the 36-hole final.

Woods then won Arnold Palmer's event at Bay Hill before finally getting beat at the WGC-CA Championship, finishing fifth, just two shots back of winner Geoff Ogilvy. The winning streak over, he was unable to get his fifth Masters title at Augusta, finishing behind Immelman.

"In all the time I caddied for Tiger, he had more of a fascination with this event than any other tournament," says Steve Williams, who caddied for Woods from 1999 through 2011. "When he had a chance to win the Masters and hold all four [majors] at the same time [in 2001], the Tiger Slam, you would think there would be a lot of talk about it. He hardly mentioned it.

"From the moment [in 2002] the USGA announced they were going to hold that tournament at Torrey Pines, he had a complete fascination with that event. And it was fascinating to me. I understand he grew up in that area, he won there, he loved the course. A complete fascination. I was actually bemused by it."

There was no misunderstanding what Williams encountered when he saw Woods for the first time: a golfer who looked nothing like one who could win the U.S. Open, certainly nothing like Tiger Woods.

Haney had already alerted him that the situation was dire. They met for a practice round on the Sunday prior to U.S. Open week, and as they played Haney's words echoed in his head: "Tiger's got no right to be playing in this tournament."

"I could absolutely see the discomfort he was in," Williams says. "The golf was not of the quality you would expect from Tiger Woods. No doubt, he was struggling."

While the outside world knew that Woods was dealing with a knee issue—and that he had withdrawn from the Memorial Tournament two weeks earlier—nobody had any idea about the stress fractures. The knee problem was bad enough, but the stress fractures in his left tibia were the main source of excruciating pain—with every step and upon impact.

The tibia runs from the knee to the ankle, and walking was difficult, let alone the pain that emanated from swinging a golf club. For a time while practicing, Woods wore a knee brace, which proved to be too bulky. And it certainly wasn't helping his golf.

Haney saw that up close when he accompanied Woods to California eight days prior to the start of the tournament. Woods played nine holes using a golf cart at Torrey Pines with no fanfare. He was wearing the knee brace that Rosenberg had given him, with instructions to limit the number of balls he hit.

Then they drove to Newport Beach to play at Big Canyon Country Club, where a Saturday morning round could not have gone worse.

"He played nine holes and lost like every ball," Haney says. "He had six or seven balls and lost them all, shot 47 or something. It was terrible. Didn't even finish the last hole. That was the last day of the brace."

Woods put the score at "50-some-odd" and decided on his way back to Torrey Pines he was over the brace. "I threw it in the trash and was done with it," he says. "I said I'm going to have to figure out how to play without a knee brace."

The good news was Woods' short game was still there. He could still putt. It was simply a matter of trying to find a swing that would allow him to manage his way around the golf course.

"He'd hit a few, try to manufacture something, then he'd go to the putting green, the chipping green, and all that was still perfect," says Rob McNamara, vice president of Tiger Woods Ventures (TGR). "Then it was an awful lot of guts and willpower. Almost every day, I was concerned for him. Once he realized he couldn't hurt himself any further, it was simply an issue of pain, and he decided he could manage the pain. It was just hard to watch."

So why put yourself through this ordeal? Why bother? The idea of walking 72 holes seemed ludicrous. Woods had barely walked, period. But walk and play golf with a game that appeared in shambles?

Woods, of course, had a strong reason for wanting not only to compete, but to win.

"That was the first professional tournament I ever went to," Woods says. "My dad took me to the old Andy Williams [what is now the Farmers Insurance Open]. To me, Torrey Pines, the U.S. Open there, was special, because that's where I learned about professional golf. I remember driving with my dad down to Torrey Pines [from his home near Anaheim], and I'll never forget Andy Bean hit a 1-iron to the last hole. I remember watching John Cook, Marco [Mark O'Meara], all the SoCal boys. To me, the 2008 U.S. Open at Torrey Pines was like going home. It meant more to me."

A FIRST-ROUND 72 WAS MORE NOTABLE BECAUSE IT WAS THE first time that Woods had walked 18 holes since the Masters. The 1-over-par score was far more eventful than the number suggested. He made two double bogeys and was four strokes back of first-round leaders Justin Hicks and Kevin Streelman. Woods played his last nine holes without a birdie.

For the first two rounds, Woods was grouped with Phil Mickelson—who was playing a U.S. Open in his hometown—and Adam Scott. The United States Golf Association, for the first time, decided to group several of the players based on their world ranking, so No. 1 Woods, No. 2 Mickelson, and No. 3 Scott were together.

Understandably, almost predictably, the scene with Woods' group was madness.

"Going to the first tee Thursday was probably one of the unforgettable moments in my career," Scott says. "I don't think I've seen a scene quite like it. It was like twenty-five deep the entire hole. It was something else. It was more like the energy of a football game than teeing off at any golf tournament. There was real atmosphere there."

Woods opened the tournament with a double bogey on the first hole—something he'd do in both the third and fourth rounds as well. And it was clear from the outset he was struggling.

"The shot that changed his entire tournament was at the fourth hole [a 488-yard par-4 that runs parallel to the Pacific Ocean]. It's probably the toughest hole on the course," says Jim "Bones" Mackay, who was Mickelson's caddie at the time. "He's in the right fairway bunker off the tee. The pin is front right and he hits a 4- or 5-iron to about five feet and made a birdie. I remember thinking, 'Holy cow, that's some way to right the ship on the hardest hole on the course.'

"I remember being impressed with how composed he was. Of the shots I remember other people hitting over the years, that probably has to be top five all time."

As the day wore on, Woods' struggles became more apparent.

"The grimacing in his face, the look in his eyes. But the treatment he was getting from his trainer Keith [Kleven] allowed him to get a little bit better each day. It was such a fascinating event," Williams says. "Particularly being the U.S. Open. It's not the greatest amount of good shots, it's the least amount of bad shots. It's more penal than any tournament in general. All of the majors have difficult characteristics, but generally the U.S. Open is played on the toughest of the four courses, and even par is usually a good score, especially in those times.

"But I thought the scoring was going to be lower. And whatever Tiger was doing, they just couldn't break away from where he was. He probably knew he wasn't playing his best 'but I'm still in this thing.'"

The second round began poorly as Woods bogeyed two of his first three holes, but there was an eagle, two more bogeys, then a front-side run that saw him make five birdies for a score of 68 to trail Stuart Appleby by a stroke, tied with Rocco Mediate and Sweden's Robert Karlsson.

But the same theme reigned: Woods suffered, and all who watched wondered if he'd be able to continue.

"We had been paired with Tiger before when he was hurting, but never like this," Mackay says. "I remember him driving off the eighteenth tee, and he looked ill because he was in so much pain. It was hard to watch in a sense; and yet, there he was near the top of the leaderboard. You had too much respect for what he was doing. He was just finding a way. He had a look like, 'They are going to have to carry me out of here.'"

Saturday's third round was surreal. Woods again double-bogeyed the opening hole and was 3 over par for his round and three strokes back of Mediate through 12 holes.

Then came an amazing stretch of six holes that included an eagle at the 13th, a bogey at the 14th, a chip-in for birdie from an awkward lie at the 17th, and then another eagle at the 18th, where Woods drained a 60-footer that had the place in full-throated hysterics.

He shot 70, hitting just 6 fairways. Throughout the round with Karlsson, Woods had his painful moments. "I was honestly trying not to have the gap widen," Woods says. "I make the putt on 13, I bogey 14 with a tee shot way right, and then 15—that was the one when it really hurt. There were a couple of shots where I could feel the bone in my leg break. And the tee shot on 15 was one of them. I felt it crack."

No matter—Woods was right there again to win a major championship. Somehow, he had willed himself into the 54-hole lead, a place where he had never failed to win a major. None of it made sense. Those who witnessed it in person could not believe what they were seeing.

Karlsson and his caddie, Gareth Lord, could not comprehend it all, either. They were as dumbfounded as any, including the long bomb on the 18th.

"The putt on the green, I watched the whole thing, and halfway there, I knew it was in," Lord says. "We came off the course, Robert and I looked at each other . . . and we went straight to the bar and each had a huge Johnnie Walker Blue. That was it. It was about ninety dollars a shot, I promise you."

Woods needed something stronger than that.

His left leg was getting worse, and despite the efforts of Kleven, walking miles upon miles every day on a golf course and the inherent torque and pressure exerted with a golf swing were simply going to be difficult to overcome.

The stress fractures were the main source of the pain, and getting ready to play was work in and of itself. But there was no thought of quitting, Woods says. "Whatever backswing I made, whatever downswing I made, the pain only got me just after impact. My whole focus for the week was to virtually try and hit perfect shots, because nothing was going to stop me from making quality impact. Now, post-impact, I may not be able to walk for a bit or it may throb, but the impact part of it I could control. So all my focus was on making proper impact, and if it hurt, it hurt."

Woods' daughter, Sam, was days away from her first birthday. "She had her little wooden club and she was hitting it against the floor and it kept me from thinking about the pain. It was just constant. The treatment was constant throughout the night. I slept on the massage table, I had my knee drained, iced, elevated, worked on, just trying to get as much inflammation out as I could. Then, I would somehow start activating it in the morning, and that was the hardest part because it was so wobbly. Once I finally got going, it was okay."

WOODS LED BY ONE SHOT OVER LEE WESTWOOD, TWO OVER Mediate, and four over Geoff Ogilvy and D. J. Trahan. He was paired with Westwood for the final round, with Mediate a group ahead alongside Ogilvy, the 2006 U.S. Open champion.

The day dawned with immense anticipation. Woods was on the verge of another major, but all who observed him knew this was a different quest, a different circumstance. So many times, Woods had made it look easy. Now he was clearly struggling. He winced with pain on several tee shots. He showed vulnerability in several aspects of his game.

And while Mediate might not have seemed the adversary he turned out to be, Westwood and Ogilvy certainly were formidable players.

Woods was the favorite with the oddsmakers and the spectators, but Mediate certainly had his supporters, too. His story as the feel-good underdog had legs. At 45, Mediate would have surpassed Hale Irwin as the oldest U.S. Open champion. Just a week earlier, he had to go through a 36-hole qualifying to make it. And to beat Woods would have been among the all-time upsets.

Things were looking good for all of the challengers as round four began.

For the third time in four days, Woods double-bogeyed the first hole. He bogeyed the second, dropping three shots in two holes. He parred six straight holes before birdies at the 9th and 11th holes helped him claim a share of the lead.

But then came a crucial mistake: a bogey at the par-5 13th. While it wasn't an easy par 5, it was not a hole where you would expect him to make a bogey. And when he added another at the 15th hole, he fell a shot behind Mediate with just three to play.

"You could see Tiger was in a bit of agony," says Alastair McLean, Westwood's caddie. "He chopped it about a bit. It was around the seventh hole—he hit a tee shot and nearly collapses. I remember saying, 'I don't think this guy can finish.' He winced on every single shot, and I can't remember any physios coming around. He soldiered on, got it around and did what great players do."

Woods needed a birdie on the 16th or 17th hole to tie, thinking that Mediate had the 18th to play, where a birdie was a very strong possibility. Playing in the group ahead, Mediate was unlikely to hold the lead in the U.S. Open, as Woods was playing in it. And he could have likely sealed the title if he could birdie on the last hole. But his par left Woods a chance, and Woods—who had eagled the hole a day earlier—needed a birdie to tie.

That task became far more difficult when Woods not only missed the fairway off the tee but also found a bunker to the left. He then hit a poor layup shot with a 9-iron that missed the fairway and left him with 101 yards to the hole.

"I didn't know he'd come out of the rough," Ogilvy said later, thinking that Woods had played from the fairway. "It's ridiculous to make a birdie from there."

This approach shot to the green became one of the more scrutinized of Woods' career. He needed to get it close in order to have a makeable birdie putt to tie Mediate. But missing the fairway caused problems; it's never easy to judge how a ball will react out of the rough, leading Woods and Williams to debate how to play the shot.

With 95 yards to the front of a green that was guarded by a pond, Woods believed the shot called for a 56-degree sand wedge. His other option was a 60-degree wedge, which was probably not enough club to cover that distance.

But Williams believed it was the correct one anyway. "Everything in my gut told me it was a lob wedge," Williams says. "Tiger didn't see that rationale. Usually in that situation, you want to be decisive. You don't want to be debating back and forth and create any doubt. But I was fully convinced, and I don't think we'd ever discussed a shot for that length of time."

Williams' resolve in that moment remains underrated. How do you go against Tiger Woods at such a crucial time? How do you allow for any doubt? And yet, Williams, a veteran caddie who had his own confidence and swagger, was true to himself. He wasn't going to allow Woods to hit a club that Williams believed to be the wrong one.

So he sold him on the idea of the 60-degree wedge. Williams correctly determined that going all out with the 60-degree wedge—instead of the 56-degree club, which Woods could hit farther but which also might present difficulties getting it to stop closer—would mean a harder swing with more spin, even out of the rough.

And that's the shot Woods hit, the ball bouncing into the green, then spinning back to the 12-foot range.

Westwood had a 20-footer to also tie and force a playoff, but missed on the low side, leaving the stage to Woods. Make it, and there's an 18-hole playoff on Monday. Miss it, and Mediate is the U.S. Open champion.

"The impressive thing about Tiger is when he's not playing well, not even feeling well, he can still find a way to get it around, and that is what great players do," Westwood says. "He hung in there, gave himself a chance on the 18th. And it's funny, but after I failed with my effort, I never felt for a second that Tiger was going to miss his. Seriously, if it had been match play, I'd have almost given it to him. Why was I so sure? Well, just because he was making everything around that stage of his career, and especially that day. It was one of those classic Tiger moments."

Woods went into celebratory mode after his putt hobbled along the green, ever-so-slowly inching toward the cup and finally dropping as those around the green erupted. Woods arched backward, shook his fists with the putter in hand, and screamed to the sky.

"I vividly remember one thing about that celebration," he says. "I remember screaming and I remember realizing I was screaming at the sky. I was looking straight up. And I put my head down quickly because I was wondering what I was doing."

For the third time in his career, Woods was headed for a playoff in a major championship. That was the good news. The bad news: one more day walking the course when it was unclear if his left leg had one more day left in it.

Mediate played the perfect foil. He had no business being in a U.S. Open playoff at this stage of his career, having endured the qualifer a week earlier that he barely survived. He also barely flinched.

Had Mediate been able to birdie the 18th hole on either Sunday or Monday, he'd have had the trophy. But Woods trailed again with one hole to play, and again Mediate could not put him away. This time, Woods hit the green in two shots, then two-putted from long range to force sudden death, both players having shot even-par 71.

How big of a deal was the playoff? Work all but stopped around the country. It began at noon ET, 9 a.m. local time, and the sports world was desperate for updates. If you couldn't watch it live, you used every means necessary to try to find out what was occurring.

A number of players who competed in the U.S. Open were leaving on a charter flight out of San Diego that morning for Hartford, location of the Travelers Championship.

"Every person on the plane—the players, their families—was watching the playoff on their TVs," says Streelman, who shared the first-round lead. "When we land in Hartford, Tiger and Rocco are going into the playoff hole and no one got off the plane. I looked out the window, saw the courtesy cars waiting for us, and no one got off the plane until the playoff was over. I'll never forget that."

The sudden-death playoff began at the par-4 7th, and was to continue to the 8th hole and then the 18th if necessary. Woods was on the green in two shots, 20 feet away, but Mediate ran into trouble, hitting his approach from a fairway bunker into a grandstand. He got a drop, pitched onto the green, but had a long par putt that missed.

Woods lagged his birdie putt close and tapped in for the most unlikely of victories. At the time, he called the win his "hardest, by far." There was a Masters victory by 12, a U.S. Open by 15, and an Open by 8. Those were dominant wins.

This was anything but easy. He couldn't practice. He couldn't swing without pain. He could barely walk. There were double bogeys and errant shots and cringeworthy reactions. Through it all, Williams kept thinking what Woods had said from the outset, even during the worst of the pain: "I'm going to win this fucking tournament."

Woods, somehow, overcame the four double bogeys (three on the opening hole) and ten bogeys. He also made three electrifying eagles.

"The thing that stood out the most—that week showed you how tough Tiger was in those days," says Butch Harmon, Woods' coach from 1993 to 2002 and who worked for Sky Sports that week. "That was a typical moment for Tiger Woods, being able to will the ball in the hole. I've never seen anybody like him in my entire life. He just had that ability. When it came down to hitting a shot or hitting a putt or a pitch, he just knew that he could do it, and he pulled it off every time."

Two days after the playoff, Woods' amazing victory came into more remarkable focus. He announced that he had played the tournament with a double stress fracture in his left tibia. While it was clear Woods was in distress through the week at Torrey Pines, all that was known was the knee issue. It turned out to be a far worse situation.

The stress fractures would heal over the next several weeks. But Woods needed to get the knee fixed. It was completely shredded and required a reconstruction. ACL replacement surgery was scheduled for a week later, ending his season after just seven events—five of them victories, one of them on the list of his greatest of all.

It would be nine months before Woods returned to competition.

And, as it turned out, it would be among the many times that Woods had to endure a lengthy layoff filled with rehab and doubt, only to try to come back again.

5

The Scandal

For the first time in his professional career, Tiger Woods was going to miss a major championship. The dramatic U.S. Open victory at Torrey Pines in 2008 would be his last event of the year. The knee surgery a week later that Woods knew was inevitable meant a lengthy rest period and significant rehabilitation.

The Open at Royal Birkdale and the PGA Championship at Oakland Hills went on without him. Padraig Harrington won them both, overtaking a 53-year-old Greg Norman on the final day in England and then dueling Sergio Garcia a month later in Michigan.

Woods watched from afar, his year done after just seven events. But Woods put together a remarkable run that would make a career for mere mortals. A blowout win at the Buick Invitational. A tense victory over Martin Kaymer, Ernie Els, and Graeme McDowell at the Dubai Desert Classic. An easy win in the final of the WGC Match Play over Stewart Cink.

Another victory at the Arnold Palmer Invitational, where a final-hole birdie to shoot 66 saw Woods rip off his cap and fire it to the ground in celebration. He won by a stroke over Bart Bryant and captured his sixty-fourth PGA Tour title.

A tie for fifth at the CA Championship at Doral finally ended his winning streak, and then came the second-place finish at the Masters prior to his winning the U.S. Open.

When Woods had to skip The Open, it was the first time he was not participating in a major since the 1996 PGA Championship, where he was not eligible because he was still an amateur.

The golf world moved on, but Woods was unable to defend his FedEx Cup title from the year prior and missed the U.S. victory at the Ryder Cup, its first since 1999. Woods emerged at his own Target World Challenge in late December, the event that later became known as the Hero World Challenge, and offered no time frame on his return to competition.

But it was coming.

And Woods did finally emerge, in February of 2009 at the WGC-Accenture Match Play Championship. Throngs of people followed him in practice rounds, but he was knocked out in the second round by Tim Clark.

His next event, the CA Championship at Doral, saw him make progress as Phil Mickelson overcame food poisoning to win, while Woods finished tied for ninth.

The next event happened to provide a front-row seat to history that was nearly as good as it gets for someone not part of the action: a spot on a hill to the left of the Bay Hill Club's eighteenth green, with only a bunker separating me and dozens of others from Woods, who was stalking a winning birdie putt on the final day.

Unfortunately, this view of another memorable Woods moment was distorted by darkness. From watching the approach shots of the final threesome at the Arnold Palmer Invitational and then seeing Sean O'Hair attempt a 40-foot birdie putt with his caddie, Paul Tesori, tending the pin, you had to know from experience where the cup was located for the final round of the tournament.

But when Woods stood over his ball, just 15 feet from the hole, it was difficult to see the cup. I was sitting on a hill, looking down on the green, no more than 50 yards away. It was 7:45 p.m., already a few minutes past sundown. Television pictures of the dramatic scene made it appear as though there was plenty of light, but that wasn't so. The scoreboard across the pond was illuminated and cars parked in the grass across the way had their lights on. Flash-bulbs were flickering throughout.

So this wasn't like Tiger's historic strolls to victory at the Old Course or Hoylake, where in the United Kingdom you could play until 10 p.m. And it wasn't like his previous wins at Bay Hill, including two other tournament-clinching victories with birdies on the final hole, both putts struck in daylight.

The weather forecast on this March day was for morning thunderstorms, so PGA Tour officials decided to group the players in threesomes and send them off both tees. The rain came, as predicted, but lingered longer than expected. Tee times ended up getting pushed back nearly two hours.

And all day, it was a toss-up as to whether the tournament would conclude on time. Adding to the difficulty was the tense nature of the happenings in the final group, with Woods cutting into O'Hair's five-stroke lead quickly, pulling within one through ten holes, finally catching him at the 15th, taking the lead at the 16th, giving it back at the 17th, then coming to the 440-yard par-4 18th tied.

The scene at this point was about as cool as it gets in golf, with the gallery ropes packed tight with spectators who by this late in the day had plenty of time to indulge—giving them more courage to shout various words of encouragement. One moment raucous cheering, the next complete silence as the players hit their tee shots.

All three, including Zach Johnson, hit the 18th fairway, with Woods playing last. As he was about to hit his 7-iron approach from 164 yards, there was some laughter that echoed across the water, amplified when just a few people stand out while thousands of others are silent. Woods backed off, went through his routine, then knocked the shot on the green and spun it back to 15 feet below the hole.

Now the tension was really building. It was clear that O'Hair's birdie putt was not one you would expect to make. A two-putt for par was more certain, although it would have been a shame if either player stumbled at this point simply because they could not see properly.

But nobody complained. In fact, O'Hair described night golf as "kind of cool."

By now, tournament host Arnold Palmer was positioned atop the same hill, peering out onto the green to see if Tiger would win his tournament again. Dozens upon dozens of photographers crammed all around. The grandstands that surrounded the green were suddenly silent. Tiger examined the putt, looked at it from every angle, and when it was his turn to play, went into his usual putting routine and stood over the ball.

Then someone yelled out, "Playoff."

Nervous laughter ensued, and Woods backed away, flashbulbs going off.

This was not the same putt Woods faced to defeat Mickelson in 2001 on this same green, or Bart Bryant the year prior. In those instances, he was above the hole, with a curling putt that broke from left to right.

This time, he was below the hole, a left-to-right breaker that was shorter.

"This was totally different," Woods said. "I kept telling myself, obviously with the temperature getting a little cooler, this putt is going to be a little bit slower. The putt is uphill and into the grain, left to right; make sure you hit it hard to get it up to the hole. If anything, if you make a mistake, miss it left so at least it has a chance.

"I hit a pure putt. I hit it really solid and it held its line all the way there."

As the ball tracked toward the hole, it was difficult to determine if it was going in or not. You couldn't tell if it was on line, too fast, too slow. Then I saw Tiger start moving to the left, and that was a clear sign that he thought it was going in.

Then the white object disappeared, and bedlam ensued.

Of course it went in, and of course Woods ripped out the heart of O'Hair in the process, and of course the golf world stood by in amazement—again.

"There wasn't any question about it, was there," said Palmer, the then-79-year-old golf legend who three times had stood by the eighteenth green of his tournament and watched a man who shattered all of his records make a winning birdie putt in dramatic fashion.

"This is the way. It's habit. It's happened every time."

Unless you were O'Hair—who held a five-shot lead at the beginning of the round—or someone who likes to root against Woods, it just didn't get any better.

"I'm in serious disbelief. I don't think I've ever seen him make a putt when he had to have one. And that was the epitome of sarcasm right there," Johnson said. "The guy is amazing. I am in awe. I don't want to say shock. I'm in awe.

"It was unbelievable drama. I tried to stay in my own world . . . It's kind of hard when you're seeing what you're seeing. Obviously Tiger, when he needs to step up, he does it. It was impressive to watch."

Woods matched the biggest final-round comeback of his career on the PGA Tour—he came from five back at Pebble Beach in 2000—to win for the 66th time, just six behind Jack Nicklaus.

It was also his sixth victory at the Arnold Palmer Invitational, the third tournament he had won six times.

And his return from knee surgery could not have gone much better, leading to plenty of speculation about the upcoming Masters. There, Woods and Mickelson played together in the final round, but he could not make up for lost ground. Woods tied for sixth.

He followed with a fourth-place finish at the Wells Fargo Championship, an eighth at the Players Championship, and then a victory at Nicklaus' Memorial Tournament, where he made seven birdies and an eagle on his way to a 7-under-par 65, which saw him birdie the final two holes after stellar approach shots capped what was his most complete tournament since returning.

"If he drives the ball like that, it won't be a contest," Nicklaus marveled after Woods won his tournament for a record fourth time.

Woods hit all 14 fairways during the final round using a combination of drivers, 3-woods, 5-woods, and even irons—a 3-iron off the final tee set up a 7-iron approach that stopped 14 inches from the hole for the birdie and final margin of victory.

"This should give him a lot of confidence heading into The Open," said coach Hank Haney, referring to the U.S. Open at Bethpage, where Woods had won in 2002.

But Woods again tied for sixth, and another opportunity to win that 15th major passed. He won in his next start, the AT&T National at Congressional, but stunningly missed the cut at The Open, played at Turnberry (where Tom Watson, at age 59, lost in a playoff to Stewart Cink).

Somewhat surprisingly, Woods entered the final Buick Open because of his longtime sponsorship deal with Buick. He won. The following week, he dueled Harrington at the WGC-Bridgestone Invitational at Firestone and won again.

That was five victories, and next up was a major championship at Hazeltine for the PGA Championship.

It was there where the unthinkable occurred.

PERHAPS THE STRAIN OF CONTENDING FOR THREE CONSECUTIVE weeks took its toll. Maybe it was simply the law of averages catching up with him outside of Minneapolis that week. But for the first time in his career, Woods failed to convert a 54-hole lead in a major championship.

The lesson had always been simple, even if it took some time to grasp. For all of the consternation over the lack of challengers to Woods in his career, we often failed to look in the proper place.

The biggest threats would come from those who are household names only in their own households, who are given odds of prevailing that are longer than Lake Superior, who somehow muster the moxie at the moment when others melt.

Y. E. Yang was the one to do that, in 2009, when he was a shocking major winner at Hazeltine National, playing in the final twosome with Woods and thumping him by five shots.

His victory was no fluke, as the South Korean golfer executed under duress and took advantage of a poor putting day by Woods to become the first Asian-born player to win a men's major championship.

The PGA was Woods' to win, the Wanamaker Trophy all but packaged and sealed for delivery to Florida. He led by four strokes after 36 holes and by two over Yang with a round to go. He was 14-for-14 in this position in major championships in his career—make it 14-for-15 after that disappointing day.

It would have been a record-tying fifth PGA for Woods and a fifteenth major title, putting him just three behind Jack Nicklaus' eighteen. It would have been a third straight victory on the PGA Tour, the 71st overall. It would have been an incredible cap to what still was a remarkable season for Woods, who despite the long layoff came back to dominate.

But on that championship Sunday, it was a 37-year-old golfer, who didn't take up the game until age 19 and needed to go to the qualifying tournament each of the previous two years just to make it to the PGA Tour, who brought down the guy who had never failed to win with a 54-hole lead in a major.

"My heart nearly pounded and exploded, being so nervous," Yang said of learning he would be paired with Woods, who shot 75 during the final round.

Six times to that point, Woods finished second in a major championship and nobody—nobody—would have picked the eventual winner who beat him.

He lost by a shot to Rich Beem at the 2002 PGA on the same Hazeltine course, by two to Michael Campbell at the 2005 U.S. Open, by two to Zach Johnson at the 2007 Masters, by one to Angel Cabrera at the 2007 U.S. Open, by three to Trevor Immelman at the 2008 Masters, and then by three to Yang.

Throw in Bob May at the 2000 PGA Championship, Chris DiMarco at the 2005 Masters, and Rocco Mediate at the 2008 U.S. Open—all playoff losers to Woods in those majors—and you have three more guys who did not win a tournament in the aftermath of those close calls.

After opening the tournament with rounds of 67–70, Woods lost his putting touch. He made just a single putt outside of 5 feet after the 16th hole of the second round, a birdie that came at the 14th Sunday just after Yang holed his eagle chip to take his first lead.

"I made absolutely nothing, a terrible day on the greens," Woods said. "And I had it at the wrong time."

But he had praise for the winner, too.

"Y.E. played great all day," Woods said. "I don't think he really missed a shot all day."

And that is often what it takes to beat Woods, a guy coming out of nowhere doing the unthinkable.

Consider this: Woods had finished ahead of Yang in each of the twenty-one previous PGA Tour events in which they had played, winning nine times.

The closest Yang ever came was a fifth-place finish two weeks earlier when Woods won the Buick Invitational. In terms of shots, Yang's closest call was a two-shot difference at the Quail Hollow Championship earlier that year, where Woods finished fourth and Yang was tied for 11th.

But none of that mattered in the end. Yang held the trophy, and Woods was left to wonder from which direction the most unlikely of long shots would be fired in his direction. And nobody, absolutely nobody, saw where the biggest threat to his career at that point would emerge.

IF THERE WAS A HANGOVER AFTER THAT SHOCKING PGA CHAMPIONSHIP defeat, Woods didn't suffer long. He tied for second and tied for 11th in his next two starts, then won the BMW Championship by a whopping eight shots. The following week at the Tour Championship, he finished second to Mickelson, a frustrating result but one with a big consolation prize: He was the season-long FedEx Cup champion, worth a $10 million bonus.

It was, by all accounts, an incredible year for Woods on the PGA Tour. He won six times. He captured his second FedEx Cup in the first three years of the competition. All after returning from serious knee surgery and a nine-month absence.

And while it was disappointing that Woods wasn't able to add a major championship—with excellent chances at two of them and a blown opportunity at a third—the prospects for 2010 brought great anticipation.

In addition to the Masters, where he had won four times, Woods would get another crack at Pebble Beach, site of his historic U.S. Open victory in 2000, and St. Andrews, where he had won the previous two Opens.

Adding another victory late in the year at the Australian Masters to cap a seven-win season only heightened the anticipation. All the momentum was on his side heading into 2010.

Until it wasn't.

A Thanksgiving run-in with a fire hydrant outside of his Orlando, Florida, home completely changed Woods' world, leading to a tabloid feeding frenzy and headlines around the world. Some of it was tied to a tabloid report that emanated from his time in Australia, leading to an infidelity scandal that led to weeks and months of inglorious headlines.

Yang might have been the biggest on-course diversion in Woods' quest for history, but these off-the-course personal woes proved to be far more problematic.

Woods went into hiding, and his golf career was on hold. Events he was expected to play were skipped. Who knew when he would return? He made an awkward public apology at PGA Tour headquarters in February. There were brief television interviews with Golf Channel and ESPN, which aired during the final round of the Transitions Championship, won by Jim Furyk. On March 16, 2010, Woods announced he'd be returning at the Masters, which would be nearly five months after his last competitive round, on November 15, 2009, in Australia.

"The major championships have always been a special focus in my career and, as a professional, I think Augusta is where I need to be, even though it's been a while since I last played," Woods said in a statement. "I have undergone almost two months of in-patient therapy and I am continuing my treatment. Although I'm returning to competition, I still have a lot of work to do in my personal life."

The Masters was already a media spectacle, and Woods' return there would ramp that up considerably. It didn't matter whose game was trending, whose game was not. It was going to be all Tiger Woods.

Given what had occurred and the unrelenting scrutiny, a return to competition would be difficult enough. To do so at the most famous golf tournament and course in the world was both terrifying and brilliant. All eyes would be on him. But Woods would also be protected from poor fan behavior, which wasn't tolerated there. And the media, while abundant, would be only the usual accredited variety.

Augusta National was also a familiar place. He had those four victories, contended often. It was a place of fond memories. And being that this is Tiger, he believed he could win.

But the lead-up didn't look good. Not even close. Woods was more than rusty. During his time away, he likely went months without swinging a club. He certainly wasn't practicing with any kind of focus.

"Steve Williams [Woods' caddie] hadn't seen him in months and he showed up in Orlando and we played eighteen holes one day and he said to me, 'Why are we even going there?'" says Haney, Woods' coach at the time. "I said, 'I don't know, but we're going.'"

Both caddie and coach were concerned. They believed Woods, after all the embarrassment off the course, might now embarrass himself on it.

Woods did his first news conference on the Monday of the tournament, the only player to do so that day. The room, understandably, was packed, with outlets having to limit their attendees. The world watched on live TV.

He admitted that the game which had given him so much glory and acclaim was not fun due to what was occurring in his personal life.

"Look at what I was engaged in," Woods said. "When you're living a life that is a lie, life isn't fun . . . That's been stripped away. It feels fun again."

Woods' news conference before more than 200 reporters lasted 34 minutes and included questions covering all aspects of his life, with little to do with golf. Among those questions was why he chose to receive treatment from a Canadian doctor linked to performance-enhancing drugs.

For the first time, Woods disclosed that in addition to recovering from reconstructive knee surgery in late 2008, he also tore his Achilles tendon in his right foot late that year.

He said he'd had a procedure known as platelet-rich plasma (PRP) therapy, which helps speed the healing process. Woods said he chose Dr. Anthony Galea because of his work with other athletes. The procedure is legal under the PGA Tour's drug testing policy. "I've never taken any illegal drug in my life," Woods said.

Woods' world had changed greatly in the four-plus months since the mysterious accident just yards from his driveway. The accident led to considerable negative publicity, including reports of extramarital affairs. He left the game, had undisclosed rehab, and gradually attempted to return to public scrutiny.

Typically, Woods would have fielded all manner of inquiries in a pre-tournament setting with topics related to his game, his quest for a fifteenth major, and his close calls at Augusta National.

But after a long break from golf, those questions and answers would wait. Woods said he wasn't "in the right place" to discuss his complicated situation sooner.

"A lot has happened in my life in the past five months," Woods said. "I'm here at the Masters to play and compete and I'm really excited about doing that."

Earlier that day, Woods played a practice round with former Masters champion Fred Couples. They were joined by Jim Furyk on the 13th hole and played the rest of the way together. Although the crowd was cordial, it was not overly enthusiastic.

Woods made an attempt to interact with spectators—not typical for him—and even engaged in the tradition of trying to skip a shot over the pond at Augusta's par-3 16th. Nobody ever remembered Woods doing that.

"I was more nervous out there," Woods said. "I didn't know what to expect. To be out there in front of the people, where I've done some horrible things . . . for them to want to see me play golf again felt great . . . Today I took it in more."

TAKING CARE OF HIS MEDIA OBLIGATIONS WAS A BIG STEP IN THE process of returning to competitive golf. And now he needed to get ready. Woods' game was not to the sharpness he preferred heading into a major championship.

During the days leading up to the first round, Woods tried his best to cram as much into preparation as possible. There's no approximating tournament play, and the time away from the game was one of the most difficult periods of his life. And then came the Wednesday news conference on the eve of the tournament.

Woods was nowhere near the media center when club chairman William Porter "Billy" Payne made his annual pre-tournament remarks. In his fourth year as Masters and club chairman, Payne was a well-known figure in the sports world, having been president and CEO of the Atlanta Committee for the Olympic Games in 1996.

He later became a member of Augusta National, got involved in various committees, and on May 5, 2006, was appointed to the all-powerful role of Augusta National chairman, becoming just the sixth in club history to hold the position.

Payne is hailed for many positives that occurred during his tenure, including the admittance of Augusta National's first women members, the use of digital technology to help promote the tournament, and the creation of various grow-the-game initiatives such as the Drive, Chip and Putt Contest and international amateur tournaments in Asia and South America that offered spots in the Masters field.

But his remarks on April 7 were surprising.

"It is simply not the degree of his conduct that is so egregious here," Payne said of Woods. "It is the fact that he disappointed all of us, and more importantly, our kids and our grandkids. Our hero did not live up to the expectations of the role model we saw for our children."

Payne's comments were the most outspoken of anyone in an official capacity in golf. Woods was a four-time Masters champion, a revered figure in the game. And Augusta National had accommodated his return news conference, at the club's insistence staging it on Monday to better cut down on distractions related to the tournament.

Woods had already played a nine-hole practice round with Mark O'Meara and had left the course prior to Payne's news conference.

"Is there a way forward? I hope yes. I think yes," Payne said. "But certainly, his future will never again be measured only by his performance against par but measured by the sincerity of his efforts to change. I hope he now realizes that every kid he passes on the course wants his swing but would settle for his smile.

"We at Augusta hope and pray that our great champion will

begin his new life here tomorrow in a positive, hopeful, and constructive manner, but this time with a significant difference from the past. This year, it will not be just for him, but for all of us who believe in second chances."

As shocking as the revelations about Woods were in the previous months, Payne's words were harsh, a right hook to the jaw. Nobody saw that kind of diatribe coming, and it seemed out of character for Augusta National. Woods had done plenty to harm himself, his reputation, and his family. But that had not impacted the Masters; indeed, he was bringing more attention to it with his presence. Payne's heavy-handed reaction was coming from a place that had not dealt with its own issues, ones that were all too apparent when Woods became the first Black man to win the tournament in 1997.

"It was disgusting," said longtime broadcaster Bryant Gumbel as part of an HBO documentary about Woods. "It was a whipping." Gumbel suggested that Woods' then-wife had reason to be mad, and that so did his family. "But the chairman of some golf club? Who the hell are you?"

Woods wasn't about to get into any kind of back-and-forth over Payne's comments. When asked about them following the first round, Woods said: "I was disappointed in myself, too."

But it was a painful blow.

"That caught Tiger by surprise," Williams says. "That was a bolt of lightning out of nowhere."

THE ANXIETY WAS HEIGHTENED BY A LATE FIRST-ROUND TEE TIME. Woods did not begin play until 1:42 p.m., one of the final times of the day. He was grouped with K. J. Choi and Matt Kuchar for the first two rounds.

Haney was nervous about how the first round would play out.

And yet, Woods split the fairway on Augusta National's first hole and went on to shoot a 4-under-par 68, the first time in his sixteen Masters appearances to that point that he broke 70 in the opening round.

"All of a sudden, he shoots 68," Haney says. "How did this happen? He's Tiger Woods."

In his four victories to that point, Woods had never opened with a score better than 70. He trailed 50-year-old Fred Couples by two shots.

It was Woods' first round of tournament golf in 144 days, and the long layoff had many understandably wondering how well he might perform at such an exacting venue.

Woods shot his tournament lows for the first round on both the front nine and overall, had two eagles in a round for the first time, and even pulled off a remarkable ninth-hole hook shot around trees to set up a birdie.

"He's good on that course if he doesn't three-putt," Haney says. "So that's one thing that worked to his advantage. A little room to wander. If we get lucky and hit our bad shots on the holes where we can recover, it's on the right course. That's kind of how it works out, to be honest with you. It could happen there.

"If you hit your three bad shots on the right holes at the right time, you can make some magic happen. If you get a little something going, you are Tiger Woods. You can kind of ride and put yourself there."

Woods was understandably pleased about his first official round since November. "If I putted well today, it could have been a really special round," he said.

Woods needed 31 putts and had several lip-outs, keeping his round from being even better. He hit fourteen greens in regulation and missed just 5 fairways.

"To be surprised by a guy who won a U.S. Open on one leg . . .

you kind of stop being a little bit surprised," said Kuchar, referencing the No. 1 player in the world's 2008 U.S. Open victory at Torrey Pines.

After admitting he was nervous about the reaction he would encounter from spectators when he played his first practice round earlier in the week, Woods received a warm, although not boisterous, ovation as he approached the first tee.

"The people were just incredible, incredible all day," he said.

Although there were no negative incidents on the course, there were two planes that flew overhead pulling banners that referenced Woods' off-the-course transgressions.

Woods said he did not notice them, and when pressed, said he was not surprised.

"It wouldn't be the first time," Woods said.

All in all, it was a good day: Woods was in a tie for seventh, trailing Couples by two and one behind Mickelson, Tom Watson, Lee Westwood, Yang, and Choi. He was tied with Anthony Kim, Nick Watney, Ian Poulter, and Ricky Barnes.

Perhaps that opening round set the stage for some ridiculous expectations. Woods had no business playing well, let alone contending. The mental anguish he put himself through was enough to keep it from happening. The lack of competitive golf and the flaws in his game were a considerable amount to overcome.

Woods shot 70 in the second round to sit two shots behind Westwood and Poulter and tied with Mickelson. He was in great shape, and again, perhaps thinking too big as Westwood surged ahead with a 68 on Saturday and was joined in the final-round group by Mickelson, who shot 67 to stand a stroke back with 18 holes to play. That included a run of eagle-eagle-birdie at the 13th, 14th, and 15th holes.

Another 70 by Woods left him four strokes behind—and lamenting his missed opportunities. He three-putted three times during the round, among other things, but he did birdie the final hole to at least give himself a chance.

"I was fighting it all day," he said. "My warm-up wasn't very good. I was struggling there. I really struggled with the pace of the greens and fighting my swing. It was a tough day."

Woods was struggling, period. He was three days into his comeback, and just being there and competing wasn't enough. He was angry he had not played better. He was angry Mickelson was leading. He was angry. Period.

It didn't get much better on Sunday. Haney could tell that Woods—for one of his rare times—was not into it. His warm-up sessions were typically "works of art," but Woods was off.

"He was not good that week," Haney says. "And he valued how good Phil was. He knew Phil Mickelson was a great player. No matter what anybody said about Phil and his game, Tiger totally respected Phil's game—and his short game, especially. If things get shaky, your short game will bail you out. Phil had that so well.

"Tiger overachieved to be in it after three rounds. But on the practice tee he felt there was no way he could beat Mickelson that day. His attitude would not have been like that if it had been anyone else. On this golf course, you've got room to wander. He's a high ball hitter, great touch, great imagination. And these things Phil has . . . and I'm spotting him a lead."

Woods was undoubtedly frustrated he wasn't closer to the leader through three rounds. But it was nonetheless unlike Woods to give in to anyone—no matter the opponent, no matter his own level of preparedness, no matter the situation.

A final-round 69 was a good score, but he could never get close enough to the leaders, with Mickelson ultimately prevailing to win his third Masters and fourth major championship.

A respectable and even encouraging tournament for Woods somehow turned into defeat. He should have been thrilled with his tie for fourth. Given all he had been through, and how little he had been able to prepare, breaking par in all four rounds was an impressive achievement, and even having a chance should have been viewed as a victory, something to build on.

But Woods could not view things with such a big-picture outlook. He was pissed. To him, there were no moral victories, and putting forth such a strong week meant little. He saw it as an opportunity squandered.

His news conference with reporters afterward suggested anything but satisfaction.

"Yeah, I finished fourth. Not what I wanted," he said. "I wanted to win this tournament. As the week wore on I kept hitting the ball worse. I hit it better on Friday, but after that it was not very good."

And Woods wasn't giving himself a pass, or lowering expectations.

"I entered this event, and I only enter events to win and I didn't get it done," he said. "I didn't hit the ball good enough and I made too many mistakes around the greens, but after that it was not very good."

Earlier in the week, Woods expressed a desire to enjoy golf more. To show a brighter, happier side. To interact with spectators. It was meant to try to soften his image and seen as a way forward after all the turmoil.

But by Sunday, that was gone. Perhaps it was too soon. Certainly it was too much to ask, especially under such circumstances. And to be honest, it was a rather ridiculous expectation. Woods had spent his entire life playing and preparing one way. Now he was supposed to smile on the course to satisfy everyone else?

"I think people are making way too much of a big deal out of this thing," he said. "I was not feeling good. I hit a snipe [hook] off the first hole and I don't know how people can think I should be happy about that. I hit a wedge from 45 yards and basically bladed it over the green. These are not things I normally do.

"So I'm not going to be smiling and not going to be happy. And I hit one of the worst, low, kind of low quick hooks on 5. So I hadn't hit a good shot yet. I'm not going to be walking around there with a pep in my step, because I hadn't hit a good shot yet."

And so it was for Woods. An amazing return to competitive golf was marred by his own incredible expectations. Despite all that had occurred, the drive never left, for good or bad.

6

THE 85

The 2015 season turned out to be the most trying of Tiger Woods' career on the course. The microdiscectomy from the spring of 2014 was, in retrospect, not the cure for Woods' back problems. It turned out to be a remedy that simply masked his lower back issues in the short term but hardly provided the kind of remedy he needed long-term.

The year began with a chipping yips issue (a malady, sometimes neurological, that causes tension and leads to errant shots) followed by lower back issues that caused him to take more than two months off. Somehow, he returned and tied for 17th at the Masters, a rather remarkable accomplishment given his struggles.

But in just eleven tournaments, Woods missed four cuts, including three major championships. He withdrew from the tournament at Torrey Pines in the first round. His best finish was a tie for 10th in his final tournament of the year, one that gave false hope that he was making progress.

All along, he talked a good game and put in the work, as best he could, to improve. And in another example of resiliency, he fought through some of the worst rounds of his career.

Bad days are inevitable in golf. It is the nature of the game, as nearly all who play it can attest. The sweet swing that had struck so many pure shots somehow is gone, leaving one to wonder if the good can ever be recaptured.

With that as a backdrop, professional golfers typically understand that some of those tough days are going to lead to some unsightly numbers. The scorecard doesn't lie, and it is the greatest indicator of one's success.

And sometimes, that can be a harsh assessment.

That scorecard doesn't know how much or how little you've practiced, if you're ill or have a bad back or a sore elbow or any number of other maladies. It doesn't know if the weather is warm, if the wind is blowing, if the course is long, or if the greens are fast.

It simply shows a number, and that number is often how a player is judged.

Sometimes those bad numbers can't be helped, and it is simply a matter of pride that keeps it from going even higher.

And pride is all Woods had during the third round of the Memorial Tournament in Dublin, Ohio. As he pondered his fate during his dark days of career purgatory, he could look back on this occurrence, one that showed his fortitude when he was far from his best and playing with the bad back he was trying to get fixed.

Muirfield Village Golf Club, the one built by Jack Nicklaus and whose tournament he lorded over, was a favorite place for Woods. He had won five times there. He was on a winning Presidents Cup team there. One of his Memorial victories there in 2012 tied him with Nicklaus' seventy-three PGA Tour wins.

If ever a venue could help restore confidence, it was the one that Jack built.

But Woods was in the midst of his most trying year as a pro.

The back problems that first became well-known in 2014 were

giving him fits. Woods did not let on the extent of his issues, but hindsight provides a mighty view.

Earlier that year, Woods developed the yips, which typically surface in putting and sometimes with the driver. But chipping is its own issue altogether.

Basically, a golfer becomes afraid to hit the delicate shots around the green. It can lead to chunked shots or skulled shots or significant misfires. And all of that was happening to Woods at the Phoenix Open.

"It's a technical problem, but then it becomes mental," says former Tour pro and longtime Golf Channel analyst Brandel Chamblee. "I've never seen anybody overcome it until Tiger did. Never, ever. Not once did I see a person in my life who had the chipping yips overcome it."

But it wasn't so much the chipping issues that plagued Woods in early June. It was everything, especially that day. Sure, he made the 36-hole cut, but he seemingly did so with masking tape and glue. His swing was off, and his short game was poor, and he wasn't helping himself on the greens, either.

"I didn't want to have anyone watch me play the way I was playing," Woods said.

The numbers would have been ugly for any pro golfer. Woods' 85 included a career-first 40 or worse for both nines, as he shot 42–43. Through seven holes, he was 2 over par, then played the remaining 11 holes in 11 over par.

His round included a quadruple-bogey 8 on the last hole, as well as two double bogeys, six bogeys, and a single birdie.

Zac Blair, a rookie on the PGA Tour in 2015, played with Woods for the first time and beat him by 15 strokes, shooting 70. Woods would have liked to forget that day, while Blair said, "It was the coolest round of golf in my life."

A few years later, Blair recalled that he could see a possible

Saturday pairing shaping up with Woods after both barely advanced to the weekend through 36 holes. And that was both an exciting and excruciating proposition.

Who wouldn't want to play with Tiger? And yet, are you prepared to deal with all that comes with it: the huge galleries, the media inside the ropes, trying not to get caught up in Tiger's game?

Blair seemingly had the right approach. He was going to enjoy the moment.

"From the first hole on, I couldn't have been more blown away," Blair says. "My favorite athlete of all time, and to get paired with him was really cool. Everything exceeded my expectations. He was my idol, and I tried to not expect much but he was really nice, talked to me all day, talked to me about fishing in Utah; the Chambers Bay U.S. Open was coming up and we talked about that because I had played in the U.S. Amateur there."

Despite Woods' poor score, Blair was still impressed.

"I remember some of the shots he hit and thinking how unbelievable this guy is and why he is on another level as far as talent from anybody else," Blair says. "To hit some of the shots he hit . . . I had played a year out here and played with a lot of good players, but some of the things he could do with a golf ball made me realize why he was the best. He was still able to do some good things. He hit some iron shots that I couldn't believe how flush they were."

And that's shooting 85.

"Unfortunately, that's all I had," Woods said. "I take pride in throughout the years, of never bagging it. I've tried in every single round to fight to the end, and unfortunately that week I shot eighty-five. I've had rounds in the eighties in my career and unfortunately that was the highest one I've ever had.

"It didn't feel very good. But it is what it is. I tried and unfortunately . . . hitting it as bad as I did it just wasn't good enough."

The 85 is one of just four scores Woods has shot in the 80s as a pro. His first came in 2002 at The Open at Muirfield, where he shot a third-round 81 in horrible weather conditions. He shot an 82 at the WM Phoenix Open in 2015, and then two weeks later he opened the U.S. Open with an 80.

In 2015, Woods had those three rounds in the 80s and missed the cut at four tournaments, including three major championships. At the Memorial, after a final-round 74, he finished last among those who made the cut—by eight shots.

"Whenever I tell people the story about playing with Tiger, I always try to tell them how amazing he was toward me," Blair says. "He could have easily walked off. He wasn't playing his best, and after nine he could have just gone in. He stuck through it all day and really grinded it out and was still really nice. That was the coolest round of golf in my entire life."

NOBODY WAS EVER GOING TO FEEL SORRY FOR TIGER WOODS, but it was nonetheless a bit disconcerting that he struggled so much on such a big stage. It was simply another example of how trying the year was for him and perhaps just how tough things were with the back problem.

Still, the numbers were shocking.

Not only was Woods bad—he was exceptionally bad. To add further insult, the field had been cut to just seventy-one players, meaning Woods would have to tee off, alone, first on Sunday morning.

While it was the second time that year Woods shot in the 80s, the circumstances were far different from those in Scotland at The Open, in 2002, coincidentally played at Muirfield—the course for which Nicklaus named his Muirfield Village—where Woods shot 81. Woods was attempting to win the calendar-year Grand Slam, having won the Masters and U.S. Open that year. Heading into the third round at The Open, Woods found himself just two shots off the 36-hole lead—and fortuitously paired with his good friend Mark O'Meara.

It was a seemingly ideal situation, one that suggested the stars had aligned for a historic run at golf's holy grail.

Then the weather came in off the Firth of Forth, and it was one of those days where nobody would be on a golf course unless it was absolutely necessary.

The wind blew extremely hard and the rain pelted down sideways, sending temperatures plummeting and scores soaring. Woods and O'Meara got the brunt of it, as the weather hit just as they were teeing off and did not subside for more than 3 hours.

By the time things finally calmed down, the damage was done. Woods didn't make a birdie until the 17th hole, when he mockingly held both arms up in triumph, smiling. The final day, well out of the tournament, he bounced back with a 66 as Ernie Els won in a playoff.

When Woods shot the 85 at Muirfield Village, it was natural to search for the same kind of difficulty that Nicklaus might have encountered in his career, regardless of how dubious.

Nicklaus shot 16 scores in the 80s as a pro, with eight of those coming before he turned 40. His highest score was an 85 at the 2003 Masters, when the Golden Bear was 63. His highest scores before turning 40 were 82s at the 1976 Pebble Beach Pro-Am and the 1979 Players Championship at Sawgrass Country Club.

"He's just kind of working through some things; obviously it takes some time to work through some swing changes and stuff like that," Blair, who listed Woods as part of his dream foursome, said that day. He met him for the first time before teeing off.

"He's the best player to ever play, in my opinion. He'll get back to playing good."

It was an odd way to experience the memory of a lifetime, but Blair nonetheless felt fortunate to witness even the bad stuff. Woods needed 32 putts and missed five putts inside 5 feet. And that was only the front side.

"I'm staying committed to what we're working on," Woods said. "And I've gone through phases like this, rounds like this before in the past where, yeah, it's easy to revert back and go ahead and hit some old pattern, but it doesn't do you any good going forward.

"And I've done it—sometimes it's taken me about a year and then it kicked in and I did pretty good after that. And as subsequent years went down the road, I did the same thing.

"Got to suck it up. If you believe in it, do it. And eventually it will start turning, and when it turns, I've had periods where I've played good for four or five years, where I've won close to twenty tournaments in that stretch."

Woods, talking swing changes, was not acknowledging that his back was the real culprit. As he would later say, he was trying to "swing around pain," and the back issues he tried to minimize were more than a mere nuisance. They were a huge detriment to his success, impacting his swing, perhaps more severely his short game—as bending over at the waist was even more painful.

"I don't remember much of the round, but clearly we know now he was hurting back then," says caddie Joe LaCava. "He had a lot of troubles, but I know I can tell you that he was trying hard."

All of that did not make the early-Sunday tee time any easier.

Playing solo before thousands of spectators, Woods tried to treat as normal as possible a round of golf that was surreal for both him and those watching.

Never before had Woods been in such a position—first off, alone, the penalty for being last in the field—and left to finish off a tournament that went down as one of his worst.

He shot an otherwise meaningless 2-over-par 74—11 strokes better than his career-highest 85 the day prior.

He played the last two holes in 3 over with a double bogey at the last—to complete his fifteenth Memorial Tournament in 302 strokes, 14 over par, his highest 72-hole total ever.

And yet, he showed the typical Tiger resolve. There was little to play for other than pride, and Woods did his best for the thousands who came out to follow him.

The round took 2 hours, 51 minutes. At one point on the seventeenth green, Woods took out the flagstick, putted, and put it back in while LaCava raked a bunker. There was no one else there to do it.

"Just trying to shoot under par, just go out there and shoot the best score I possibly can," Woods said when asked what was at stake in a tournament where he finished more than two and a half hours before leader Justin Rose was to tee off—and 29 strokes behind him. "Just because I'm in last place doesn't change how I play golf. Whether it's the first day or last day doesn't matter—play all out."

Woods did just that. He studied putts, checked his yardage book with LaCava, got frustrated at the bad shots, and tried to make the best of the situation. Only pride was at stake.

He got to 3 under par for his round with a birdie at the 11th hole, looking far better than he did shooting the big number on Saturday. But he couldn't finish. The back nine gave him fits all week, especially the final two holes, playing them in 12 over par for the tournament.

His six double bogeys or worse were the most of any tournament in his career.

The 18th was particularly gruesome—two doubles, and a quad. The only par came on Friday, when he needed to get up and down to make the 36-hole cut on the number.

"I had to go through [the 85]—I had to go through those painful moments, just like I did at Torrey and Phoenix, to be able to make the leap I did at Augusta," said Woods, who took nine weeks off to work on his game following those first two events of 2015 before returning at the Masters.

"Yesterday was the same thing. It was just unfortunately on a golf course like this where you can't get away with much. It kicked my butt pretty hard."

Woods said the 85 "felt a lot higher."

"It's hard. It's real hard," he said, when asked if the 85 was humbling. "This is a lonely sport. The manager is not going to come in and bring the righty or bring the lefty [relief pitcher]; you've just got to play through it. And that's one of the hardest things about the game of golf and it's also one of the best things about the game of golf—when you're on, no one is going to slow you down. Also when you're off, no one is going to pick you up either.

"It's one of those sports that's tough; deal with it. For us, unfortunately, you have those days, they're five hours long. Those are long, tough days.

"You have moments where you go backwards, and then you make big, major strides down the road," he said. "That's just the way it goes. You have to look at the big picture. You can't be so myopic with your view and expect to have one magical day or one magical shot and change your whole game. It doesn't work that way."

Said Nicklaus: "You go up and down and shoot a snowman [a score with an 8] and all of a sudden you say, 'Gosh, how did I do that?' Then you go back and the next day you shoot a sixty-eight or a sixty-seven and find out why you did that.

"That's part of the learning experience, and even at age 39 years old that's still a learning experience. He'll be fine."

Unfortunately for Woods, he wasn't.

He shot an 80 during the first round of the U.S. Open a few weeks later and missed the cut. He went to St. Andrews for The Open, hitting his second shot on the opening hole in the burn that fronts the green, and went on to miss the cut. He missed the cut at the PGA Championship as well, marking a first in his career—missed cuts in three straight major championships.

Surprisingly, Woods entered the Wyndham Championship, the regular season–ending tournament, in a last-ditch effort to try to qualify for the FedEx Cup playoffs.

There, he found some form, tied for the 36-hole lead, and had a chance on Sunday before faltering on the back nine, some chipping woes coming into play and his back problems again apparent.

Woods talked a good game afterward, suggesting this was something to build on. His season was over, but some rest, rehab, and the fall offered promise for a new season.

Then news came out about another microdiscectomy in September. Six weeks later, another one? Yep. Two such surgeries to alleviate disk pain suggested an ominous situation.

And it would only get worse as Woods headed to the Bahamas in late November, where he could not play in his own tournament and where he said he saw "no light at the end of the tunnel."

That ominous time just weeks before his 40th birthday seemingly spelled doom. It would not be his lowest point on the way to another major, but at the time it sure seemed like it.

Visiting some of the other players while riding a golf cart with his daughter, Sam, and son, Charlie, Woods was in extreme distress. Big soccer fans, Sam and Charlie were asked by *USA Today*'s Steve DiMeglio if they would rather be soccer star Lionel Messi or Tiger for the day.

Sam started giggling, and Charlie said, "Messi," before pausing and adding, "He's playing."

Tiger roared with laughter, acknowledging the situation. He

had several times noted that his kids called him the "YouTube golfer" because that is the only way they ever saw him play.

It was a light moment in a time of darkness.

Throughout 2016, Woods was barely seen. He went to the Tuesday night Champions Dinner at the Masters. He spent a couple of days at his foundation-hosted tournament at Congressional Country Club a week after the U.S. Open. He made plans to play the tournament in Napa, California, only to pull out on Monday of that week.

The Hero tournament came with so much promise, only to be scuttled just a few weeks later when Woods could barely walk while in Dubai.

More pain followed, along with his biggest decision in framing the rest of his career.

7

The Bahamas

The wind whipped across the mostly isolated landscape, the warm, salty air providing a slight breeze off the nearby Atlantic Ocean on a December afternoon in the Bahamas. It was just a few days after Thanksgiving in 2016, and out in the distance was Tiger Woods, hitting golf balls at the back of a driving range, caddie Joe LaCava the only other person in sight.

Witnessing Woods striking golf balls in any setting was jarring in itself. It had been more than a year since I had seen him hit a single shot, the last time coming at a PGA Tour event in Greensboro, North Carolina, in August of 2015. That was some fifteen months prior, and nobody knew then the dire turns of events that would unfold in Woods' life, ones that would put serious doubts in the minds of all those who followed his prolific career as to the viability of his continuing.

The situation would ultimately become even more harrowing, but this Sunday in Nassau provided hope. Woods had arrived from his South Florida home a day earlier and set up camp nearby at a marina where his yacht, *Privacy*, was docked.

Woods had established ties to Albany, the golf development in the Bahamas where his longtime annual charity golf tournament had relocated a year earlier. He owned property at the club and could zoom down a short side street on a golf cart from his boat.

Now he was to begin preparations for the Hero World Challenge, an offseason money grab for the game's top players that also served as a fundraiser for the Tiger Woods Foundation (now TGR). Started in 1999 with the help of Woods' late father, Earl, the tournament attracted players based on their place in the Official World Golf Ranking. And while they were certainly there to support Woods, it was also a nice way to earn some extra holiday cash.

While a week in the Bahamas for some low-key golf with a guaranteed payday was a nice perk, Woods' motives were far different. It was a busy week anyway, as he had all kinds of demands centered on an event meant to raise funds for his foundation: photo shoots, interviews, pro-ams, auctions, a poker night—you name it. Woods did a good bit of shaking hands, kissing babies, posing for photos—anything to appease the title sponsor, Hero MotoCorp, an India-based motorcycle and scooter manufacturer, and the various other sponsors who were there supporting his foundation with big-money donations and a week of soaking up the sun.

But Woods was also using the event to launch a much-awaited comeback, and the early signs were promising.

After arriving in the Bahamas, I visited Albany that afternoon, thinking LaCava might be walking the layout to gain insight into a course he had yet to see. A golf reporter for ESPN at the time, I was with colleague Steve DiMeglio from *USA Today*, and both of us were surprised to see Woods hard at work.

We somewhat guardedly approached him to see if we could observe, and after a few pleasantries, we settled in for a riveting couple of hours. It had been months since either one of us had been in contact with Woods, and while he warmly greeted us, he did not leave the work at hand for long. He was busy testing equipment—and looking pretty good doing so.

"I'm not dead," he deadpanned.

A month shy of his 41st birthday, Woods looked for a majority of this practice session like the guy who'd won fourteen major championships and seventy-nine PGA Tour titles to that point but was more than three years past his last victory. He sweated profusely as he attempted to figure out how far the ball was traveling and hitting to various spots, with LaCava there to help him crunch the numbers. It was cool to witness Woods in this setting, even more so knowing that for most of the year, he'd been unable to stand properly, let alone swing a club with such authority.

(Quick aside: For any golf geek, watching Woods hit golf balls up close is the stuff of dreams. Over years and years of his doing this, there is nobody quite like him when it comes to striking a golf ball, particularly with his irons. The sound at impact is unique, one that can be identified without looking among those who play and follow closely. Time flies by as he goes through the bag, neatly hitting shots in a perfect divot pattern. His divot etiquette on a driving range is actually something to behold. "The way he hits his irons is unbelievable," says PGA Tour pro Joel Dahmen, who played one round with Woods in 2018. "He was hitting at pins that would be dumb for me to go after. All of them are just so incredible. Moved it different ways. All landed in the right spot. Not many people have that.")

He shaped shots, spending time not only on the driving range but in a nearby testing center, gauging various aspects of his swing speed, ball speed, and distance. As part of this session, he was testing a new ball—a Bridgestone—that was about to become big news because he was signing an endorsement deal.

In the time he was away, Nike—his longtime equipment manufacturer—had left the golf equipment business, leaving Woods with numerous choices. Manufacturers sent him so many samples that "my head was spinning," he said. Woods said he had a living room at home with clubs strewn all about. For the rest of us, that's Christmas. For Tiger, it was decision time.

To the casual observer, it didn't matter. Woods could have been swinging a broom handle and it would have looked glorious. Since a tie for 10th at the 2015 Wyndham Championship, Woods had not played a single competitive round of golf. A month following that tournament, he underwent a microdiscectomy that was termed "minor." Of course, it's only minor to those not having to endure it.

Woods had been plagued by lower back pain since at least 2012, and it became keenly acute in 2014, when he underwent his first microdiscectomy, knocking him out of that year's Masters and U.S. Open. It was the first time since Woods played the Masters as an amateur in 1995 that he missed the year's initial major championship. The simple explanation for the procedure was that it was meant to treat a herniated disk and relieve nerve pressure.

But throughout his return late in 2014 and for all of 2015, Woods never seemed right. He shot his highest score ever, an 85, during the third round of the 2015 Memorial Tournament—one he had captured five times. He shot an opening-round 80 at the U.S. Open. He chunked a ball into the burn fronting the first green at the Old Course and missed the cut at The Open. And so it went.

Things became more dismal when it was learned that he needed another microdiscectomy in September. They grew even more dire when the procedure was repeated a month later. And when Woods showed up in the Bahamas at the end of 2015 to host his event but not play, the mood could not have been more depressing.

After years of playing the tournament in Southern California with a one-year stop in Florida, a new beginning was supposed to unfold in the Bahamas, with Woods the star and his foundation the beneficiary. Instead, the proceedings turned somber, and Woods was strikingly blunt.

"I can't see the light at the end of the tunnel," he said, putting his future in troubling doubt, as it was clear he had a difficult time walking without pain.

"I have no answer for that, and neither does my surgeon," Woods said when asked about a rehabilitation time line. "There is no timetable, so that's the hardest part for me. There's really nothing I can look forward to, nothing I can build towards."

Asked what he is able to do, Woods said, "I walk. And I walk and I walk some more.

"It's just taking it literally day by day and week by week and time by time," he said. "It's different from any of the other surgeries and procedures that I've had in the past, where, okay, you blow out your ACL, which I did and I had ACL reconstruction and okay, you're back in nine months. That's the timetable.

"For nerves, there are really no timetables, and therein lies the tricky part, because you can come back earlier or you can come back later, it just depends on how the nerve heals and how it settles."

The calendar turned, and into 2016 Woods went, never saying he was sitting out the entire year, leading everyone on up to each major before deciding he was not going to play.

An entire year passed, and here was Woods at the end of 2016, hitting the ball beautifully and moving about like the guy golf fans had seen dominate the game for so many years.

Woods had no trouble carrying drives more than 300 yards, shaping shots in both directions with his various clubs while showing no pangs of discomfort. His participation and his being able to engage without pain were followed with intense scrutiny.

During his absence, Woods—who had been ranked No. 1 in

the world for more weeks than any other player in history—had slipped to 879th in the Official World Golf Rankings.

Woods admitted to being nervous. "But I'm nervous for every tournament I play in, whether it's after a layoff, or six in a row, or a major," he says. "I care. If I care, I'm nervous. And it's good to be that way. To have that nervous energy and channel it into aggression, into focus, concentration—that's good stuff. If I wasn't nervous, that would mean I didn't care. I don't want to be out there flat."

Woods said he understood the thinking that he shouldn't care, that just being back after an extended absence was more than enough.

"I get that, and that part is great, too," he says. "I'm out here playing and competing. That part is really neat. Then there is that part of me that is the competitor who wants to beat these guys. I want to compete."

Less than two months prior, Woods had announced he was not ready to do that. He first committed to the Safeway Open in California, then three days before the tournament decided to pull out, describing his game as "vulnerable" and saying that he was not ready to compete against the best in the world.

That set off a new wave of doubts about his game and his future, and while Woods said he understood and badly wanted to play that week, "It was a good decision in the end. The competitor inside me wanted to go so badly and was itching to go. I had been playing at home. I thought if I have only a few shots [in his repertoire], it's good enough to get it around. I had played feeling worse. But what's the point in rushing back when I've waited over a year to begin with?

"I've waited this long; it's not going to hurt to wait just this much longer."

Still, there was a sense that, for one of the rare times, Woods was loath to put his game on display. He had gone through a chipping yips issue in 2015, due mostly to back pain, that was at times embarrassing. Now he was about to compete in front of the world for the first time in more than a year.

Woods was, perhaps, uncomfortable with the idea of not being Tiger Woods.

Few people could understand what that must have been like. One who had a chance was Mickey Wright, the LPGA legend who has since passed away. Wright won 82 times in her career and was admired throughout the game for a beautiful swing and amazing ball-striking ability.

Thinking she might be among the few people who could relate to Woods' plight, I reached out to her in advance of the Hero tournament.

"Most people just don't understand how mental and emotional great golf is," said Wright, who was 81 at the time and had more or less stopped playing competitive golf at age 34 because, among other issues, she had difficulty with the idea of being less than her best.

"They think purely about athletic ability. Tiger will always be the great athlete he's been, but for a while he'll be thinking about playing shots rather than just stepping up and hitting them. There are a lot of new good players who have built their confidence over the last couple of years who are in their early twenties and at their strongest. Big difference being in your forties."

The back problem first began bothering Woods—at least outwardly—in late 2013, a year in which he won five times. He tried to manage it through a fall in which there were some hints of discomfort. He contended at the Barclays tournament—where he fell to the ground due to back pain after hitting a shot during the final round, and still tied for second. He contended at a European

Tour event in Turkey. He lost in a playoff at the last Hero World Challenge to be played in California.

Rest and rehabilitation were supposed to take care of the issues heading into 2014, but after just four tournaments, Woods shut it down. He withdrew from the final round of the Honda Classic with less than nine holes to go and announced on April 1—there were many who wondered if it was an April Fool's joke—that he had undergone a microdiscectomy, a word that all who followed Woods would come to know well.

He returned after just three months, and in retrospect that was probably a mistake. And he was not the same.

In the fifteen official tournaments he played following the March, 31, 2014, surgery, Woods missed six cuts, withdrew twice, and posted a best finish of a tie for 10th. The only consistency was surgery. He had the same procedure twice more.

Another prominent player who had difficulty putting his game on display after a lengthy layoff was the great amateur Bobby Jones, who quit on top after his historic 1930 season. He went on to compete in the Masters twelve times, but was never a contender, citing the difficulty of putting his game on display. "I realized that this return to competition was not going to be too much fun," Jones wrote. "I realized that I simply had not the desire nor willingness to take the punishment necessary to compete in that kind of company."

Annika Sorenstam retired from competitive golf in 2008, still possessing the skills to be competitive. Always a perfectionist, Sorenstam said she had to learn to not be so hard on herself, even in post-career events where she was meant to enjoy the atmosphere.

"I was extremely dedicated and practiced so hard for so long, and then basically I stopped completely," she said. "I moved on and became at peace with my level of play."

Woods never emitted a vibe that he would just be happy to be there. He took enormous pride in his game and wasn't keen on showing any struggles. His situation most clearly mirrored that of Wright, considered by many to be the best female golfer of all time.

Wright quite possibly had years of competitive golf left in her career when she played her last full season, due in part to foot problems, but also because she felt burned out from the competitive grind, as well as being the face of the LPGA Tour. You think Woods couldn't relate to that burden? Wright won her last tournament in 1973.

"I was too demanding of myself," she said. "Playing badly was intolerable. When I was in my 40s and playing fewer and fewer tournaments, I found myself disappointed often. [That] had something to do with my stopping full-time competing at quite a young age. I really never played golf casually.

"If I could go back and do it again, I would hope to be a little kinder to myself and probably enjoy the game more."

At that point in time, Woods was far from the mindset of playing to enjoy. He was desperately trying to play around his injuries and figure out a way to do more with less. He knew he couldn't grind and practice like in the old days. But in order to compete with the younger generation, his otherworldly skills were not going to be enough. He needed to find a way.

LaCava twice went to Florida to work with Woods following the Safeway withdrawal, mostly to get Woods in tournament mode and off a golf cart. His instructor, Chris Como, had also been there.

Two weeks prior, Woods and LaCava played rounds on four consecutive days, walking—which seemed simple enough until Woods explained he had not been doing that enough.

"It's weird to say, but I have to get my walking legs," he said about a seemingly simple task that would become a big part of his ability to compete going forward. "It's a 5-mile walk. You forget what it feels like to be in golf shoes versus tennis shoes. To be on an uneven lie versus a flat lie. I can walk for two or three hours on a treadmill and it's not the same as walking on a golf course. It's so different, the standing around [between shots].

"The rhythm of playing in a golf cart versus walking and playing. I had forgotten that, because I had been away for over a year. Joey really helped me . . . Normal tournament talk—I had to get used to that again."

Never was there so much scrutiny of a player in an offseason charity event in which many of the players were there to enjoy the scenery and pick up an easy paycheck. Woods beat just two players in the eighteen-man field (another withdrew). And he finished 14 strokes back of winner Hideki Matsuyama.

But his second-round 65 had the place buzzing, and a final-round 76 hardly took away from the excitement.

"Getting back to this point is beyond anything that I've ever experienced in my lifetime," Woods said. "The pain issues that I had, it was rough. To battle back, to battle through it. Frankly, there were some pretty dire times where I just couldn't move."

The positivity was short-lived. Woods announced an ambitious early-season schedule for 2017 that included the Farmers Insurance Open in San Diego, the Dubai Desert Classic in the Middle East, and the Genesis Open, a tournament where his foundation was again involved.

But Woods made it through just those three rounds of golf in early 2017, his season coming to an abrupt end after just one round of golf in Dubai. The back acted up again, and Woods was clearly in pain after a first-round 77 that saw him fail to make a birdie.

Nobody knew how bad it ultimately would become. There was still hope he might return in a few weeks for the Genesis tournament. Or maybe the Honda Classic near his home in South

Florida. Or the Arnold Palmer Invitational, where he had won eight times. Certainly he'd be ready for the Masters, right?

Nope.

Woods went to that Champions Dinner on the Tuesday night of Masters week and thought his career was likely over, the pain-killing shot just another reminder of what he had to do merely to exist.

The flight across the Atlantic had to be lonely and distressing, with no answers forthcoming. Winning the Masters could not have been further from his mind, and yet the journey was just beginning.

If there were any positives to draw on, any hope for the future, Woods had plenty of career highlights that allowed for reminiscing and revisiting. After all, his career was filled with extraordinary moments and stretches that required the same kind of strength and fortitude that would be required for this next journey.

There would be countless moments for reflection and a bevy of accomplishments to draw on that offered examples of his dedication and desire.

8

The Doctor

When Tiger Woods left Augusta National on the evening of April 4, 2017, there could be no visions of future Masters glory. No thoughts of wearing another green jacket, lifting championship hardware, reveling in the sights and sounds of success.

His goal was to find some relief.

His golf career was the furthest thing from his mind. Earlier that day, he met with CBS's Jim Nantz for what turned out to be a somber reflection on his Masters career. Nantz recalled Tiger speaking in the past tense, as if his career was over.

Why would he think otherwise? For the better part of four years, Woods had been in pain. The lower back area where back problems first surfaced in 2012 and again in 2013 had required microdiscectomies. The idea was to alleviate the pressure on a herniated disk, a procedure that is called "simple" and yet is anything but.

Woods said after the March 31 operation that he immediately felt relief. And yet it's all relative. What was relief?

Notah Begay, Woods' longtime friend dating back to their college days at Stanford, recalled visiting Woods a week following that surgery. He said Tiger had complained about the stitches from his surgery and wanted him to take a look. Begay chuckled.

"I've read a few medical journals, but shouldn't we have a doctor look at that?" he recalled saying, before making an appointment.

"Honestly, he couldn't get up out of the chair under his own power," Begay says. "This is a guy who I'm helping, one of my dear friends in the world, just to walk to the car. His arm is draped around my shoulders using me for support to help him get step by step. I'm thinking this guy will never play golf the way he ever played before. A sadness came over me. Maybe we'll never see him play golf again.

"I just kept thinking of that image of helping him into the car. How is he ever going from this to holding up to a major championship trophy? Wearing a green jacket? I just didn't see it."

Only the most optimistic of supporters could see Woods returning to golf as the first major championship was about to play out in 2017—the optimists, and perhaps those who had no idea just how dire Woods' situation was at the time.

He headed to the airport that night in pain, having endured plenty just to see his fellow Masters champions at the dinner held in their honor. And now he was about to fly across the Atlantic to meet with consultants who would try to figure something out. Woods just wanted to play with his kids, to kick a soccer ball, play catch, maybe be well enough to swing a golf club for fun.

Competing, being anything like *the* Tiger Woods, appeared out of the question.

Dan Hellman had started working with Woods late the previous year. Hellman is a physical therapist and trainer, a job title that does not do justice to his various areas of expertise. I met Hellman briefly at the 2016 Hero World Challenge. He was a new face in Woods' world, and his role soon became clear.

Like just about all who work for Woods, Hellman approached his duties with an abundance of caution and without an abundance of fanfare. That week, he spent time watching the action alongside Tiger's mom, Tida. It was probably two years before I learned his last name, and long after that before I could understand exactly what he did. It was simply clear that his knowledge was being used to help Woods navigate the back problems that were sure to surface.

At the time, Hellman had his own practice, called "Hellman Holistic Health of Fort Lauderdale," later changed to "H3 by Dan Hellman." In 2017, *Golf Digest* had recognized Hellman as one of the country's top fifty golf-fitness professionals.

For nearly twenty years, Hellman offered physical and osteopathic therapy, personal training, counseling in nutrition, and lifestyle management. And as part of all those duties, he became quite proficient in dealing with back pain, especially as it related to disk injuries and rehabilitation.

Hellman was introduced to Woods through Chris Como, who coached Tiger for a period of time and was keenly aware of the back problems he faced. The entire time Woods and Como were together, from late 2014 until Woods' comeback in 2018, Como had only a fragile golfer with back issues to try to help.

Aside from the golf-swing part, Como sought medical knowledge and came to know Hellman through other clients. Eventually, Como met with Woods and Hellman, and they began working together during the time in 2016 when Woods was not competing.

Hellman agreed to speak to me only due to his immense respect for Woods. Some five years had passed since he'd last formally worked for Woods, but Hellman understandably wanted it made clear that he still marveled at what Woods endured—and accomplished.

The idea was to avoid surgery. Hellman, through various

techniques, manipulations, and perhaps some hope for divine intervention, did all he could to keep Woods upright, allowing him the freedom to swing a golf club without searing pain. Or, even more important: to live a normal life.

But the Dubai tournament proved to be too much.

There had been so much promise at that first tournament a few months earlier in the Bahamas. Woods had plans for an ambitious start to 2017, including a trip to the Dubai Desert Classic, a European Tour event he had won twice and for which he'd be getting a seven-figure appearance fee.

But there were ominous signs when he made his first official PGA Tour start in seventeen months at the Farmers Insurance Open, played at the Torrey Pines course in San Diego where Woods had enjoyed so much success. He had won there eight times, including the 2008 U.S. Open.

It had become his typical starting point for the year, and Woods looked forward to getting back and relaunching his career on familiar turf. But Woods opened the tournament with a 76, and the cool mornings and brisk temperatures made for a bad combination with his back. Woods looked far from the limber, speedy golfer he'd seemed in the Bahamas. He added a 72 to his opening score and missed the cut by a mile.

The thought was that the long course, cool conditions, and lack of competition all contributed to the poor showing. Always with Woods, there was a search for optimism. Man, those iron shots still look good. Or the short game did. Anything to avoid the reality: Too much golf, too much cold weather, too much activity was going to catch up with him.

The positive take was that at least Woods would be getting some rest before embarking on a 17-hour journey to the Middle East.

But the long trip to Dubai proved to be a waste of time. He was paid well, but that's about it. Despite saying otherwise, Woods did not look right during the opening round on Thursday. Frankly, he hadn't looked all that great at the Farmers Insurance Open a week prior, either.

From the moment he hit his first tee shot, Woods appeared different. He walked gingerly and did not swing freely. On the first hole he emerged from a greenside bunker so awkwardly that Golf Channel commentator Brandel Chamblee said the golfer "looked like an old man."

Woods didn't make a birdie on his way to a score of 77, and looked bad. And it made his words on the eve of the tournament more ominous. When asked about the latest reincarnation of his golf swing, Woods said: "The simplest thing is just to play away from pain."

That was never going to work. And, sadly, Woods had been doing that for three years with little success. It's one of the reasons he often struggled. Bad habits resulted from trying to avoid pain. It's what the body does. It compensates, which leads to other issues, some of them poor swings, others making matters worse for other parts of the body.

And then you add it all up. Three microdiscectomies. Virtually two years without competitive golf. Rest, rehabilitation. Nothing worked. And that night at Augusta National could not have been darker.

IT WAS APPARENT THAT SURGERY WAS INEVITABLE. AFTER returning home from Dubai, Woods rested and then began the process of trying to get golf-ready again. The idea of playing at the Genesis Invitational was a long shot. The tournament deadline came and went. Same for the Arnold Palmer Invitational. There was still hope for the Masters—at least publicly—but when Woods tried to ramp up to get ready, it just was not possible.

That is why Hellman had already begun the process of searching for answers. Perhaps more than anyone, he knew how dire the situation Woods faced was, and its intricacies. And he knew that Woods needed surgery.

And that brought on other issues. Who would Woods trust to handle it? What kind of surgery was required? "I knew just about everybody would want to operate on Tiger Woods," Hellman says.

That led to their clandestine trip to the United Kingdom, where Woods met with consultants, including Dr. Damian Fahy, a surgeon who "functions more like being a patient advocate," Hellman says. "The goal was to find an advocate who would look after Tiger and not just want to cut on him. Someone who would be in his corner."

Almost as soon as the plane landed, Woods was on his way to various appointments, spanning three days.

It was during that testing period that Hellman learned the obstacles Woods faced, the pain he endured. Woods had always described the pain he felt as the feeling of bone on bone, something that puzzled Hellman. "That's not possible, because you've got a disk there," says Hellman, who described it as "a feat of human determination" that Woods endured three microdiscectomies on the same level of the spine. "To see that, even playing three rounds of golf with his spine like that . . . it's just amazing."

Fahy was just as astounded. The consultant spinal surgeon at the Fortius Clinic, Fahy, who also advised tennis star Andy Murray before a hip surgery, said Woods reminded him of the Scotsman as it related to the careful management of his treatment.

In an interview with *The Daily Telegraph* after Woods won the 2019 Masters, Fahy expressed his surprise over how arduous the process had been. He spent several days with Woods trying to decide on the best course of action, with the main goal to return him to a good quality of life, with golf as a bonus.

"People don't realize just how much pain Tiger was in," Fahy said in the *Telegraph* interview. "When he came to see me, his first thought was to get to a place where he would be able to spend time with his kids without breaking down in agony. The pain was twenty-four/seven.

"You never know how a person will recover—most of it will depend on the patient's strength of mind—but if he was to get back to playing golf at all, we saw that as a bonus. To get back to the point where he could win the Masters is incredible.

"It took a tremendous amount of courage to go through what he did. He had achieved everything in the sport. A lot of people would have accepted that and retired to a quiet life, but that wasn't enough for Tiger."

Fahy could have done the surgery he was proposing. So could another doctor in London he recommended. But for obvious reasons, Woods wanted to return home and not be stuck overseas. Hence, the need for a different recommendation, which led Woods to Dr. Richard Guyer, the spinal surgeon outside of Dallas, who had more than thirty years in the field.

The surgery was scheduled for April 17, barely two weeks later. Nobody knew. In fact, Woods attended a news conference near Branson, Missouri, in conjunction with a design project he had at the nearby Big Cedar Lodge. While there, he answered several questions about his future, never once letting on that the next day he'd be under the care of Guyer.

While a spinal fusion is a common procedure, it's not a simple one. It requires a lengthy recovery, and it is not conducive to swinging a golf club at a high rate of speed.

Although due to privacy reasons Guyer could not speak specifically about Woods' surgery, the doctor was clearly a fan. Woods' team named him in news releases about the surgery. Guyer was picked due to some impressive credentials, including cofounding the Texas Back Institute along with Dr. Stephen Hochschuler, now retired, who said, "Tiger's people really did their due diligence."

"I have always believed in Tiger," Guyer says. "If anyone could do this, it was him. His ability to will himself is really amazing, and that has nothing to do with his spinal fusion. He's just a remarkable example of someone who has unbelievable will."

Part of Guyer's work has involved convincing patients that they can have a normal life after a fusion surgery, as well as convincing insurance companies of the need to cover the procedures.

While they might appear drastic for athletes, especially golfers, spinal fusions are actually quite common, in practice for more than fifty years. They are performed in various ways, some more invasive than others.

Officially Woods' procedure was called an anterior lumbar interbody fusion, in which an incision is made through the belly button. The disk that had been giving him so much trouble was removed, and a bone graft and screws helped bring the bones together, ultimately "fusing" them over time.

Whether Woods expressed any trepidation is unclear.

"Everybody is different," Hochschuler says. "The procedure can be done in many different ways. Where society is going is minimally invasive surgery. Outpatient surgery. People want to go outside the hospital because there is less bureaucracy.

"In terms of doing a fusion, one of the questions you ask [of a doctor] is how many of these have you done? I always for forty-five years would say to you I'd get a second opinion. It never hurts. Treat the patient the way you'd want to be treated. Make it simple. This is what we do, this is how we do it. So they can understand it and ask a question. When they meet with you, they're nervous. Write down your questions. And if you do and go home, call back. But write down your questions."

Hochschuler says that a majority of patients do not need spinal fusion surgery, and that they should try everything possible first: "Rehab, physical therapy—trying to deal with it," he says. "But you have to be realistic. We happen to be surgeons, not plumbers."

So how many of these procedures has Guyer done? "Probably two or three a week," Hochschuler says. "Over a lot of years. So that's thousands."

It would seem Woods was in good hands.

SCORES OF GOLFERS HAVE ENDURED BACK PROBLEMS OVER the years, but few have had surgery that dealt with the spine and returned to any high level of success. Retief Goosen, the two-time U.S. Open champion, had a degenerated disk (L3-L4, higher up on the spine than where Woods had trouble) and elected to have disk replacement surgery in 2012. Although he said afterward that the surgery "has given me a second life," he did not win again on the PGA or European tours.

Dudley Hart, who starred at the University of Florida before turning pro, won twice before his back issues really began to hamper him, at the 1996 Bell Canadian Open and the 2000 Honda Classic.

Not only did he have his own spinal fusion surgery—he had two of them.

When he was considering his options due to back and nerve pain, Hart was told by several doctors that he should quit golf. "That's not something I wanted to hear when you're not qualified to do anything else in life," he quipped.

His trouble began in 2000, when he was on a golf trip in Ireland prior to playing The Open at St. Andrews. He ended up withdrawing from the championship during the third round and had issues on and off for the next several years, finally figuring enough was enough after limping through the 2009 Masters.

"I had a herniated disk and I was having the worst pain I ever had," he says. "I finally went and saw a doctor, and I didn't have any disk left—basically bone on bone. I went and saw three or four more doctors, and two of them told me I should stop playing golf."

Hart had the spinal fusion surgery in 2009, although he said it did not work. When he was still having issues two years later, he consulted with another doctor, who determined that the bone had not properly fused.

Like Woods, Hart was dealing with an issue with the lowest lumbar vertebrae (L5) and the highest vertebrae in the sacrum (S1). The fusion removes the disk, and then fuses the bones together with screws.

Hart's second surgeon discovered two screws that were not attached.

"And so I started the process all over again," he says, having the second surgery performed in 2012 after playing no tournaments over two seasons.

"After that surgery, to be honest, I could tell a difference in pain immediately upon waking up compared to the first one," Hart says. "But it took a long time. I was told I couldn't do anything for six months, except walk. No working out. No lifting. No chipping. No twisting. They want it to grow and they want to be careful. Then after that you start the rehab process."

Despite all the setbacks, Hart managed to earn more than $12 million in official prize money, had fifty-five top-10 finishes, and when he turned 50, was able to play on the PGA Tour Champions circuit.

"For me, once I started the physical therapy part, it was kind of trial and error," Hart says. "Not sure anybody who had a lower back fusion had tried to come back and play. If you tear your ACL, there's a protocol. That is what I struggled with the most, trying to find out what I needed to do to get back where I needed to. Is yoga good? Is Pilates good? Some things worked, some things didn't. I don't think there is a manual for a professional golfer after a back fusion.

"I don't think your back is ever the same. I don't have a ton of painful days. But every day is uncomfortable to some degree. It doesn't necessarily hurt to swing, but you just know it's not always normal. I had a day recently where I felt like I could make about a half backswing and that was it. It wasn't painful. There are just days where you don't move as well."

PERHAPS THE PLAYER WHO CAN SPEAK TO WOODS' PLIGHT BEST is Greg Owen. The English pro who competed on the PGA Tour and European Tours also had a spinal fusion—performed by Guyer.

"Without Dr. Guyer, I'd be mostly crippled right now," Owen says. "That's a slight exaggeration. But I owe everything to him."

Owen was back trying to compete in senior golf in 2023 after some twenty years of dealing with back issues and a career that saw him win three professional tournaments.

"In 2004, I just won my first big tournament," he says, "the British Masters in 2003 on the European Tour. Everything was going great. Best part of my life, the best time. I was practicing and hit a shot and basically collapsed. Tried to stretch it out. Tried to work it out. I thought by the end of the week it had gotten better.

"But I was home on that Saturday and I picked up my daughter and I felt this little twinge in my lower back and two hours later I couldn't move. I had a ruptured disk trapped in the spinal column. I had injections—needed surgery. And in May of 2004 I had a microdiscectomy.

"But I was losing muscle. My left leg was withering away. There was nerve damage. I was quite happy with the surgery, but I rushed the rehab. We didn't have quite the facilities in the U.K. that we have here in the U.S., and I just wanted to get back playing.

"So I was playing in the Memorial and I remember hobbling off the last green. A lot of people trying to get autographs. And I could barely stand up. I was nearly in tears. Things got worse and worse. I saw chiropractors, physios, therapists, trainers. I was literally just managing the pain and putting up with it for years.

"I actually sat down with Tiger at one of the [FedEx Cup] playoff events for lunch and asked him for some advice. What needs to be done? . . . It just got to the point where practice was no fun. And enough was enough."

Owen consulted with several doctors and teams. Some suggested just doing therapy. "I was really at a loss, really getting down," he says.

Finally someone at the PGA Tour, Owen said, gave him Guyer's number. The year was 2018, when Woods was in the midst of his comeback. So Owen went to Dallas.

"He was the only surgeon who said let's figure out exactly what is wrong," Owen says. "We'll come up with a plan for what needs to be done."

Owen's surgery took place in January of 2019. A day later he was up and about. But it was far from easy. "I was at home a week later in tears, wondering if I had done the right thing," he says. "It was painful."

Like Woods, Owen was told to be patient, to not extend himself, and certainly to stay away from swinging a golf club.

"I felt like it was my last chance for having a normal kind of life, never mind playing golf," Owen says. "I didn't want to mess this up. I just didn't want that nagging, lingering ache anymore. If I was sitting still or standing still for more than three or four minutes, it would just become unbearable. It was awful. And since I couldn't play or practice properly, that turned into mental problems as well. It got very frustrating. I just didn't see any light at the end of the tunnel."

Sound familiar? Woods used those same words to describe his plight late in 2015.

But after the surgery and a period of recovery, "I had gone from being totally defeated to optimistic," he says. "Now there's nothing I feel I can't do. I used to struggle to tie my shoelaces. It's night and day."

Owen says it took him nine months before he could hit full shots, a longer period than that endured by Woods, who reported about six. But Owen was determined to be careful. And he marvels at what Woods did afterward.

"I knew Dr. Guyer had worked on Tiger before my surgery, so I figured if Tiger is going to see him, who am I to argue with that? He's got the contacts and finances to go to the best people for whatever he needs," Owen says.

"But you can't get your head around winning a major after it. Playing and competing, yes. But to actually win a major after all the things he's been through on top of that? He just took it in stride. I'm amazed at what he did. What he does for the game of golf. What he continues to do. And after what he's been through. A different human being than me, that's for sure."

Hochschuler, too, was impressed.

"It's amazing," he says. "I'm sure Rick [Guyer] did not guarantee him he'd get back. He probably said there is a chance you'll get back. Tiger was treated properly, and he had amazing results. Part of it is Tiger's own discipline. Following the rehab. Doing the right things. It's a combination of all that. Could another surgeon have gotten him to where he is? I'm sure that's true.

"But he's lucky he's found Guyer. He's the whole package. It's unbelievable what Tiger has done. Unbelievable. He had the right surgery at the right time by the right doctor who treated the whole person."

Still, in April of 2017, there were no guarantees. Woods reported immediate relief, but he had said similar things after previous surgeries, only to have golf set him back.

And then he had humiliation to overcome. A mere six weeks after the surgery, Woods made headlines. Bad ones. Headlines that would lead to ridicule and all manner of scrutiny.

On May 29, 2017, Woods was asleep at the wheel of his car in the early-morning hours of Memorial Day. Driving a black 2015 Mercedes-Benz AMG S65, Woods had come to rest on the side of a road called Military Trail, less than 10 miles from his Jupiter, Florida, home. It is unclear how he ended up there, and no reports surfaced of him being out that night. Speculation centered on the possibility that he was "sleepwalking"—and given what was discovered to be in his system, it's a good if unconfirmed guess.

The driver's-side front and rear tires were flat, the rims damaged. So was the front bumper, which had scrape marks, according to the police report. No other vehicles were involved.

The first instinct was to believe that Woods was intoxicated, but lab reports would later show he had no alcohol in his system. He did, however, have enough prescription medication to cause him to fall asleep at the wheel, and possibly do further damage had he not been so fortunate.

Woods struggled to get out of his car, and he told the officer who questioned him that he was in Los Angeles, on his way to Orange County. His speech was slurred, and he nearly fell.

There was a twelve-page police report. And there was police video that made its way onto YouTube. It was not pretty. A toxicology report released nearly three months later reported he had painkillers, sleep drugs, and an ingredient active in marijuana in his body.

The five different drugs that were traced in his system were: hydrocodone, an opioid pain medication; hydromorphone, another type of painkiller; alprazolam, an anxiety drug whose brand name is Xanax; zolpidem, a sleep drug, brand name Ambien; and delta-9 carboxy THC, which is found in marijuana.

Weeks before the report was released, Woods announced he would take part in a rehabilitation program.

"I'm not at liberty to say where he is, but he is receiving inpatient treatment," Mark Steinberg, Woods' agent, said at the time. "Tiger has been dealing with so much pain physically. And that leads to insomnia and sleep issues. This has been going on for a long time."

The difficulties Woods endured during those years led to quality-of-life issues. He was in constant pain. He had difficulty engaging with his kids. Golf was nearly impossible. There was a lot going on.

When he was arrested, Woods failed multiple field sobriety tests, but he blew a 0.00 on a breathalyzer after being taken into custody.

"Was the night in question a tipping point?" Steinberg said. "He's now gone and checked himself into a facility . . . He's been in pain for so long. He's had to handle the pain which then potentially leads to the lack of sleep because you're in so much pain."

Woods agreed to enter a diversion program that allowed his charge of driving under the influence to be dropped later in the year; he also pleaded guilty to a lesser charge of reckless driving.

And it was yet one more issue to overcome, physical as well as mental.

But if it were not for the spinal fusion surgery performed by Guyer—and for Hellman's steering Woods in that direction—who knows if even Tiger's immense drive would have been enough to overcome what he faced.

9

The Comeback

The spinal fusion caught the golf world by surprise. Like nearly everything with Tiger Woods, nobody outside of his closest friends, family, and advisors was aware that he was even having any sort of medical procedure, let alone one as serious and possibly career-ending as the operation to fuse his spine.

Golf was secondary at this point. . . . It was all about relief. Woods had been in pain for so long and had endured so many setbacks that figuring out a way to live peacefully and productively was the goal.

A few years earlier, as Woods neared his 40th birthday, he gave a rare glimpse into his personal struggles in a *Time* magazine interview. This was a period after three microdiscectomies in which he still struggled to find comfort and acknowledged the idea that his career might be done.

Woods has a practice facility in his backyard at his South Florida home, and he described how one day he was hitting flop shots over a bunker. Something he did set off the nerve issues and caused a sudden rush of pain in the area of his lower back. Woods fell to the ground. He could not get up.

And there was nobody around.

Without a phone, Woods could not call for help. Yelling out would do him no good on such a vast piece of property. Woods lay there, helpless, unsure what to do next.

He needed his 8-year-old daughter, Sam, to come to the rescue. Sam was born in June of 2007, just a day after Woods narrowly missed a playoff with Angel Cabrera at the U.S. Open. Had Woods tied Cabrera that day at Oakmont Country Club, he would have been involved in an 18-hole playoff around the time Sam was born.

"Daddy, what are you doing lying on the ground?" she said upon finding him.

"Sam, thank goodness you're here," Woods said. "Can you go tell the guys inside to try and get the cart out, to help me back up?"

"What's wrong?" she said.

"My back's not doing very good."

"Again?"

"Yes, again, Sam."

That was just a single moment, and Woods shared very few of them. How many more were there? How many times did Woods, behind the scenes, out of sight, away from a golf course, go through such agony?

Now here he was less than two years later, the same issues having plagued him to the point that he'd resorted to a last-ditch surgery. When it was over, everyone pronounced it a success. But don't they always do that?

So a few months went by without a public word from Woods. There was the very public Memorial Day scene just miles from his home where he was found by police by the roadside, having fallen asleep behind the wheel of his car, a bevy of painkilling drugs in his system. But aside from that, nothing.

He finally emerged at the Presidents Cup, where he was an assistant captain for Steve Stricker at Liberty National in Jersey City,

New Jersey. It was there that during a pre-tournament news conference Woods shared a rather ominous outlook.

"I don't know what my future holds for me," he said.

The week prior, Woods had released a lengthy statement in which he said he had started hitting 60-yard shots but was not yet cleared to hit full shots due to the limitations still in place. He was nearing the six-month mark since the surgery.

"Overall, I'm very optimistic how I'm progressing," he said. "Like I said, the pain's gone, but I don't know what my golfing body is going to be like because I haven't hit a golf shot yet. So that's going to take time to figure that out and figure out what my capabilities are going forward. And there's no rush."

Woods—who had downplayed any issues when he withdrew earlier in the year from the Dubai event—acknowledged that he was in considerable pain that day and continued to be as he hoped to make a return at the Masters before ultimately deciding on surgery.

"I've been out of the game for a while," he said. "First things first: Get my health organized, make sure the pain goes away. Then, basically, just as I said, just keep waiting for what my surgeon says. I've given you guys the updates on what I can do as I progress, and that's all I'm doing.

"I'm still training. I'm getting stronger. But I certainly don't have my golf muscles trained, because obviously I'm not doing anything golf-related."

Asked why he wanted to return given all he'd accomplished, Woods said: "I think it's fun. I've been competing in golf tournaments since I was, what, four years old. From pitch, putt, and drive to playing major championships, it's always been fun for me."

What he did not discuss was the May incident that occurred

roughly six weeks after the surgery. It was but one more issue that he had to overcome on his way back to competitive golf.

WOODS REPORTED FEELING BETTER IN THE DAYS AND WEEKS after the surgery, but he would actually have to get worse before he could move forward. Who knows what led to all manner of medication being in his system and being found asleep in his car on the side of the road on May 29, 2017? Was it the pain from the spinal fusion? The previous issues with the back? The personal issues that led to his divorce all those years later? The stress of being Tiger Woods?

It wasn't long before Woods resumed his recovery process from the surgery. He did not discuss the guilty plea for reckless driving during his brief media interactions at the Presidents Cup, and soon after that, he began posting photos and video on Twitter of him swinging a club or hitting a shot. It wasn't much, but it piqued considerable interest nonetheless.

Woods said that when Dr. Richard Guyer gave him permission to finally hit driver shots after his spine had been fused six months earlier, the first ones he hit carried barely 90 yards. "I was a little bit apprehensive," Woods said.

Soon he was putting those fears behind him. Woods was again digging deep, figuring out a way, plotting his return—one that nobody could have ever seen coming.

After he emerged at the Presidents Cup, his next event was the Hero World Challenge in the Bahamas, where he once again used his foundation's event as an opportunity to gauge his game in a low-pressure situation.

And each step of the way, Woods showed more promise than expected, to the point where in just his fourth official event, he contended.

For the better part of an hour during the second round of the 2018 Valspar Championship, Woods' name graced the top of a golf tournament leaderboard. Alone. All by himself. It's where he always used to be, and where many never expected to see him again.

A week prior? A month prior? A year prior?

How about the previous September, when he told everyone at the Presidents Cup that he was uncertain about his golf career? It was difficult to envision at any of those points Woods being in this position, on this day, so soon afterward.

And so it was that on a Friday morning, Woods faced a 5-footer on the 5th hole (his 14th of the day) on the Copperhead course at the Innisbrook Resort in Palm Harbor, Florida. He rolled it in for a birdie to take the outright lead.

A final-hole bogey (his only one of the day) knocked him off that perch and into a tie, but no matter how it ended for him, Woods leading a golf tournament just four events and twelve rounds into a never-assured comeback was a surprise even for him.

"Could I have envisioned myself being here? No," he said. "My surgeon told me I was fused. If I'm not fused, this is a totally different game. Am I going to feel what I did for the last four, five years? Or am I going to be like this?"

"Like this" is showing signs of the previous version of Tiger Woods. The powerful tee shots. The sharp short game. The clutch putting.

All of that had been missing for most of the previous four years as Woods underwent the three microdiscectomy procedures to deal with a disk issue in his lower back and the spinal fusion that—remarkably—was just eleven months in his past.

To that point, Woods had played just sixteen rounds of competitive golf, including the four in the Bahamas at the unofficial Hero World Challenge. When there was fear he might not break

80 for a time, the highest score he had shot was the 76 in the second round of the Genesis Open, where he missed the cut three weeks previously.

He had shot five rounds in the 60s, three of them in the Bahamas, but managed to stay around par for all but three rounds.

When making the cut was a reasonable goal at the Farmers Insurance Open, he tied for 23rd. He regressed at Riviera a bit, the eight-hole stretch to end the second round a matter of not trusting his swing and being unable to save himself with his short game.

The Honda Classic seemed a risk, with all the water and sand dotting the PGA National in Palm Beach Gardens course not far from his home, but Woods saw himself as a weekend contender, although he missed a playoff by eight strokes and ended up finishing twelfth.

The decision to add the Valspar Championship at the last minute proved to be beneficial, the extra rounds of competition he was seeking turning into a chance to be in contention. He beat Jordan Spieth by nine shots and Henrik Stenson by ten through 36 holes—and those two guys were the last two Open champions.

"I left that Sunday at [Valspar]," says Brandt Snedeker, who played with Woods in the final round. "I was like, 'He's got every opportunity to win the Masters.' There were a few bad shots due to rust. But the way he flighted the golf ball, he was working it both ways with his irons. I was really impressed with everything he was doing.

"He got up to the 18th hole and had to make a birdie to tie. He hit a beautiful 2-iron down the middle. His iron shot [approach] came up a little short, but man, I thought, 'He's back.'

"What people don't realize when Tiger was playing his best, he always hit the proper golf shot under the most intense circumstances. Like when he got to 12 Sunday at the Masters [in 2019]. He was able to hit it over that bunker on the left side of the green.

That's when you know you're in control of what you're doing. Not going at that pin. And that's what I saw in Tampa [at the Valspar] that Sunday."

A few cringeworthy moments occurred in each tournament, including a first-round brush with a pine tree—Woods slammed his forearm into the tree trunk—and an instance during the second round when he aggressively went after a shot out of the rough on the 18th hole.

The Tiger of the past few years simply could not do that. His body would not allow it. The signs of distress were often there, no more so than the hobbling gait in Dubai just more than a year earlier. Thinking of that image of Woods, and then to see him at that point near the lead of a golf tournament, was simply remarkable. Dubai was the picture of a hobbling old man; Valspar was a confident, vibrant golfer who projected not an ounce of vulnerability.

"I am not surprised one bit," says Sean Foley, Woods' former coach, who worked with him from 2010 through 2014. "After the Hero, I was very optimistic. Very glad for him. He is Tiger Woods, so good play is never surprising."

In the end, Woods came up short. Two and a half feet short, to be exact. But who in their most positive moments could have ever envisioned Woods coming to the 72nd hole of a golf tournament at this point in his comeback with a chance to win the Valspar Championship?

Woods' birdie putt on the 18th hole from nearly 40 feet stopped short—a theme throughout the day—and left him a stroke shy of Englishman Paul Casey, who fired a final-round 65 to claim his second PGA Tour title in addition to thirteen European Tour wins.

Casey sat in the clubhouse while Woods and Patrick Reed still had a chance to tie him, and it was Reed who faltered with a bogey while Woods could not muster the birdie he needed.

"I was close," Woods said after a final-round 70 left him in a tie for second, his best finish since he'd tied for 10th at the 2015 Wyndham Championship. "I had a chance today. Unfortunately, I just didn't quite feel as sharp as I needed to with my irons, played a little conservative because of it.

"I just needed to handle the par-5s a little better. Missed a short one there on four for par. Should have two-putted fourteen. I know that was a long putt, but I was trying to leave it below the hole. I overdid it. I missed it."

IT WAS REMARKABLE TO THINK THAT WOODS WAS GETTING IN the weeds with his golf just four tournaments into his comeback. In many ways, it seemed like old times. Talking about cleaning up the par-5s. Chipping better. Hitting more fairways. The highs and lows of tournament golf. Just like everyone else, dissecting various aspects of his round. It was a jolt to the game to have him back, and clearly Woods enjoyed being in the mix.

For perhaps the first time in his career, Woods was learning what he meant to people who'd followed him for so many years, and he appreciated having another chance. He had made the game look so easy—it clearly wasn't, but he made it appear that way—and now he seized more upon the ideas that time might be short and showing himself to be a more mortal figure on the golf course.

Woods seemed to take more time with people. He was more engaging with fans, with media, certainly with fellow players. But though maybe some of the edge was off, certainly the competitiveness was not. That still simmered like it always did. The difference now was that he could live with the results better, smile when things went awry, and maybe actually swing a golf club without the maddening discomfort that had plagued him for the better part of four years.

Woods followed his tie for second at the Valspar with a tie for fifth at the Arnold Palmer Invitational—where he was announced, surprisingly, as the captain of the 2019 U.S. Presidents Cup team. And he briefly fought his way into contention during the final round before pumping a tee shot out of bounds on the 16th hole.

Those two results probably raised expectations higher than was realistic. It was still just five events—although with three top-12s.

That meant enormous hype heading to Augusta National, where Woods had not played since 2015. And it was simply too much to ask for Woods to go after a fifth green jacket that week. Woods was never really in it, tying for 32nd.

Over the next couple of months, he showed flashes of his old self, but he never really got into serious back-nine contention. He tied for 11th at the Memorial but missed the cut at the U.S. Open. He had the crowd roaring all weekend at the Quicken Loans National, a tournament he then hosted, as he tied for fourth in Bethesda, Maryland—but he was still eight shots back of winner Francesco Molinari.

And it was Molinari whom Woods would see a few weeks later in Scotland.

The Open was back at Carnoustie, the brutish links that had claimed so many victims over the years. Woods had played the tournament in 1999, the year Jean Van de Velde imploded, finishing tied for seventh with a score of 10 over par—four shots out of the playoff. When the event returned in 2007, he tied for 12th and was never really in the tournament, which was won by Padraig Harrington.

After missing the previous two Opens, you could forgive Woods if he was just happy to be there, but clearly it was about more than that. With his name atop the leaderboard, Woods reached into the past for the magic that had been missing for so long, a push to a major title that even he at times wondered if it was possible.

And for a time, he led on Sunday, carnage occurring all around him, his two early birdies and some deft par saves putting him in position for a fifteenth major championship.

But the golf gods did not comply, and Woods was unable to sustain what would have been one of golf's all-time tales, his major hopes derailed by the long, rough fescue on one of the hardest links in the world.

Woods settled for a final-round 71 and finished three strokes behind Molinari—with whom he played the final round—ending up in a tie for sixth.

A consolation was moving to 50th in the world for the first time since January of 2015 and qualifying for the WGC-Bridgestone Invitational two weeks later.

"A little ticked off at myself for sure," said Woods, who held the lead alone when he stood on the 11th tee. "I had a chance starting the back nine to do something, and I didn't do it. I thought nine [under] would be the number.

"Next thing, lo and behold, I'm tied for the lead, and then I'm leading it."

But Woods, who led the field in driving accuracy through three rounds, misfired with a 3-iron off the tee at the par-4 11th.

Playing from tall, wispy rough, he experienced what many do when finding that type of grass on a links: It grabbed the shaft, his clubface closed, and his approach sailed well left of the green.

The ball bounded into spectators, and actually caromed back toward the green. But Woods was behind a bunker, tried to cut it too close with a flop shot, and missed the green. He ended up with a deflating double bogey that knocked him out of the lead. And then followed it with another missed fairway with an iron at the 12th, leading to a crushing bogey.

There was plenty of room to debate his strategy. Another club off the tee? Pitching back to the fairway instead of going for the green? Playing a safe shot from behind the eleventh green?

But Woods would not go there, saying, "I did everything the way I thought I needed to do it to win the championship. There were a bunch of guys with a chance to win, and I was one of them."

Woods began the final round three strokes behind Jordan Spieth, Xander Schauffele, and Kevin Kisner. Amazingly, all three of those players made double bogeys over the first seven holes. Spieth, the defending champion, shot 76 to drop to a tie for ninth. Schauffele ended up in a tie for second, two shots back of Molinari, as did Kisner.

It was Molinari who didn't make a mistake, shooting a final-round 69 and playing the final thirty-seven holes of the tournament without a bogey.

Woods was there for all of it, and it's a tribute to Molinari that he did not flinch in the presence of one of the game's most popular—and followed—players.

"It was a blast," Woods said. "I was saying earlier that I need to try and keep it in perspective, because the beginning of the year, if they'd have said you're playing The Open Championship, I would have said I'd be very lucky to do that.

"I talked to Serena [Williams, the week prior at Wimbledon]. I'm sure she'll probably call me and talk to me about it, because you've got to put things in perspective. She just had a baby and lost the Wimbledon finals. Just keep it in perspective.

"I know it's going to sting for a little bit here, but given where I was to where I'm at now . . . blessed."

Woods had not played The Open since missing the cut at St. Andrews in 2015. This was just his ninth major championship in the last four years. He tied for 32nd at the Masters and missed the cut at the U.S. Open but now had six top-12 finishes in as many events.

When he birdied the 14th hole Sunday, that gave him an outside chance at getting back into the tournament, as he trailed by just two. But the closing holes are treacherous, and despite flinching on a tee shot at the 18th due to a spectator bellowing in his backswing, he managed to give himself a 5-footer for birdie, which he missed.

As it turned out, that birdie would have just briefly brought him to within one shot—as Molinari made his putt for birdie to seal the tournament.

"It didn't feel any different," Woods said. "It didn't feel any different to be next to the lead and knowing what I needed to do. I've done it so many different ways. It felt great to be part of the mix and build my way into the championship. Today was a day I had a great opportunity."

Bidding to win his fifteenth major forty years removed from Jack Nicklaus' doing the same thing in 1978 at St. Andrews, Woods had not been in such a position in years. The three-shot final-round deficit was his closest to the lead in a major since the 2013 Open at Muirfield, where he was two back but tied for 6th. Also that year he tied for 4th at the Masters.

As it turned out, he was not done.

IT WAS A SWELTERING WEEK IN ST. LOUIS FOR THE PGA CHAMPIONSHIP, and Woods waited near the scoring area after posting his best final round in a major, ready to offer congratulations to the winner, Brooks Koepka—the man he could not reel in that day at Bellerive Country Club.

Koepka won his second major championship of the year, and

though Woods finished second, for the ninth time in a major, it was hard not to view the fourteen-time major champion in a positive light after he'd stirred the masses to the verge of hysteria.

"I could hear it," Koepka said with a smile as Woods hugged him afterward, acknowledging just how boisterous it was up ahead as Woods was making eight birdies in a round of 64.

It didn't bring a fifteenth major championship, and you could certainly quibble about the lost opportunities along the way. But when you consider that 64 was Woods' lowest final round in his eightieth major championship, and that his score of 266 was his lowest 72-hole total, it was an impressive performance.

Gary Woodland, who played with Woods in the final round, saw it up close.

"The ball flight—he controls it," Woodland said. "The putter was awesome. He hit a lot of good putts that didn't go in as well. Sixty-four, and it looked pretty easy to be honest with you.

"The energy in the crowd—that was as big a crowd as I've seen and to play in front of, and he just kind of ho-hummed a sixty-four there. I think he could have shot a lot better than he did."

Woods struggled off the tee, however, making the score all the more remarkable. He didn't hit a single fairway—0 for 7—on the front nine but still made four birdies and shot 32, his 9-iron from just off the cart back at the ninth hole to 10 feet for a birdie among his more remarkable feats.

"I didn't drive it good all day," said Woods, who hit just five of 14 fairways and 12 of 18 greens. "I was struggling with my golf swing. I warmed up hitting it left; I was hitting it right with every single club; even my sand wedge I wasn't doing very good. So I knew this was going to be a struggle to try and piece together a round, and I did."

Despite missing the fairway at the first, Woods hit his approach to 7 feet—and missed the birdie putt. But he stuffed iron shots to 4 and 2 feet at the next two holes, then after a bogey at the sixth he birdied the eighth and ninth and for a time was within one shot of Koepka.

Woods finally found his first fairway at the 10th, left a birdie putt on the lip at the 11th, then birdied the 12th and 13th holes with approaches inside 10 feet. A bogey at the 14th was the result of a missed fairway, but he rebounded with a birdie at the 15th.

If Woods was going to have a chance, he had to have a birdie at the 17th but again he couldn't find the fairway, nearly knocking his drive into a creek that borders the right side, from where he was only able to advance the ball 60 yards. Woods had to get up and down from a bunker to save par.

But at the 18th, he nailed his tee shot 320 yards, knocked his approach to 19 feet, and made the putt, giving a fist pump and getting a huge ovation as he left the course and walked across a bridge to the scoring area.

Joe LaCava, his caddie, noticed the emotion, the fire.

"It's been a while, to be honest with you," he said. "Even in '13—when he won five times, player of the year—there weren't a lot of fist pumps. I think from all the hard work he's put in, he's starting to reward himself, so to speak. He's pretty pumped for himself. He's put in a lot of hard work."

Woods was happy to get that closing birdie, knowing that he needed to at least tie Adam Scott and give himself an outside chance, which he realized was unlikely.

"I posted [minus] fourteen, and that meant he [Koepka] would have to shoot something in the sixties. He couldn't make a bunch of pars and win the golf tournament. He went out there and made a bunch of birdies."

Woods had played fourteen tournaments in 2018 and made a remarkable rise. When he began the season at Torrey Pines that

January, he was ranked 656th in the world. He had moved up to 27th. He was also 20th in FedEx Cup points, meaning he was a lock for the first three FedEx Cup playoff events and in good position to make the Tour Championship for the top 30.

He needed a victory to move into the top eight automatic qualifiers for the U.S. Ryder Cup team, but still moved to 11th and was all but certain to get one of captain Jim Furyk's at-large picks.

A year prior, Woods had yet to begin swinging a golf club due to the spinal fusion surgery. When he was an assistant captain for Steve Stricker at the Presidents Cup, he noted that he was only hitting chip shots.

Now he had contended at two major championships, and posted five top-10 finishes and moved back among the top 30 in the world.

"This has been a process on building," he said. "I didn't know when I was going to start this year and how many tournaments I was going to play, how well I was going to play. I didn't know what swing I was going to use, either. I'm in uncharted territory. Because no one's ever had a fused spine hitting it like I'm hitting it.

"So I had to kind of figure this out on my own, and it's been really hard—it's a lot harder than people think. And I'm just very pleased at what I've done so far, and now to be part of the Ryder Cup conversation, going from where I've come from to now in the last year, it's been pretty cool."

BY NEARLY EVERY MEASURE, WOODS' COMEBACK WAS A ROUSing success. He finished second at the Valspar Championship. He contended at two majors. He gave himself chances. And if he was in pain, Woods did not let on. Remarkably, a year-plus removed from the spinal fusion surgery meant to improve his quality of life but which provided no golf guarantees, he was playing among the best in the world.

The only thing left was to win, and it had been a long time since Woods' name finished atop a leaderboard. That happened to be five years prior, in 2013, at the WGC-Bridgestone Invitational, his seventy-ninth PGA Tour victory.

His eightieth was on the way.

10

The Coronation

The clubhouse at East Lake Golf Club in Atlanta is a shrine to Bobby Jones, the great amateur golfer who honed his game at the Georgia club, accumulating numerous trophies, prizes, mementos, and photographs, many of which adorn the walls and hallways.

But in September of 2018, it became Tiger's place.

Tommy Fleetwood was among several peers standing on a rooftop off the locker room from that clubhouse, witnesses to a bit of history before their eyes. Woods was strolling toward the eighteenth green, thousands of spectators rushing behind him, ropes and security and officials helpless to do anything about the spontaneous celebration that was taking place.

Woods still had a few more shots to play, but it was obvious he was about to accomplish what just a few months earlier would have seemed preposterous: that eightieth PGA Tour victory.

"It was special," Fleetwood says. "Just very, very special. A special moment in golf, a special moment in sport. And we were all out to watch it. An incredible comeback. It's just one of those moments where you stand back and watch it and be grateful to be there to witness it. It was amazing. Those scenes will be played for a long, long time."

The coronation was a long time coming for Woods, given all he had been through. Woods had started 2018 in San Diego with little idea how the year would unfold, with hardly anyone believing it could go as successfully as it did. Even without a victory he was, remarkably, ranked 20th in the FedEx Cup standings heading to the season-ending event.

Despite an opening-hole bogey, Woods got off to a great start, shooting a first-round 65 that included an eagle at the last hole. It tied him with Rickie Fowler atop the leaderboard. He played with Fleetwood during that first round.

"I remember it quite well," Fleetwood says. "I went on Twitter afterward and said something like, 'Tiger Woods is good at golf.' It was my most liked tweet ever.

"He was clearly back, playing really, really well. I had played with him a few times that year and his iron play had been really great. It's always been about if he puts it in play, he's still the best iron player in the world. And he was driving it in play. He was hitting his fades in play, he was confident, playing great. You could tell that week he had it going for sure."

Paired with Fowler in the second round, Woods added a 68 to his opening-round 65 to complete 36 holes tied for the lead with Justin Rose, who shot 66–67. Rose was coming off consecutive runner-up finishes in the FedEx playoffs—he had lost in a playoff at the BMW Championship—and had risen to No. 1 in the world.

In the third round, Woods got off to a hot start, and it wasn't until late that Rose was able to close the gap, shooting a 68 that left him three strokes back after Woods shot 65.

"The crowds were electric because of it," Rose says. "He was running the tables there. He was hitting good shots and making the conversion putts."

SOMETHING SPECIAL WAS UPON US. WOODS WAS IN THE LEAD and victory, finally, seemed near. But it had been five years. A long, hard five years. Nothing was a given at this point.

And the chaos that constantly surrounds him can never be overstated, an incessant combination of cheers, chatter, and combustion that follows him from green to tee, down the fairway, and onto the green, only the moments during shots providing peace.

It was fair to wonder again how Woods could manage to deal with it, such is the level of noise and distraction that dots his golf world, sometimes at earsplitting levels that even the greatest of minds would have difficulty pushing aside.

But there he was during that third round, doing it again while leading a golf tournament and dealing with an old, but new, set of emotions, that elusive eightieth victory just 18 holes away.

For so long, and in so many instances, that story could have already been written, with just the mundane details to fill it out. Woods was money with third-round leads, especially of three shots or more. He had never failed to deliver to that point, thirty-two times going on to victory when in that position.

His overall record of 53–4 on the PGA Tour with at least a tie for the lead was mind-blowing in and of itself. Imagine getting to that position fifty-seven times. The first one? Way back in 1996, when as a 20-year-old making his third start as a pro, Woods led by one, only to get beat by an aging veteran named Ed Fiori, who possessed a strange grip and who to this day Woods still refers to as "The Gripper."

Woods' last blown lead after that was perhaps his most crushing loss, a shot at a fifteenth major, denied at the 2009 PGA Championship by Y. E. Yang—who never won on the PGA Tour again.

That was likely a reminder to Woods that nothing is certain, especially at that point. As much as he had done that year, posting six top-10s in a comeback season that defied belief, Woods still struggled to put four complete rounds together, and simply had not been in this good of a position.

How would he handle it?

"I felt very comfortable when I got in the mix there at Tampa [the Valspar Championship] even though it was very early in the start to this year," Woods said after the third round in Atlanta. "And because of that, I felt comfortable when I got to Bay Hill, when I grabbed the lead at The Open Championship.

"Things didn't really feel abnormal, even though it's been years, literally years since I've been in those spots. But I think I've been in those spots enough times that muscle memory . . . I guess I remembered it, and I felt comfortable in those spots."

Woods sure looked it on that Saturday, when it might have been easy to get caught up in all the hysteria. He birdied the first hole, then ran off five in a row starting at the third. He made it look simple, and you wondered if Sunday was just going to be the coronation to that long-awaited victory.

Of course, it was never going to be such a stroll. A bogey at the ninth followed. Another at the 16th. He was unable to birdie the par-5 18th, despite an excellent approach that just traveled too long into a back bunker.

Rory McIlroy was paired with Woods for the final day, and there was the feeling that a good bit of killer instinct would help him play the foil. A four-time major winner, McIlroy, 29, had played with Woods just once in a final round, back at the 2012 Masters when both were well out of contention.

Rose showed his resolve after opening with consecutive bogeys, then rallying to shoot 68 to stay in touch with Woods. He'd seen plenty of the fourteen-time major champion of the year and was just as curious as the rest of us as to how it would play out.

"I'm sure it will be hard for him tomorrow," Rose said. "It will probably be for him, trying to win for the first time again. It's been a long time. But he has so much experience to draw on that he's going to be a hard guy to chase down tomorrow."

Woods was in a familiar spot, but it was a long, arduous path back. Throughout the year, even after shooting an opening-round 62 two weeks prior at the BMW Championship, Woods found himself trailing heading into the weekend, fighting to get in contention.

There had been some good play and some solid chances, but aside from the Valspar Championship, where he was just a stroke back going into the final round and couldn't make up that difference, it had mostly been a matter of trying to prevail from too far back.

"You certainly want to be leading regardless—simple mathematics—but he's been a pretty good front-runner his whole career and obviously that's going to help," said Woods' caddie, Joe LaCava. "In the past he's been chasing, chasing, chasing, and people want him to win so badly and he gets close, but you have to remember there are people behind him who are capable of going low.

"It'll be nice to know that everybody will be in front of us for a change. That will help a little bit. But he's got two great players behind him. I'm not saying it's going to be a piece of cake. But you'd rather be leading by three than be three behind."

McIlroy and Rose didn't promise to make it easy. Both were more than capable of putting together the low round that would ruin Woods' plans.

But it was always likely to be more about Woods. How would he deal with the cauldron, that one he handled with so much ease for all those many years? It was a different time, a different Tiger.

AND YET A LOT OF DOUBTS WERE PUT TO REST QUICKLY. WOODS birdied the first hole to stretch his lead to four strokes, a daylong celebration commencing. In much the same manner he'd won numerous titles over the years, Woods played smart, methodical golf, eliminating mistakes while letting the others falter.

His lead was never less than two strokes, and it only got that close at the 16th hole, with Billy Horschel already in the clubhouse. An important par-save from over the green at the 17th allowed Woods to play the par-5 18th with a freedom that let the raucous scene unfold.

"I was very happy for him," said McIlroy, who shot a final-round 74 and was well out of it over the closing holes, settling for a tie for seventh. "I feel like the whole scene coming down eighteen was pretty cool, and I definitely took that in, and I realized what it meant for golf and what it meant for the people. It was obviously a great moment for golf, and good to be a part of."

At times, the situation looked a bit dangerous, fans scurrying for position, walking fast and sometimes running for position, with nowhere near the number of security personnel and tournament officials needed to hold them back. Woods took it all in stride, but McIlroy saw fit to scurry ahead, as did LaCava.

Woods had hit his second shot into a greenside bunker, and his only concern at that point was to play it onto the green to assure victory.

"After Tiger hit his approach shot to the front of the green, as he and Rory made their way around the lake, fans engulfed them, and I said to myself, 'This isn't supposed to be happening,'" says PGA Tour commissioner Jay Monahan, who was to the right of the green looking back toward the tee.

"I walked down the fairway towards them, and it was one of the coolest and most natural responses to a championship moment in our sport that I'd ever seen. I kept on thinking to myself, 'This is really cool to be here, to know all of what Tiger had gone through, to get himself in contention throughout the course of the year and be in position to win the final event of the year.' Like everyone else, I was happy I was there."

For Woods, the victory was as satisfying as any in his career. For the first time in five years, he had won again. And he'd beaten back the likes of McIlroy and Rose to do it. If he never won again, Woods could have happily and understandably gone out with that incredible memory, the fans swarming him as he traversed the final hole.

"I was pretty emotional when Rory was tapping out, he was finishing out," Woods said. "I looked around and the tournament was over. I'd won eighty. Eighty is a big number."

Another big number awaited him.

11

The Admirers

Among the many traits that Tiger Woods has possessed throughout the bulk of his career is the ability to intimidate his opponents. He's done nothing on purpose to perpetuate the advantage, but he's done nothing to dissipate it, either. Woods knows that you know that he knows that his aura means something. And it can make it hard to play with him or against him.

Think about it. You're in contention and Woods' name is on the leaderboard. You know you have to try to beat him, but how do you do it? The name has elicited such respect that there's often a misguided notion that you have to play perfect golf to beat him.

In truth, Woods has not always played perfect golf himself. But he's been a master at managing his game and letting others make the mistakes. The belief that an opponent has to play without error has undoubtedly led to more issues. It's impossible to be so precise at golf; trying to be so meticulous means even more pressure. And in trying to keep up with Woods, it simply plays right into his strengths.

"So many guys who say, 'I don't have that,' meaning they couldn't hit the kind of shots Tiger did," says longtime TV analyst David

Feherty. "But they felt they had to try. And sometimes that led to mistakes. In trying to catch Tiger, they fell further behind."

It's one of the reasons Woods is so good with a 54-hole lead. Before South Korea's Y. E. Yang came from two strokes back in the final round of the 2009 PGA Championship at Hazeltine in Minnesota to win, Woods had been a remarkable 14-for-14 in such situations. He got out in front and didn't let anyone beat him. It spoke to his ability to navigate and plot his way around a golf course with an advantage, forcing others to catch him. It worked nearly every time.

Woods' record in that category is just as impressive in overall tournaments on the PGA Tour, where he is 54–4 in such situations and 43–2 with an outright 54-hole advantage.

For years, Woods' counterparts have struggled with the various ways in which they've had to deal with him. Vijay Singh, Ernie Els, Phil Mickelson, Retief Goosen, and any number of his contemporaries were good enough and accomplished enough to beat him several times. They are all in the World Golf Hall of Fame. But they have also played in an era where they've seen him win a majority of the encounters and gotten beat up pretty good trying to make their mark.

But as Woods has suffered through injuries, this mindset has slowly begun to change. Tiger still has an incredible presence and throughout his struggles has remained a world-class iron player. And yet, he's shown vulnerabilities. He's proved that he, too, can make mistakes. The chipping problems in 2015 come straight to mind. So do the issues with getting the ball in play off the tee at various junctures. Woods' short game has become less reliable, his putting far more ordinary.

And so he's become less intimidating. At least to those who for years have struggled with the idea of trying to beat him.

And this became another aspect to Woods' return in 2018. The focus was understandably on his ability to recover from serious surgery and put his game back together. But would Tiger be different? Less intimidating? More approachable? Just as intimidating?

The younger generation of players didn't have the scar tissue of getting beat up by Woods. They hadn't suffered through his greatness. They emerged while Woods was either out with injury or barely playing. And many had grown up watching him and idolizing him. They were in grade school or high school or maybe even younger when Woods was racking up all those major wins, scoring records, and the like. For some, it's the reason they took up the game. And the idea of getting to compete with him was inspiring.

For many, they were in awe. And it didn't much matter that they might feel inferior or be intimidated. The idea of getting paired with him or even just getting to meet him was a cool career objective.

ON A SWELTERING SUMMER DAY THAT SAW HIM SWEAT THROUGH a couple of golf shirts, Woods emerged from the scoring area to a scene he has encountered hundreds of times in his career: fans screaming his name at the top of their lungs, imploring him for an autograph, a photo, a golf glove, a ball.

Woods headed toward a group of people waiting for him and posed for photos, shook a few hands, signed a few autographs.

He was doing it all for Bronson Burgoon, who with his family was waiting for Woods—after just having played with him. Burgoon at the time was a PGA Tour player whom Woods likely could not have identified in a lineup.

Burgoon played with Woods during the final round of the Quicken Loans National in Bethesda, Maryland, in early July of 2018.

While that development might seem a bit odd, it was one that played out several times as Woods saw his comeback mesmerize not just golf fans, but fellow competitors who were just as thrilled to see him back—and play with him.

"My generation grew up watching him," says Burgoon, who was in his third full season on the PGA Tour at the time. "When he came on the scene, he was the young guy and beating everyone's brains in. Now it's different. We're getting to play with a guy we idolized growing up. It's different than one of his contemporaries. We were all watching him break records we thought would never have been possible. It's a different feeling. I think he understands that. He was more than gracious to take pictures and talk with my wife, my caddie. He was so cool about it."

When Woods emerged as a force, the phenomenon was often referred to as "Tiger Mania." In many ways, that returned in 2018, as many were genuinely stoked he was back and enjoying the moment. A rock star–like scene greeted him nearly every step of the way.

Who knew a bunch of young players in the game would be just as on board with the hysteria?

"It just means I'm old," Woods says. "I've been around the tour for the better part of twenty-five years now, so I've been out here a while. That's one of the neat things about our sport: It can cross so many different generations.

"I remember playing with Jack [Nicklaus] in his final PGA [Championship], and he said he played with Gene Sarazen in his final PGA. You don't get to hear that in any other sport. We cross so many different generations, and this is one of them." (Woods played the first two rounds of the 2000 PGA Championship with Nicklaus, who was playing it for the final time. In 1972, Sarazen played in his last PGA and withdrew after a first-round 79, having played with Nicklaus.)

So keen was Burgoon on wanting to play with Woods that he

nervously watched the scores come in on that Saturday afternoon, figuring that a Bill Haas birdie on the final hole would set up such a scenario based on the scoreboard.

"And my heart sank because [Haas] had a wedge in his hand, tugged it, and dropped the club in the middle of the fairway," Burgoon says. "Then he knocked in about a 40-footer, and I swear, I was so happy. I thought it was fantastic. I wasn't going to be afraid of the moment. What a cool opportunity. Just embrace it and have some fun with it."

Burgoon did, shooting a final-round 67 to finish tied for sixth—his first career top-10 on the PGA Tour while playing alongside Woods.

Not only did that round give Burgoon a boost of confidence (he would have a career-best runner-up result at the John Deere Classic just two weeks later), but he came away with a strong appreciation for what Woods endures every time he plays, as well as a learning experience that would help him in the future.

"I know that the moment is not going to get any bigger than that," he says. "That is as big as I'm ever going to see in terms of people. Even if I'm in the final group at a major, I'm not going to see as many people as I saw that day. It was a ton. My brother flew out to watch, and he had to hang out a hole behind. It was crazy.

"It's kind of cool, because he elevates your adrenaline. Sometimes out here, you're finishing up late, fans have left. You can get a little complacent. No way you can do that in that environment. It was electric. The hair actually stood up on my arm on the first tee. He started walking and everyone on the hill started cheering. And I thought, 'Here we go.'"

It was one of several occasions where Woods ended up being paired with a player he otherwise might not have known. Between him and caddie Joe LaCava, there had to be some googling occurring prior to several first-tee meetings.

From Sam Burns at the Honda Classic to Brandon Harkins at the Wells Fargo Championship to Mackenzie Hughes at the Players Championship to Joel Dahmen and Burgoon at the Quicken Loans to Shaun Norris at The Open to Austin Cook at the Northern Trust to Cody Gribble and Peter Malnati at the Genesis Invitational in 2019, Woods saw no shortage of unfamiliar faces—many of whom were mere kids when he was dominating the game.

Back then, Woods was not much for small talk on the golf course, especially among his so-called rivals. But these encounters showed a softer side, one where he was more willing to engage with his peers, recognizing that many of these younger players were truly ecstatic over the opportunity to play with him.

"It was like a dream come true," says Dahmen, who was in his third full season on the PGA Tour and played with Woods during the third round of the Quicken Loans. "That night [before] was kind of wild. Didn't sleep well. Thought about what I was going to say to him. Should I come up with some jokes? I was kind of stunned, basically.

"I was probably as nervous as I've ever been on that first tee. Walking from the putting green to the tee and I got out there before he did and it was loud. And when I walked through, it got louder and louder. It was the coolest moment. It was crazy.

"He teed off and then the mob ran off after the golf ball. I made sure I got my tee in the ground as quick as I could so I didn't have anybody watching that. And I swung as hard as I could. It took me a few holes to settle down."

During that round, Woods at one point birdied four consecutive holes to get into contention. Dahmen said he tried to take it all in.

"My caddie [Geno Bonnalie] was standing right next to me on the green, and he yells, 'This is fucking awesome!' Screamed it, right next to me. Nobody could hear it. The roar was so loud. We were just laughing. To be in that moment with him was incredible."

Even a few years later, the memory brought a smile to Dahmen's face, and he said playing with Woods helped his career.

"I remember shaking. I could barely get the ball on the tee," Dahmen says. "But I remember thinking if I could play in front of that, I could play in any environment. I played really well after that result. It helped me. And you can look at my career on the PGA Tour and it was straight up since then.

"Sam Burns did the same thing. Beat him at the Honda in the last round. Nobody knew who he was. And you look at these little moments. A lot of these nobodies play with Tiger and ended up playing well right after."

Burns had the presence of mind to try to break the ice, walking off the first tee with Woods at the Honda Classic during the final round and quipping, "Can you believe all these people are here to see me?"

"It was a very cool day, something I'll always look back on and be thankful it happened," says Burns, who was a year old when Woods won his first Masters in 1997.

Hughes was paired with Woods at the Players Championship in 2018, where Woods had made the cut on the number, then went out early Saturday and began piling up birdies on his way to a 65.

"I know it's ninety degrees," Hughes, 28, said that day. "But I can assure you, for me it was goose bumps and shivers out there hearing all the noise and playing with him."

These types of pairings happen based on scores after the first two rounds, when Woods is typically grouped with other major champions or highly ranked players.

Groupings are done in tiers, with major winners and multiple tournament winners put together, followed by regular PGA Tour members, and then qualifying school grads, sponsor exemptions, and Monday qualifiers.

So a player such as the relatively unknown Cook, who in 2018 was in just his second season, would need some good fortune—and relatively decent scores—to get paired with Woods.

It finally happened at the Northern Trust for the final round, and "when I saw the message come through that I was paired with him, I had to take a deep breath," Cook says. "I knew I'd be nervous.

"I was going to be teeing off in front of the guy I had always looked up to, my idol on the golf course. I will always remember that.

"He was a really nice guy. He answered my questions, started some conversations, never big-dogged me, and for a guy in his position, I understand. It was pretty cool."

And it was just as much of a thrill for Cook's caddie, Kip Henley, a veteran who had never been in Woods' group.

"I was like a kid in a candy store playing with him the first time," Henley says. "I spent eleven years with Brian Gay, and he wanted no part of playing with Tiger. I always thought that was funny, and as far as I know I don't think he ever has, and he's been on tour for twenty-plus years."

Henley has worked for a slew of players who'd never got grouped with Woods to that point when he was with them: Eric Axley, Boo Weekley, Vijay Singh, Jeff Overton.

"I have always just been a huge Tiger fan," Henley says. "He was awesome to go out with and very considerate of us and he was as cool as I had hoped he would be. He knew me and my little brother Brent were loopers [caddies] and has always been nice to us, but pinning him down on a conversation is very tough unless you're in his group, because so many people want a piece of his time."

A few common themes from those who were asked about Woods was that they were not surprised he won again.

And, of course, there were the moments in which Woods' full talents were on display. Even for professional golfers who are used to doing what the rest of us cannot fathom—and who are not typically impressed by others who play the game—the wonder at seeing Woods up close was inspiring.

From the sound of his shots to the flight of his ball to the way he hit his irons . . . even mishits were applauded, as was his ability to simply think his way around a course.

"Nobody hits their irons like he does," Burgoon says. "Nobody. It was so unbelievable. The sound his irons make is so much different than the sound other people's irons make. And that's not to say that other people aren't good ball strikers.

"It's just different. I don't know how to describe it . . . just different."

"His irons are unbelievable," Dahmen says. "He was hitting at pins that would be dumb for me to go after. All of them were just so incredible. Moved it different ways. All landed in the right spot. Not many people have that. Obviously he's one of the few who ever had that."

WHEN WOODS RETURNED IN 2022 TO THE MASTERS JUST MORE than a year removed from the car crash, many were trying to wrap their heads around the idea that he was playing in the tournament.

He ended up playing just nine official rounds of golf with just nine different players. Joaquin Niemann, who played the first two rounds with Woods at the Masters, could not have been more impressed, especially under the circumstances. "It was amazing, some of the shots he hit," Niemann said. "He's still got it."

Perhaps that was a bit optimistic. Certainly Woods' performance was impressive. But a cold morning greeted the competitors for the third round on Saturday, and Woods was understandably running out of energy. The more he walked, the worse it got, leading to his worst round ever as a pro at Augusta National: a 78. He did it again on Sunday, but playing alongside Jon Rahm, the reigning U.S. Open champion, who was born with a clubfoot and had to learn to swing differently because of it.

"We see the reality afterwards that the cameras don't see," says Rahm, who would go on to join Woods as a Masters winner in 2023. "He puts on a bit of a show for the camera, like he's not going to show how much he's really hurting. When we finished scoring, just seeing him stand up and move around that room when there's nobody watching, there's a difference, especially after playing eighteen holes and after sitting down; when your legs cool off a little bit, it changes.

"It's really inspiring. How many surgeries has he had where he was written off? He was done, he's not playing again . . . He's not only come back but won tournaments, right? It seems right now that we might be reaching that point, but I don't put anything past him. He surprised me before, and he surprised a lot of people before."

Woods returned again when he was not expected to at the 2023 Genesis Invitational. It was nearly two years to the day from the car crash that occurred just a few miles away from Riviera Country Club in suburban Los Angeles, site of the tournament.

As tournament host, Woods was going to be there anyway—just as he had been in 2021 in the days leading up to the crash. But he dearly wanted to play. The tournament benefits Woods' foundation, the one he founded in 1999 along with his father. While the event was likely to do just fine without him, having him compete is always an added boost.

Woods opened the tournament with a 69—his first competitive

round in seven months. He hung on to make the cut. Shot a third-round 67. Then struggled in the final round. It was all inevitable. But Kramer Hickok was duly impressed.

A former college golfer at the University of Texas, Hickok was 30 years old and had never played with Woods. He marveled at how accommodating the famous golfer was—and how good his game looked under the circumstances.

"I think it's unbelievable he's doing what he's doing," Hickok says. "I saw him leaving the clubhouse [the night prior] and he was limping pretty good. The work just to get up walking is a lot . . . Being able to walk up and down these hills and hitting golf shots—it's insane. Just to be out here and playing again shows his heart and determination.

"And he hits all the shots. Some parts of his game are rusty, sure. But you can see him plot his way around the course. He's thinking where to hit it and not hitting it in some of the places I did. I really watched to see how he did that. And hitting all the shots. Amazing experience.

"But he's still got so much game. I wouldn't be surprised if he wins again this year."

Perhaps Hickok was analyzing Woods with his heart and not his head. Nonetheless, he was not alone. Woods has had numerous admirers throughout his various comebacks, and the sentiment to see him succeed has always been strong.

It was far different from the early days, when pros who competed against Woods had sometimes had enough of him. Now, the appreciation was real. So was the realization that what he was doing—even if he didn't win—was simply another example of his greatness.

Many of them now were among his biggest fans. And as the 2019 Masters played out, those not trying to beat him—and even some of those who were—were offering up cheers.

12

The Speech

Tiger Woods pulled into the parking lot at the Savannah Rapids Pavilion without an entourage, arriving early at the banquet hall that rests on a wooded bluff 80 feet above the Savannah River in Martinez, Georgia, six miles from the home of the Masters, where a day later he would begin his pursuit of the most unlikely triumph.

Woods had driven alone—he often insists on driving, no matter whom he's with—from his Augusta, Georgia, rental home, pulled into a random parking space, and was greeted by a couple of Columbia County police officers, who had easy duty protecting him from invisible stalkers. One of the most famous people in the world strolled seamlessly toward the facility, like any random person might, bothered by no one and eventually greeted by a few friendly people who escorted him to the building.

Within the next 30 minutes, Woods—on the eve of the 2019 Masters—would be receiving an honor for which nobody wants to be eligible.

At another point in time, Tiger might have seen this as folly. The great Tiger Woods—who trained unlike any other golfer, who put in hours upon hours in the gym, running on the hot Florida pavement, hitting balls at sunrise and again at sundown—was not the player who would one day be honored for overcoming pain and injury simply in order to return to his sport.

And yet, that is exactly what was about to unfold.

The following morning Woods would make his twenty-second appearance in the world's most famous golf tournament, and at age 43, fourteen years removed from his fourth and most recent victory at Augusta National, there was still doubt he would ever be physically or mentally equipped to win his fifth green jacket.

Woods had seriously contended at The Open Championship and PGA Championship the previous summer, nearly ending his ten-year drought in the major championships, and he had won his eightieth PGA Tour title just a few hours down the road the previous September at the Tour Championship in Atlanta, his first victory of any kind in more than five years and one that produced an iconic scene, with dozens upon hundreds of spectators swarming behind him as he played the final hole, victory secure.

But from his earliest days of accumulating trophies, Woods' mission became the major championships, and Jack Nicklaus' record of eighteen titles. As much as Woods believed he had proved something to himself and a slew of doubters at the Tour Championship, he knew he had yet to win a tournament that really mattered—at least one that mattered beyond the realm of tour golf. And the one, of course, that mattered the most.

Woods played his first major as a pro at the Masters in 1997, winning by 12 shots and orbiting golf into the mainstream at a place that had admitted its first Black member only seven years prior. Opened in 1932, the dream of the great amateur golfer Bobby Jones, Augusta National became home to an iconic tournament despite an uncomfortable backdrop that hovered like humidity as its stature grew: The club's caddies and laborers were almost exclusively Black, while the members and players were as white as the course's famously pristine sand.

The Masters did not invite the first Black player to compete until Lee Elder in 1975, and Augusta National did not invite its first Black member until 1990, in the wake of a scandal at Shoal Creek in Alabama (venue for that year's PGA Championship) that prompted all of golf's governing bodies and tournaments to make membership diversity a prerequisite for hosting events. TV executive Ron Townsend—who would later moderate many of Woods' interviews in the Augusta National media center—became that first member more than four decades after Jackie Robinson broke baseball's color barrier and thirty-six years after *Brown v. Board of Education* rendered segregation in schools unconstitutional.

So it was that as Woods traversed the grounds, the club's minority waitstaff emerged from the two-story clubhouse (it had been built more than a century earlier, when the land was used as an indigo plantation) and looked on in wonder as Woods, then 21, became the first man of color to win the Masters, shattering the tournament scoring record in the process, nearly fifty years to the day Robinson made his major league debut for the Brooklyn Dodgers.

The victory emphatically announced the arrival of a global superstar, a golfer known well outside of his sport who would perhaps become the most recognizable face on earth. He would dominate the game like no one had ever seen, putting together winning streaks in regular events and knocking off major championships at a pace to rival Nicklaus', accumulating fourteen in an eleven-year-plus span that had prognosticators wondering when, not if, the record would be broken.

But it was Woods who would be broken first. The late author Dan Jenkins, of *Sports Illustrated* and *Golf Digest* fame, had once said that the only things that could slow Woods down would be "a bad marriage or a bad back." And he turned out to be plenty prophetic. A personal scandal that led to divorce evoked a mental toll that resulted in Woods' not winning for two years. But injuries were just as debilitating, and it wasn't just his back.

Initially it was replacement ACL surgery on his right knee, knocking him out of action for eight months in the aftermath of one of his greatest victories, the 2008 U.S. Open. Then came the infidelity scandal that cost him his marriage, his good name, his corporate endorsements, and his aura of invincibility. Then more crippling injuries piled on, his body betraying him again, leaving him bedridden and unable to play golf, just yearning to walk and play with his young children after three failed back procedures.

A desperate back surgery was recommended, a final hope to save his golf career but even more so to save his chance at a quality of life. Woods was no longer thinking about Nicklaus' records; he was just hoping to be able to enjoy his years as an elder statesman, just like the Golden Bear. Less than a month into life after another surgery in April 2017, Woods was found asleep in his car by Jupiter, Florida, police, who released embarrassing roadside video of the disoriented golfer mumbling and stumbling, his problems again playing out in front of the world. A rehab stint followed, with hopes of breaking an addiction to painkillers, not long after Woods had confided in a few fellow Masters champions at their annual Augusta National dinner that his career was over.

Just to attend that dinner, Woods needed a painkilling shot so he could walk up the stairs in the Augusta National clubhouse. But somehow, the spinal fusion surgery he had just a few weeks later allowed Woods to return to competition in 2018 and arrive at the Masters describing himself as a "walking miracle." Woods stunned everyone, including himself, with how consistently he played throughout 2018. By his fourth tournament, he was already contending, finishing second at the Valspar Championship, followed later by those close calls in the majors and the victory at the Tour Championship and a spot on the U.S. Ryder Cup team.

That comeback season earned him the Ben Hogan Award from the Golf Writers Association of America (GWAA) and a trip to the banquet on the Savannah River that would serve as good karma preceding the most memorable days of his golf life.

Wearing a blue sports coat over a black shirt, Woods posed for a few photos with various attendees, chatted easily with GWAA's Player of the Year and swaggering major championship force who defeated him at the PGA, Brooks Koepka, and even made small talk with a few media folks he had sometimes disdained and always kept at stiff-arm distance. He sat at a corner table with his longtime agent, Mark Steinberg, and public relations man, Glenn Greenspan, and a small group of writers, and watched the large screen nearby as a video tribute to Koepka's season played to the song "Unstoppable" by The Score. Koepka received his award, said thanks, spoke for a total of 53 seconds, then headed for the door to prepare for the Masters.

For whatever reason, even though he wasn't teeing off until 2 p.m. the next day, Koepka didn't stick around to watch and listen as the next award recipient, Woods, delivered his acceptance speech. It was an opportunity missed for Koepka, who admired Woods growing up and might have gleaned something from the greatest player of his generation. While the move was curious, it is only fair to point out that a younger version of Woods would have undoubtedly done the same thing.

But the old Tiger wasn't this Tiger, as three hundred writers, broadcasters, golf officials, former players, and corporate executives were about to find out. As is its custom, the GWAA makes video tributes to its Player of the Year winners, with other award recipients introduced with a verbal presentation. Woods had been honored ten times as Player of the Year previously, and apparently had gotten used to watching those highlights.

As a longtime Woods observer and GWAA member, I was

asked to introduce Tiger, giving a bit of background on the Hogan award as well as outlining several of the reasons why Tiger had been voted the recipient and recapping his dire injury situation. Then I called him to the stage. Tiger adjusted the podium microphone upward and asked, "How come I didn't get a video? . . . I got Bob Harig."

The audience laughed heartily at Tiger's dig, and Woods delivered like it was the 2000 U.S. Open, with no video necessary. He confirmed that he thought he was indeed done as a golfer two years earlier, and dropped a previously unknown nugget that he had flown to London to meet with medical consultants, who suggested that spinal fusion surgery was his only hope. Woods spoke of the operation performed by Dr. Richard Guyer—for the first time acknowledging him publicly by name—in Texas, and how the spinal fusion allowed him to walk again, to take his kids to school, to watch their soccer games. "I was able to participate in life," Tiger said.

The packed room barely made a sound. Woods had spent his entire dynastic prime with an invisible "Do Not Disturb" sign hanging from his neck, not letting anyone get too close. There had been times when he relished giving the shortest of answers to media inquiries, feeling the less conversation the better. And yet here he was opening a vein, making himself human, showing his vulnerabilities in a speech that was being taped before hundreds of strangers.

Woods recalled that, at one point during his recovery, Guyer gave him the go-ahead to begin swinging the longest club in his bag. The first time Woods hit the driver, he said, "It carried maybe ninety yards." Woods told the audience that practice rounds with the likes of Justin Thomas, Rickie Fowler, and Dustin Johnson near his South Florida home hastened his comeback, and he thanked his younger peers for their patience and kindness in preparing him to beat them after he returned to competition.

But Woods stunned everyone in the room when he talked about the media. "As I've come back and started playing again and being part of the game of golf at this elite level," he said, "and to see all of you, all the writers that have followed me, and have written some really nice articles and really supported me and have given me great words over the past year, I can't thank you enough."

Giving praise to the media was shocking enough, but Woods kept going. He said he was honored to win an award named after Hogan, who famously came back from a serious auto accident that nearly claimed his life in 1949 to win six major championships, including the 1950 U.S. Open. And then he returned to what had typically been among his least favorite subjects: the fourth estate.

"To all the golf writers who voted for me to be a part of this award, and for all the hard work and dedication that all of you have shown over the years—promoting the game, growing the game—we are so thankful to have all of you here."

Tiger then praised another award winner in the crowd, Johnny Miller, the Hall of Fame golfer who had been something of a broadcasting thorn to Woods at times during his tenure in the booth. He recognized longtime Associated Press golf writer Doug Ferguson, who was receiving a lifetime achievement award. "There are very special people in this room," Woods said. "And I'm so honored to be here. Thank you very much."

Woods delivered his speech, which lasted 5 minutes and 15 seconds, without notes, and the banquet room applauded as if he had just birdied his way through Amen Corner. He stepped from the stage, posed for a few photos, shook some more hands, and then headed off to prepare for his first-round tee time the next morning.

The general reaction: What did we just see and hear?

Woods came across as likeable, relatable. Shockingly so. Praising, and even thanking, the media had been far outside his realm.

Miller, during his own acceptance speech, lauded Woods for his graciousness. Geoff Ogilvy, the 2006 U.S. Open champion who was getting an award for his good relationship with the media, took notice. So did Dave Kindred, one of America's longtime distinguished sports columnists, who said, "Tiger was so good tonight, I take back everything I wrote about him."

Woods' agent, Steinberg, whispered to a reporter, "He really is a changed man." Woods, betrayed by his body, had been humbled, and he responded by opening up and letting people in. For the bulk of his comeback, he had been making more eye contact than he ever had with fans in the galleries, acknowledging their cheers.

"I don't think there's any doubt about it," says his caddie, Joe LaCava. "He has made a strong effort to connect more, to smile more." Tiger had become more willing to sign autographs, and to slap hands with kids, and to spend quality locker-room time with his peers. He was no longer the terminator in red, looking only to step on necks and walk to the next tee.

Could a kinder, gentler Tiger actually win a Masters Tournament he hadn't won in fourteen years? Did his concessions to humanity dull the jagged edge Woods seemingly required to win a major championship? Deep down, Woods did not know the answers to those questions as he stepped to the first tee at Augusta National on Thursday, April 11. He did not know if he was capable of doing precisely what he would go on to do—author one of the most incredible sports stories ever told.

13

THE 12TH

The bonefish had stopped biting, but Jack Nicklaus was getting antsy anyway. He knew the Masters was nearing the back nine and was curious about how it was playing out. And given the Golden Bear's seemingly eternal link to the legend who was contending, Jack was keen to see if Tiger Woods would finally knock off another major championship on his way to his record eighteen.

Since he'd last competed in the Masters in 2005 at age 65, Nicklaus had gotten into a routine of heading on a fishing trip during the tournament weekend with his wife, Barbara, and longtime friends Billy and Cindi Bone. Nicklaus attended the Champions Dinner on Tuesday night, played in the Par 3 Contest on Wednesday, and—since 2010—helped kick off the tournament early Thursday morning with a ceremonial tee shot, now with Gary Player and Tom Watson.

Afterward, Nicklaus typically conducted a multitude of interviews, then headed home to Florida and spent the weekend on the water. This time, it was Ambergris Cay off the Bahamas, and by early Sunday afternoon, Nicklaus had directed his skiff back to his 112-foot yacht, *Sea Bear*, where, while still on the high seas, he could observe the major championship he once owned.

"I watched it from the boat" is how Nicklaus described the crucial moments of the 2019 Masters.

And he almost couldn't believe his eyes.

"When the guys started filling up Rae's Creek on the 12th hole, I'm watching them one after another hit the ball right of the bunker, and I said, 'Really?' You just can't hit the ball right of the bunker," Nicklaus says. "How many times have you seen the tournament lost because they hit it right of the bunker?"

Nicklaus would undoubtedly know. He played in the Masters a remarkable forty-five consecutive years, dating to his days as an amateur. He won the tournament in 1963, 1965, 1966, 1972, 1975, and 1986 at age 46 when he said he "caught lightning in a bottle."

The 12th hole might have cost Nicklaus another green jacket in 1981, when he made a double bogey there and lost to Watson by two. He also bogeyed it on that emotional day in '86, the mistake lighting a fuse that ignited a sizzling back-nine 30 and final-round 65.

Years earlier, when Nicklaus was a long-bombing force in his 20s who began to dominate the game like no other, Augusta National founder and acclaimed amateur Bobby Jones famously said that Jack "played a game with which I am not familiar." Nicklaus always appreciated the compliment, and it meant even more to him because his dad, Charlie, idolized Jones, who had won the 1926 U.S. Open at Scioto Country Club in Columbus, Ohio—where Jack learned the game and heard all manner of Jones stories throughout his youth.

In 1964, as the defending champion and playing alongside Arnold Palmer, Nicklaus reached the 12th tee and noticed Jones and Augusta National cofounder Clifford Roberts sitting in a golf cart to the front and right of the tee. He proceeded to shank his shot right over their heads.

"It went so far right it didn't even go in the water," Nicklaus says. "I usually don't remember bad shots, but I couldn't forget that one."

NICKLAUS MORE THAN ANYONE IS AWARE OF THE OLD AXIOM AT the Masters: Never aim for the Sunday pin. It is perched tantalizingly on the right side of the green, the farthest point from the tee. But because the shot is hit on an angle toward the flagstick, anything that comes up short of the pin—even on the front portion of the green—almost certainly rolls back into Rae's Creek, the body of water that fronts the green.

Masters history is filled with Sunday contenders whose hopes drowned in that creek, and just as he tuned in from his yacht, Nicklaus saw Ian Poulter find the water in the group ahead of Woods, as well as Brooks Koepka—who would finish second by a shot.

There is no theater in golf quite like the one at the 12th. The tee box is roped off from the gallery, thousands of whom are perched in grandstands behind or standing on a hill, craning to see play on the eleventh green. The echoes of their cheers can be heard acres away, all the way up to the clubhouse or on other holes on the back nine. Certain applause or groans are discernible to the trained ear at Augusta National. And when Woods walked from the eleventh green to the 12th tee, he was greeted with teeth-chattering cheering.

Francesco Molinari, who had recovered from nearly every mistake he made to this point, stepped to the tee, leading Woods by two strokes—and promptly hit his ball in the water, too, eliciting some muffled cheers from spectators, who were heavily in Woods' favor. As Nicklaus noted, it was a mind-numbing mistake at the most crucial time. Tony Finau, also in contention, deposited his ball in that same body of water.

"I can tell you, I didn't leave my chair," Nicklaus says. "Tiger hit the ball, and of course he had a little cut shot over the left side of the bunker into the middle of the green. And the tournament is over."

Pressed on this, Nicklaus insisted he knew Woods would win at that point. And while it is undoubtedly where the momentum turned, there was still a tough par to make, and a six-hole stretch to the clubhouse with plenty of twists and turns.

But the 12th is where Woods found himself tied for the lead. Finally.

Inspired by a jazz song, author Herbert Warren Wind coined the phrase "Amen Corner" for the intersection of the eleventh green, 12th hole, and 13th tee at Augusta National following the 1958 Masters, won by Palmer, in Wind's account of the tournament for *Sports Illustrated*.

The song—"Shoutin' in at That Amen Corner" (which Wind years later recounted incorrectly for *Golf Digest* with the wrong name of the song)—only partially described the scene. It was full-on screaming and cheering, spectators aware something special was occurring, as Woods was now in position for the most unlikely of victories.

Through various missteps by his opponents and solid, measured play by the veteran Woods, the tournament had turned, and Nicklaus predicted how it would end. "That little stretch there I knew was the tournament," Nicklaus says. "That was the turning point."

MOLINARI STRUCK HIS SHOT POORLY, AND IT CAME UP SHORT and rolled back into the water. A few feet to the left, and it likely would have been in a bunker that fronts the green. From the sand, Molinari was unlikely to make more than a bogey-4 and still would have had a chance to save a par. Instead he made a double-bogey 5.

Woods never thought about the flagstick. He wanted something to get him over the bunker, in the middle of the green.

"That's all I was concentrating on," Woods said. "I had forty-seven [147 yards] over the first tongue in the bunker there, and so my number, I was hitting it fifty and just being committed to hitting it fifty. There's a reason why. I saw Brooksy ended up short. Poults ended up short as well. So when I was up there on the tee box and it was my turn to go, I could feel that wind puff up a bit. Brooksy is stronger than I am, and he flights it better than I do, so I'm sure he hit 9-iron and didn't make it."

(These comments from Woods came immediately after the round, and how he knew what Brooks Koepka hit—he was playing in the group preceding him—is just part of the way Tiger's mind operates.)

"So I knew my 9-iron couldn't cover the flag, so I had to play left, and I said just be committed, hit it over that tongue in that bunker. Let's get out of here and let's go handle the par-5s. And I did. Yeah, that mistake Francesco made there let a ton of guys back into the tournament, myself included."

Woods' shot ventured a bit farther left than he would have preferred, but it was safe. While Molinari and Finau were figuring out where to drop for their third shots, Woods walked across the famed Hogan Bridge to the left of the green alongside caddie Joe LaCava sensing opportunity.

The twelfth green is that rare spot in golf where you are all alone and yet still within the gaze of millions of eyeballs. There are the spectators preening from 150 to 200 yards away, their stare penetrating every moment. And, too, there are those watching on television around the world. But because of the distance, there is a slight delay in any reaction to what occurs on the green. A putt followed by strange silence, to be followed by an eruption.

Woods stalked the putt as Molinari and Finau figured to have trouble navigating a treacherous chip shot over Rae's Creek and to the pin. While a bogey was still possible for both players, any slip ends the tournament for them, too. As Jordan Spieth proved just three years earlier in 2016, chunking his third into the water—and as Woods did himself in 2020, when he made his highest score ever at Augusta National, a 10 during the final round at No. 12—that pitch is no easy task.

That is why sometimes players will elect to play farther back than would seem necessary. The turf is so tight that making proper contact is essential. And yet, trying to be so fine as to clip it just right, landing it in the correct spot, keeping it from coming up short and in the water while also guarding against hitting it too far to such a narrow green—well, there's a reason why Nicklaus long ago described it as the most difficult short hole in championship golf.

Molinari was in a daze. He'd looked invincible for so long. Truth was, his ball-striking was not up to his previous standards. He scrambled to make a bunch of unlikely pars. And it finally caught up with him at the worst possible time with that shot to the 12th.

"Just bad execution," says Molinari, who dueled Woods only nine months earlier at The Open in Carnoustie, Scotland—watching Woods blink first as the Italian prevailed to win the Claret Jug. This time, it was he who made the crucial mistake.

"I think we picked the right shot and just didn't hit it hard enough—as simple as that. And it was a tough day and with the wind gusting . . . I think I just had a couple of mental lapses on the back nine that were costly."

Hitting first, Molinari did not have the advantage of seeing how other shots reacted.

"I was trying to hit a chippy eight-iron," he says. "It was probably a nine-iron yardage, but I didn't want the wind to gust and to get the ball too much and I just didn't hit it hard enough."

Molinari had been on a strong run for the better part of a year. Eleven months earlier, he captured the BMW PGA Championship, the flagship event of the European Tour. In his next start, he finished second at the Italian Open. On the PGA Tour, he won the Quicken Loans National outside of Washington, D.C.—with Woods presenting him the trophy as host of the event.

After a tie for second at the John Deere Classic, Molinari traveled overnight to Scotland to prepare for The Open—where he found himself grouped with Woods in the final round, only his family on his side.

Woods briefly shared the lead on the back nine at the famed Scottish course, but could not avoid the crucial errors. Molinari never flinched, playing the final round without a bogey and knocking his approach shot stiff at the 18th hole for a satisfying final birdie and a two-shot victory over Justin Rose, Rory McIlroy, Kevin Kisner, and Xander Schauffele.

A missed short birdie putt on the 18th denied Woods a share of second and he settled for a tie for sixth, three shots back of Molinari. It was a bittersweet day for Tiger, whose kids, Sam and Charlie, were in attendance, the first time they could witness their dad in contention at a major championship.

Molinari, meanwhile, finished the year ranked seventh in the world. A month prior to the Masters, he won the Arnold Palmer Invitational, shooting a final-round 64 to win by two. He finished third at the WGC-Dell Technologies Match Play Championship.

And so it was no surprise to see Molinari right there again at Augusta National with rounds of 70, 67, and 66 to get in the final group with Woods and Finau.

And despite the double bogey at the 12th, Molinari was still tied for the lead with Woods. And he was still tied after both birdied the 13th hole. A costly mistake at the par-5 15th, where he missed the fairway and then hit a poor layup shot, led to another double bogey. And his tournament was over.

FINAU WAS STILL A FEW MONTHS SHY OF HIS 30TH BIRTHDAY, playing in just his second Masters. But nobody was surprised to see him near the top. Although he had just a single PGA Tour victory—and in a weak-field opposite event in Puerto Rico—Finau had established himself as one of the game's top players, if not a prolific winner.

A long hitter with a tall, lanky frame, Finau had somewhat dubiously come upon the scene a year earlier when he played in the Par 3 Contest that precedes the tournament on the day prior to the first round at the club's 9-hole par-3 course.

After making a hole in one, Finau got caught up in the delirium, running down the fairway in celebration, only to severely twist his ankle. The gruesome injury seemed like it would knock him out of the tournament. But despite X-rays showing a dislocation, Finau played with a heavily swollen ankle and went on to tie for 10th in his tournament debut. He finished the year ranked ninth in the world, and was one of the lone bright spots in a U.S. defeat at the Ryder Cup.

Although Finau did not contend in the early part of 2019, a third-round 64 put him in the final group with Molinari and Woods.

"For me, 12 was the turning point," says Finau, who was tied with Woods, two shots back at the time. "[Tiger] hit the green and I hit it in the water when Francesco had hit it in the water. I knew from then on I pretty much had a chance to make something happen. I had a birdie look on 14. I missed an eagle on 15. Had a birdie look on 17. So I still could have made something happen down the stretch, but 12 was a big swing."

Like many who looked back on that day, their own disappointment was tempered by seeing Woods come through. Finau was among them. As badly as he wanted to win, getting an up-close look at Woods doing so was almost as good a reward.

"It was pretty much everything I expected," Finau says. "The crowds were going crazy for Tiger. And I battled. We had the door open on 12, and that changed the tournament. I just needed to hit on land. I needed to put it in the bunker and just barely hit it, chunk, and it kind of rolls on me. And that line was okay. I thought I still had a chance to maybe fly on the green, and unfortunately it didn't. But not my best swing, and it ended up costing me."

Finau's plight highlighted the exacting nature of the 12th. With the pressure of the Masters coupled with the tricky wind, narrow green, water in front, and bunkers in the back, getting that shot right is no easy task. Finau hit a 9-iron that he feared might be too much club. So he tried to take a little off it—"a chip cut 9," he said—and it didn't work.

An 8-iron was too much club; a 9-iron was the right club if he hit it perfectly. "Even Tiger was fifty feet from the hole," Finau said, noting that while he found dry land, he still had work to do.

Woods completed that work. He lagged his first putt to 5 feet, leaving himself far more than he wanted. So much focus was on Molinari and Finau messing up the hole, but if either one of them had gotten their pitch shots up and down for a bogey and Woods three-putted, none of it would have mattered.

But the two players who found the water ended up with double-bogey 5s. Woods confidently struck his 5-footer into the hole for a par 3.

They headed to the 13th tee, but the tournament now had a completely different vibe, one of anxiety filled with electricity and all manner of emotions. Some 90 minutes of action remained, and for those pulling for Tiger, it seemed like hours.

Not to the Golden Bear.

"Tiger was smart enough to play the shot he played, and he could play it," Nicklaus says. "Tiger was rejuvenated by watching those balls go in the water and knowing he was smart enough not to do that. You could just see it on his face. He was back to doing what he used to do."

Woods was still six more tension-filled holes from victory.

14

The Victory

The win in Atlanta might have been the ultimate career capper, if that was the way Tiger Woods wanted to play it. The scene at East Lake, with all of the spectators flooding to the green as he walked those final steps toward victory, was as fitting as those ticker-tape parades bestowed upon the great amateur Bobby Jones, whose photos adorned the walls at the old club, the place where Jones grew up and where Woods now made history.

It was an eightieth PGA Tour victory, and capped a remarkable comeback from spinal fusion surgery that could have ended his career. That Woods was playing golf at a high level and competing spoke to his never-ending grit and determination.

Woods, exhausted, joined his American teammates on a charter flight that night to Paris, where they would get waxed at the Ryder Cup. Woods went 0–4, losing a Sunday singles match to Jon Rahm, a star in the making. Woods quite clearly was tanked, the toll of a long year and an emotional victory too much to overcome.

Remarkably, Woods played eighteen times through the Tour Championship, a number beyond the wildest of any dreams. There were years during his prime that he barely touched that many events. Just getting through them was remarkable in itself. To post nine top-12 finishes, including a victory, and contending at two majors is the kind of stuff that random tour players dream about.

Woods put so much into winning the Tour Championship that there was nothing left in France. Partnerships with Patrick Reed and Bryson DeChambeau required them to carry him, and they were unable to do so; leaning on Woods that week was a mistake, and the U.S. paid dearly. Its two most accomplished stars—Woods and Phil Mickelson—went a combined 0–6. And facing Rahm, Woods simply was going up against a determined player who was coming into his own.

Woods, afterward, was clearly spent. In a greenside interview, he talked almost incoherently, perhaps due to medication he took for his back, which undoubtedly was killing him. Woods would never let on that he was hurting, but clearly the toll of the FedEx Cup playoffs, winning at East Lake, the long trek to France, and the subsequent activities associated with the Ryder Cup were enough. He needed a rest.

Two months passed before the Hero World Challenge in the Bahamas, Woods' tournament that benefits his foundation. He finished 17th out of eighteen players, nineteen shots behind winner Rahm. Nobody cared. There was nothing to prove this time.

Woods had won a tournament earlier that year, and the glow was still apparent. This time, there was no sense in agonizing over every swing, every hole, every round. He had hosting duties for his foundation, and playing good golf in December might have been mildly of interest, but hardly a priority this time. The Masters was four months away.

But the focus after the holidays would be on Augusta National—just like the old days.

THE TRUTH IS THAT WOODS HAD NOT GONE TO THE MASTERS with a realistic chance to win since 2013, the year of his infamous drop on the 15th hole that led to a two-stroke penalty and eventually a tie for fourth, four strokes behind Adam Scott.

He missed the tournament for the first time in 2014 due to his first microdiscectomy; took nine weeks off prior to the 2015 tournament due to back and chipping woes; didn't play in 2016 and 2017; and was making just his sixth official start after spinal fusion surgery in 2018.

But the Tour Championship victory in September of 2018 provided a big boost of confidence, even though the Masters was still well into the future. The way he battled against some of the game's best, including Rickie Fowler, Justin Rose, and Rory McIlroy, is often overlooked in the telling of that story. None of them would have feared Woods at that point, and yet he outperformed them head-to-head and overall.

Serious preparation didn't begin until January, and Woods had a nice run of tournaments at the Farmers Insurance Open (tied for 20), Genesis Invitational (T15), WGC-Mexico Championship (T10), Players Championship (T30) and WGC Match Play (T5). No missed cuts, a good mixture of courses and competition, and some head-to-head golf at the Match Play to really get focused. One of those Match Play victories was over McIlroy.

The downside is that in those five tournaments, Woods never finished closer than eight shots to the winner in the four stroke-play events, and was never a back-nine contender in the final round. It left doubts as to his competitiveness at the year's first major championship.

"Personally, I wasn't quite sure he had enough tournament rounds," says Joe LaCava. "We had a pretty light schedule going in. Having said that, I know when he's not feeling well. I think he knew he needed to save up some energy and it was more important for him to be rested and get his back worked on versus playing tournament golf. Easy to say now, because he won the thing. But I thought we needed one or two more tournaments to be a little sharper going in."

A few days following his quarterfinal loss at the WGC Match Play in Austin, Texas, Woods played a practice round at Augusta National. It was the Wednesday prior to tournament week, and despite a three-putt bogey on the first hole, Woods shot 65.

That was a promising sign, but the course never plays the same a week prior to the tournament, so perhaps a more important occurrence was when Woods returned to Augusta National on Sunday evening for a putting and chipping session in the late-afternoon gloaming.

Most had left the course for the day, so Woods headed out with LaCava and Rob McNamara, Woods' friend and business associate, using just a wedge and a putter to traverse the course.

"Ball-striking-wise, he was way ahead of where he was [a year prior] coming into the last couple of months," McNamara said after the Masters. "All year he [had been driving] the ball and really struck the ball extremely well. It was just scoring. Short game and putting. I started to see a change once he started pitching it really close and tight. That was some of that work on Sunday night. Just taking a wedge around. He knew it was about pitches and chips and controlling your distance and your speed and your spin. He started getting dialed in and had a nice feel. I think that carried him through."

Woods had adopted a less-is-more approach to practice prior to tournaments, especially the majors, where a pro-am round was not required. He preferred to play nine holes, seeking the proper balance between getting ready and doing too much. There was always concern he was not seeing enough of the course, and it heightened when Woods did not practice on Tuesday. But there were also concerns about taxing his body.

"The best move I made the entire week was to not go out and play on that Tuesday," Woods said. "The rain had come in and the greens had slowed up. They didn't quite cut them. The golf course was playing slower. I knew they would speed it up come Thursday. That was the best thing I could have done."

So it was back to work on Wednesday, and Woods played a practice round with Fred Couples, the 1992 Masters champion, and Justin Thomas, his South Florida friend who would get close to Woods and his son, Charlie.

And what occurred on the ninth green came in handy during the tournament, when Woods faced a dicey two-putt from 50 feet, a downhill effort that he lagged to within inches to save par.

"It was huge," LaCava says. "He hits it way back to that top shelf. Back left, the third tier. The pin is front left. And the funny thing is when we finished up on Wednesday with J.T. and Fred, Tiger dropped a ball and they had a little closest-to contest. He dropped the ball a foot from where he hit it on Sunday. And the pin was a foot from where it was on Sunday.

"Now listen, I don't think that's ever an easy two-putt. But it's certainly way easier on Wednesday with nothing on the line than Sunday. But I think it helped a little bit. He had a good look at it Wednesday, believe it or not. You drop ten balls there, you're going to hit two that close. You'll leave one up top. You might hit one off the green. You're going to three-putt three times. And for him to hit it to like a tap-in was huge."

FOR THE FIRST TIME IN FIVE YEARS, WOODS WAS UNDER PAR following the first round of a major championship. And for just the ninth time in twenty-two Masters starts, Woods broke par on the opening day at Augusta National. A 2-under-par 70 saw him on the leaderboard as well, four strokes back of Brooks Koepka and Bryson DeChambeau.

The most recent time he had shot under par during the first round of a major was at the 2014 Open, where he shot 69 but faded.

"I felt like I played well and I did all the things I needed to do today to post a good number," Woods said. "I drove it well, hit some good iron shots, speed was good on the greens. And it was tricky, the winds as of right now—it puffs up, it goes down, it switches directions, and it's typical of this golf course, it just kind of swirls out there and it's hard to get a bead on exactly what it's doing at all times."

Woods made four birdies and two bogeys, the last coming at the par-4 17th when he found the trees off the tee and could not get up and down from the left front of the green.

That denied him a chance at just his second opening round in the 60s at Augusta. The only time he'd been under 70 in the first round to that point was in 2010, when he shot 68.

And yet, three of his four Masters victories—1997, 2001, and 2002—came after opening the tournament with a 70.

The good news for Woods was that nobody went crazy low on a day that seemed ripe for scoring, with soft conditions, warm temperatures, and manageable wind.

"I'm sort of surprised," said pre-tournament favorite Rory McIlroy, who made five birdies but bogeyed his last two holes to shoot 73. "I'm sort of surprised that there hasn't been lower scores out there. It's soft. The greens are sort of slow. It's there for the taking, and I'm surprised someone hasn't run off."

Several players who had late tee times made runs in the afternoon, including three-time major champion Koepka—who missed the 2018 Masters with a wrist injury.

But Woods had struggled with slow starts and had yet to shoot an opening round in the 60s that year. Like many, Woods often had first-tee jitters. Anecdotally, there were numerous examples over the years where a ramped-up Woods would miss a fairway badly on his first tee shot of the tournament.

There was no better example than the 2008 U.S. Open, where Woods stunningly won despite making a double bogey at the opening hole in three of the four regulation rounds.

He started slowly again this time, although he birdied the 2nd hole before missing a 5-footer for par at the 5th, and a 4-footer for birdie at the 6th. He had another chance for a birdie at the 8th from 9 feet but was unable to convert, finally getting one to drop at the 9th to shoot a front-side 35.

After a two-putt birdie from 50 feet at the par-5 13th, Woods made an impressive birdie at the par-4 14th, where his approach from the trees stopped 25 feet away and he curled in an unlikely putt.

At 3 under, that marked the most Woods had ever been under par through 14 holes of his opening round of the Masters.

But he couldn't take advantage of a big drive at the par-5 15th, knocking his approach over the green and having to scramble for par. And he'd let those other opportunities get away, particularly the sixth and eighth holes.

"It's not a bad start," Woods said. "I've only shot under 70 one time, but I've shot 70 [three of the] four times that I have won here. So we still have a long way to go. Tee off late tomorrow and the wind's supposed to be up, so I have my work cut out for me the rest of the week, and so does everyone else."

Little did Woods know that Friday's biggest obstacle would arrive in the form of a human missile.

The sliding, perhaps overzealous, security guard meant well, but for a few fleeting, scary moments during the second round, the scene appeared ominous for Woods, who was clipped in the right knee and was left hobbling to the fourteenth green.

That he would go on to birdie the hole was but one aspect of a wild day. Woods overcame the injury scare, a balky putter—at least on the short ones—a weather delay, and the pressure that comes with contending in a major championship to shoot 4-under-par 68 and put himself firmly in the hunt for a fifth green jacket.

Woods was a shot behind an all-star cast that included Koepka, Adam Scott, Francesco Molinari, Jason Day, and Louis Oosthuizen. All were major championship winners.

"I feel like I played my own way back into the tournament," said Woods, who was in a share of sixth place. "I was just very patient today, felt very good to be out there doing what I was doing. This is now three straight majors that I've been in the mix, and so it's good stuff."

Woods finished tied for sixth at The Open, where Molinari won, and was second at the PGA Championship, where Koepka won his third major. And now thirty-six holes into his twenty-second Masters appearance, he'd given himself another opportunity; his 36-hole score matched the fourth-best of his Masters career.

And for the first time in seven years—since the 2012 PGA Championship—Woods opened a major with consecutive rounds under par.

But it was far from routine. In fact, a different Woods might have lost his patience and cool, given the opportunities he let pass.

He made six birdies, including a 30-footer at the ninth, a 15-footer at the 14th after the near-accident, and another 30-footer at the 15th, where he made his only par-5 birdie of the day.

But he missed a 5-footer for par at the fifth; three-putted the eighth to bogey a par-5; had it to 5 feet after an excellent approach at the par-3 12th and failed to convert. After a nice two-putt for par at the 16th, Woods had an 8-footer for birdie at the 17th and an 14-footer at the 18th, neither of which dropped.

"I missed a few putts out there, but I'm not too bummed out about it, because I hit them on my lines," he said. "So I can live with that. I can live with days when I'm hitting putts on my line and they just don't go in; that's the way it goes.

"But I also made some distance putts there at 9, 14, and 15. They were nice to make and if I keep hitting the putts on my line, they will start dropping."

By the time Woods headed out at 1:47 p.m., scores had gone much lower. He was tied for 11th. Koepka and DeChambeau (who shot 75) dropped back, and Molinari (67), Day (67), Scott (68), and Oosthuizen (67) made their moves to the top. Koepka's 71 helped him keep a share of the lead at 137, 7 under.

They were followed by Woods, Dustin Johnson, Justin Hardin, and Xander Schauffele at 6 under.

"This is really stacked," Scott said. "I think it's going to be an incredible weekend no matter what happens now. There are so many great players in with a chance. It really is an exciting leaderboard, fun to be a part of."

Saturday's third round would be a big one in terms of the quest for a fifteenth major title. Would he stay in contention or simply fade off? There was a good bit of work to be done, and Woods managed to put himself in a position to accomplish the ultimate goal and win his first major since 2005.

And the lavender mock turtleneck was a throwback to fourteen years earlier, when the red mock took center stage in the final round as he executed the famous chip-in birdie from behind the sixteenth green before eventually winning in a playoff.

A more conventional birdie at the same par-3 during the third round stamped a 5-under-par 67 and put him within grasp of that elusive major, with a familiar nemesis in his path.

Molinari, European Ryder Cup hero and suddenly the world's most steely golfer, was there again, and to be alongside Woods and Tony Finau in a rare Sunday three-ball.

"It's been a while since I've been in contention here," said Woods, who was to begin the final round two strokes back of Molinari and tied with Finau. "But then again, the last two majors count for something. I've been in the mix with a chance to win major championships in the last two years. And so that helps."

Molinari shot 66 and did not make a bogey over his last two rounds, with just one for the tournament—at the 11th hole on the first day. Since the previous year's Masters, Molinari, 36 at the time, had amassed four worldwide victories, including The Open, the European Tour's BMW Championship, and the Arnold Palmer Invitational a month earlier.

All fourteen of Woods' major victories had come with at least a share of the 54-hole lead, but that stat discounted the fact that several times he trailed in a final round before rallying.

He would need to do that on a final day that was expected to be impacted by the weather.

"It will be interesting to see if that wind comes up like it's forecast; fifteen, twenty miles an hour around this golf course is going to be testy," Woods said. "And to be committed, hit the proper shots, and then hopefully we time it right."

Woods failed to birdie the par-5 second hole during the third round and appeared to be spinning in the Augusta sand as players like Finau, Webb Simpson, and Patrick Cantlay were having their way with the venerable course.

All three shot 64, one off the course record held by Nick Price and Greg Norman, and produced a Masters first: The tournament had never before seen more than one score of 64 or better in a round, and now it had seen three in one day.

But following a bogey at the par-4 fifth hole—his third of the tournament, after finding a fairway bunker each time—Woods had a quick talk with himself walking to the sixth tee.

"Just be patient," he said. "Very simple. The golf course is certainly gettable, a lot of scores going out there. One of the ams [amateurs] was out there earlier [Takumi Kanaya, who shot 68]. He was four or five under. Patrick [Cantlay] was going low. Tony obviously was six under through eight. Just be patient. Let the round build. We've got a long way to go."

And that's exactly what happened. Woods got going with a birdie at the par-3 sixth, rolling in an 18-footer. He knocked an approach stiff at the seventh, converting from just a foot. And he finally handled the par-5 eighth, knocking his second shot on the green and giving himself an 11-footer for eagle that he missed, but still a third straight birdie.

From there, it was all pars until Woods got a break with his tee shot on the par-5 13th. It appeared he pulled it too close to the trees that line the corner, but the ball somehow got through, and came to rest in the rough. He laid up to 70 yards, then pitched close for his fourth birdie of the day.

Then at the par-5 15th, Woods knocked his second shot just over the green from 218 yards, hitting another nice pitch to set up birdie. He added his final birdie at the par-3 16th, rolling in a 7-footer that helped him finish at 205, 11 under par.

Molinari led at 203, with Woods and Finau tied at 205. Koepka, after a 69, was three shots back of Molinari, with Webb Simpson and Ian Poulter four behind.

Woods hit 16 of 18 greens for the second straight day and was tied for second in greens in regulation, always an important factor for him: In all four of his Masters victories, he was no worse than second in that category.

"I just did everything," he said. "I drove it well and hit my irons well. I made some putts. Like I said, I just let the round just kind of build. And I don't need to go after every single flag. Just put the ball in the correct spots so I can have gettable looks and gettable putts.

"And I was able to do that, and I tried to keep the ball below the hole as best as I possibly could. And I made sure that I had those type of looks, and if I gave myself those looks, the way that I'm hitting my lines I'm going to be all right."

Woods was closer to the lead than he was in any major going into the final round since the 2013 Open at Muirfield, where he was also two back but finished sixth.

He noted that the early start would be unusual, and while Woods is a notoriously poor sleeper, he needed the extra time each day due to his back issues to prepare for a round of golf.

It was a challenge he relished.

"The day I don't feel pressure is the day I quit," he said. "I always thought that if you care about something, obviously you're going to feel pressure. And I've always felt it, from the first time I remember ever playing a golf tournament to now. That hasn't changed."

THE FINAL ROUND WAS MOVED UP DUE TO THAT DIRE WEATHER forecast, which showed rain and thunderstorms hitting the area in midafternoon. So the Masters took the unusual step of putting players out in threesomes, starting on both tees, hoping to end the tournament prior to the projected storms, meaning Woods also needed to awaken earlier and go through the process of getting ready to play golf, which for him was elaborate.

That meant his lengthy routine of stretching, physical therapy, and engagement. This likely took several hours, and was necessary for Woods, allowing him to not only loosen up his various body parts but to try to prevent injury.

As the early holes played out, Woods struggled to stay close to Molinari, who began the round with a two-shot advantage and kept scrambling to keep his lead. Woods finally got within a shot when he knocked his approach close at the par-4 seventh.

Because of the 9:20 a.m. tee time (Woods would have been teeing off shortly after 2 p.m. on a normal Masters Sunday), he had not seen his kids, Sam and Charlie, before heading to the first tee. They had made plans to arrive Sunday morning. And they almost didn't come at all.

Had Sam's soccer team won its tournament game a day earlier in Florida, there would have been no trip to Augusta, because her team would have continued on. And there would have been no Augusta for Charlie, either. They would have stayed home and watched the tournament on TV.

Instead, they had their first opportunity to see their dad in his Sunday red at the Masters—having previously been to Augusta National only one time prior, for the 2015 Par 3 Contest.

But when Woods struck his tee shot off Augusta's No. 1 hole, he was unsure if they had arrived.

"I didn't know until I got to 7 and I had that little tap-in for birdie, and I see Charlie is jumping up and down," Woods says. "And I thought, 'Good, they made it; they made it.' And I didn't see them the rest of the day until 18."

The turning point turned out to be the 12th hole, where Tiger's competitors could not keep their golf balls out of Rae's Creek. Four players, including Molinari, found the water there, dooming their chances.

One who didn't was Webb Simpson, who played in the group preceding Woods along with Koepka and Ian Poulter. Simpson felt like he didn't give himself much of a chance to win that day, despite finishing the tournament just two strokes back.

"It was cool," Simpson says. "You could feel how much everybody wanted Tiger to win. My crowd . . . There was like eight of them. When I made the birdie on 13, there were like eight claps. Everybody else was cheering for Tiger. And honestly, that was the first time at Augusta where I heard anyone cheer for a water ball. They cheered for Molinari's and Finau's water ball, because it meant Tiger had a better chance. They were all excited.

"When I was on 13 waiting to hit, I turned around to see Tiger on the [twelfth] green. That's when I think as a player, you remove yourself for a second, and you take in the moment. And I did that. I grew up watching him. In '97, I was there for a practice round. And then it's his Sunday red on the twelfth green of Augusta, maybe the most famous picture in golf. It was cool. I told myself, 'You're competing against Tiger Woods in the Masters. That is a childhood dream.' So I took that in."

Woods was tied for the first time after the 12th hole but didn't take the lead until his birdie at the par-5 15th, where Molinari ran into trouble. A wayward drive to the right, a poor punch-out that went through the fairway on the left—and then a clipped tree branch as he attempted to hit his third shot to the green. Ball in the water, double bogey, game over.

Molinari's miscues meant more gasps, but Woods had only separated by a shot. There were still three holes to play, and the par-3 16th, the site of so much drama over the years, delivered again. Woods' iron tee shot flew toward the right side of the green, landed on a slope, kicked left, and gained momentum as it tracked toward the hole.

One of the more iconic photos that emerged from that tee shot is Woods staring the ball down while chewing gum—and Olympic swimmer Michael Phelps behind the gallery rope intently watching the flight of the ball.

It stopped just a few feet away, setting up a short birdie putt that led to a comical moment amid all the tension. Woods asked

LaCava for a read on the putt, which was less than 3 feet—to which Joe replied: "Just knock it in!" Woods did, meaning a two-shot advantage with two holes to play.

"We're on the 17th tee, Tiger hits and lands it on the hill and it starts trickling," Simpson says. "We have a perfect view. Crowd is so excited. They want it to go in. It looks like it's going in. And [Simpson's caddie] Paul [Tesori] turns around and looks at me and says, 'What if this went in?' It was one of those moments you'll never forget. The crowd is so loud they're oblivious to everyone on the tee. That was a cool moment, too."

Tesori remembered just how loud it was at that time: "You could hear the crowd murmur and as the ball was getting closer to landing, you could hear the excitement," Tesori says. "Obviously when the ball landed and started to trickle, it just got louder and louder. I had goose bumps and said to Webber, 'Can you imagine if this goes in?' It was just a surreal feeling, one that I will never forget. Brooks was first to hit on our tee and he hit while the crowd was still extremely loud from all the applause."

Woods had not been in this position at Augusta National in fourteen years. Way back in 2005, he led by two shots with two holes to play, then inexplicably bogeyed both the 17th and 18th holes, nearly losing to Chris DiMarco, who came agonizingly close to chipping in for a birdie at the 18th that would have won. Woods won in a playoff.

So there was still work to be done.

"The tee shot he hit on 17 I think was everything for me," says Justin Rose, who watched the final round from home after missing the cut. "That's just a tee shot that you can't hide from. It's straightaway. It's like you either hit it straight or you're in the trees. With a two-shot lead, 17 was the only hole that could have really made it difficult for him. So that was cool to see."

Woods laced his tee shot into the fairway, and knocked his

approach to 10 feet, narrowly missing a birdie putt that would have all but ended any drama. He went to the 18th tee still leading by two strokes. Up ahead, both Dustin Johnson and Koepka had missed birdie putts that might have made things far more difficult.

A nervy tee shot ensued, with Woods flaring one out to the right, leaving him a long way from the green. But he needed only a bogey, so Woods played a shot short of the green, wedged on, and then had two-putts for a most satisfying and remarkable win.

After Woods holed the winning putt, he raised his arms in triumph and then eventually headed off the green through a chute to the scoring area, where cheering and chanting rang in his ears as he greeted his family, including son Charlie, wearing a backwards baseball cap. It brought back all kinds of memories and flashbacks to 1997, when Woods walked into the arms of his father, Earl, following his first Masters win.

"I had never, ever in all my years of going there and all my years of watching the Masters . . . I had never heard chanting at Augusta National," Woods says of the continuous "Tiger, Tiger" bellowing that followed him from the eighteenth green all the way to the clubhouse and beyond. "I get goose bumps talking about it still. The chanting. The amount of support I had. So many people that wanted to see me do it.

"It was special to have that kind of support, that kind of backing. I was going up against the best players in the world. I was trying to come from behind for the first time [to win a major]. And that support was so important."

Once he was near the clubhouse, a group of several players—including past champions Bernhard Langer, Trevor Immelman, Zach Johnson, and Bubba Watson—all waited for him wearing their green jackets.

There were other players, too, including Koepka and Poulter and Xander.

"I wanted to congratulate him," Schauffele says. "I didn't know him very well at the time, but I know him a little bit better since he was the playing captain in the Presidents Cup. It was a sight to see. Augusta is known for being very quiet and reserved, traditional, and it was a circus when Tiger came off that 18th hole. I think every green jacket [Augusta National member] loved it. It was something that hasn't occurred there too often."

Says Keegan Bradley: "I was out on the course, but I watched the end and got to see it. It was spectacular. Probably the greatest moment in the history of the game. Really. The whole celebration. Everything that went into it. It was just so perfect. Now looking back on it and what has happened, it makes it more special."

Gary Woodland, who finished earlier, said he changed his flight in order to stick around and watch the finish.

"I wouldn't do that for anybody else," says Woodland, who won the U.S. Open later that year. "I wanted to see it. The way he finished it. The way he played when everybody else was sort of folding on 12. That was epic Tiger.

"I played with Tiger when he was struggling. Back when he couldn't hit it on the planet. But he always found a way to get the ball in the hole. You want him to be able to go out on his own terms. We're all here because of him and we all look up to him. You kind of felt like you were part of it. It was special. Just so happy for Tiger."

DUE TO THE WEATHER ISSUES—WHICH NEVER MATERIALIZED—there was not supposed to be a second green jacket ceremony on the putting green, as is the custom, but only the one in the Butler Cabin, where Woods was presented the green jacket by Patrick

Reed in a ceremony shown on TV. Usually numerous chairs are set up for Augusta National members and various golf dignitaries to watch the event unfold, with chairman Fred Ridley offering various remarks before the defending champion puts the jacket on the new one. None of that occurred.

The Butler Cabin ceremony took place as scheduled for the CBS audience, but Woods did still have a semi-ceremony on the eighteenth green, Reed putting the jacket on him, being handed the Masters trophy, and a long photo-taking session to cheers.

"When I was done [playing], sitting there and waiting and watching it unfold, and then seeing Tiger make the putt to win, it was inspiring," Reed says. "To put the jacket on him was unbelievable. The only thing I could think of when I did that was to not mess it up. I reminded myself to make sure I put the jacket on him correctly. And we got that job done. But it was a special moment.

"Growing up and watching him win everything and how dominant he was and the focus and energy he had, and the talent he had was just unbelievable. It definitely drove me and others to push really hard and try to get to that kind of level. I know I grinded harder and worked harder because I saw Tiger do what he did."

After conducting his media interviews, Woods went to the Champions locker room, where he shares a locker with 1956 champion Jackie Burke, the oldest living Masters champion.

And then, in a twist, he had his green jacket tailored, a process that took about 90 minutes. During that time, Woods headed back to the Butler Cabin for a 15-minute interview with CBS's Jim Nantz that aired during the rebroadcast of the final round that afternoon. There was a cocktail party in the clubhouse and then a reception in the Founders Room that included a moving speech by Woods to the members. He later posed for photos with everyone who asked.

Because the day had begun so early, Woods emerged from all

of his obligations to a different scene from the one he had encountered at each of his previous four Masters victories. Instead of darkness, there was still light.

"I have never seen the golf course empty like that," Woods says. "I was out there with Sam and Charlie and I said, 'This is what Augusta National is like.' You see the beauty of it. The rolling hills. The perfect grass. It was immaculate.

"It's so different when nobody is out there. That's when they started to understand how beautiful the place is."

The win was mesmerizing, capturing the attention of sports people and entertainment personalities around the world. The former president, Barack Obama, offered his congratulations via social media, as did the current president, Donald Trump, who weeks later invited Woods to the White House along with his family to present him the Presidential Medal of Freedom.

Among those who could not get enough was Lee Trevino, the six-time major champion, who at age 79 watched from his home in Dallas with his wife, Claudia.

"Glued to the TV," Trevino says. "We were watching Tiger, especially that Sunday. We knew he had a chance to win. And I never thought for one second that he wouldn't win again. I felt like if he got his back straightened out, he would be fine.

"Goddamn it, it was just like [when] Nicklaus won at forty-six [in 1986]. I had just finished playing [the Masters, finishing forty-seventh] and I drove to Atlanta. I was in the airport and there was a bar across our gate where we were getting on the plane. And Nicklaus made that eagle putt on fifteen, everybody went nuts. And they were loading the plane and nobody would get on. They had to stop and wait for Nicklaus to finish. We told them to go ahead, we'll take the next one! I remember exactly where I was then.

"And it was the same with Tiger. I was at home, and it was

wonderful. I was in awe. I thought this was the greatest thing that ever happened to the game. I can't tell you the words I used but there weren't a lot of letters in them! I know he had a pretty private life for all those years. And when he got hurt and it looked like he wasn't going to play anymore, I think he realized that people really loved him. He got all kinds of letters. And I don't think he ever realized that. When he came back, the way they accepted him, it was for the better. He's got a lot of personality. He has to understand now how much people love him. Especially golfers. We respect him. He didn't fall out of bed and become the greatest golfer in the world."

Trevino said he saw Woods at a gathering of past U.S. Open champions later that summer at Pebble Beach.

"I was just so happy for him," Trevino says. "I had dinner with him at the U.S. Open at Pebble Beach. It was a great evening. He's the guy that makes me turn my TV on. Not too many people can do that. How's Tiger doing? No disrespect to anyone else. But Tiger makes me turn on my TV."

There is no doubt that Woods' win invoked some of the same feelings as the ones achieved by Nicklaus thirty-three years earlier. Neither player was expected to win. Both had long spells between major championships.

Woods, at age 43, became the second-oldest Masters champion after Nicklaus.

"I think this is one of the best sports stories we've ever seen," says Immelman, who won the 2008 Masters—when Woods finished second, the closest he had been to victory at Augusta National since his last win in 2005.

"When I was coming through the ranks and he was at the height of his game, you always got the feeling that he knew he was the best, you knew he was the best, and that's just the way it is.

"But a couple of years ago, after surgeries and everything else that happened, it was the first time I had ever seen him uncertain.

It's a word that I would have never used for Tiger Woods . . . To dig himself back from that moment to here is something that is just so special. Special for our game. This is awesome. For my mind, this goes down in the same vein as Jack in '86."

Tiger Woods chats with Paul Azinger during the second round of the 1997 Masters at Augusta National. Woods, who shot an opening-round 70, was paired with the 1993 PGA Champion and added a 66 to his total to take the lead. "If you're going to drive it great and not miss a putt inside ten feet, who is going to beat you?" Azinger said of Woods' round.

In the midst of the "Tiger Slam" that began in 2000, Woods points at his birdie putt as it goes into the cup during a three-hole aggregate playoff that he won over Bob May at Valhalla Golf Club in Louisville. The victory at the PGA Championship followed wins at the U.S. Open and The Open. He won the Masters the following April, giving him four consecutive major championships.

Playing for the first time since the Masters, a "minor" knee procedure turns out to be much worse for Woods, who shows signs of distress often, as he does here while trying to walk at Torrey Pines during the third round of the 2008 U.S. Open. A score of 70 that day, which included a long eagle putt on the 18th green, gave him the 54-hole lead.

Right: Woods celebrates his birdie putt on the 18th green at Torrey Pines in San Diego, where his 12-footer ties Rocco Mediate for the tournament lead through 72 holes at the 2008 U.S. Open. Woods, playing on what was later learned to be two broken bones in his left leg and an ACL issue that required surgery, goes on to beat Mediate the following day in a playoff that went to 19 holes, capturing his fourteenth major championship. "To me, the 2008 U.S. Open was like going home," Woods said. "It meant more to me."

ONE

Tiger Woods hits a shot during the Dubai Desert Classic in January of 2017. On the eve of the tournament, Woods said, “The easiest thing is just to play away from the pain.” Not so simple, it turned out. A birdie-less round of 77 at Emirates Golf Club and plenty of ominous signs suggested that his back was bothering him. A day later, prior to the second round of the European Tour event, Woods withdrew. It turned out to be his last competitive round of golf before spinal fusion surgery.

It’s over. Tiger celebrates on the 18th green at Augusta National at the 2019 Masters after holing his final putt for a bogey that wrapped up a one-shot victory over Brooks Koepka, Dustin Johnson, and Xander Schauffele. It was his fifteenth major championship victory and first since winning the 2008 U.S. Open. “Probably the greatest moment in the history of the game. Really,” said Keegan Bradley.

Tiger and caddie Joe LaCava embrace on the 18th green following Woods' final putt that wrapped up the 2019 Masters. It was Tiger's fifth Masters victory and the second for LaCava as a caddie—he worked for Fred Couples during his 1992 Masters win and started working for Woods in 2011.

Tiger shows off a couple of the perks of his Masters victory. He is holding the trophy given to the winner that is a replicate of the Augusta National clubhouse while wearing the traditional green jacket, given to winners of the tournament. This was during an impromptu ceremony on the putting green.

On the putting green following conclusion of the 2020 Masters, Woods takes part in the ceremony in which, as defending champion, he puts the green jacket on the new champion, Dustin Johnson. The tournament was delayed until November due to the coronavirus pandemic and played before a small group of spectators. It would be Woods' last official tournament prior to his February 2021 car crash.

Making a surprise return at the 2022 Masters just fourteen months after his horrific February 2021 car crash, Tiger Woods is set to tee off alongside Kevin Kisner in the third round at Augusta National. After shooting a 71 in the first round and amazingly making the cut, Woods runs into a difficult cold weather Saturday and struggles, shooting his highest-ever Masters score, a 78.

Tiger plays the final round of the 2022 Masters. Walking with caddie Joe LaCava, Woods would shoot a final-day 78, matching his highest-ever Masters score that he shot the day before. But making the cut and competing at all were considered a bigger victory than the final result. "I'm a little on the stubborn side," Woods said a year later when describing his drive to keep competing.

Playing his tee shot on the 16th hole of the Old Course during the second round of The Open, Woods achieved his long-held goal of returning to golf's oldest championship at St Andrews, Scotland, in 2022. He surprised the rest of the golf world by earlier making the cut at the Masters and PGA Championship but was unable to do so at The Open, which was his third and last official tournament of 2022.

Tiger walks across—but does not stop on—the Swilcan Bridge, the famous seven-hundred-year-old structure linking the 18th tee to the fairway, and where all the greats of the game waved goodbye in their final Open at St Andrews. Woods was careful not to do that as he was unsure if he would have another opportunity to play the Old Course at The Open. "You could feel the warmth, you could feel the people from both sides," Woods said of the long ovation he received while walking up to the green.

Tiger hugs his caddie, Joe LaCava, after an emotional end to the 2022 Open at St Andrews where he played the 18th hole at the Old Course to a long ovation.

Tiger plays during the second round of the 2023 Masters at Augusta National. Weather interrupted play and he would have to return Saturday morning to complete the round and ended up making the cut for the 23rd consecutive time, tying a Masters record held by Gary Player and Fred Couples. He would eventually withdraw prior to resumption of the third round on Sunday morning. Another surgery on his right ankle ended his season after just two events.

15

THE ZOZO

The glow of victory followed Tiger Woods wherever he went after winning the Masters. The win was so special, the accomplishment so impressive, it would have been hard to ever erase the smile from his face.

A few weeks after his win, Woods sat down for his first full-length interview with GolfTV, a company with which he had an endorsement arrangement. A perhaps ominous sign, a video showed him shuffling toward the interview setting, moving slowly and somewhat painfully. Was something amiss?

It was fair to wonder, because Woods had decided to skip the Wells Fargo Championship, a tournament in Charlotte, North Carolina, that he normally might have played. He'd competed there the year prior during his big comeback season, and it made sense to play another event prior to the upcoming PGA Championship—which had been moved from August to May as part of a revamp of the PGA Tour schedule.

But the lead-up to the Masters was intense, the victory itself draining, and Woods needed more time. We also came to learn months later that his left knee was bothering him. Yep, the one that he had repaired following his 2008 U.S. Open victory. Woods never said anything about it.

He also had that back to deal with, and it was at times taken for granted and certainly underestimated how much of a day-to-day issue it could be for him. There were times when he just didn't feel good. Whether it would be soreness or a lack of flexibility or general discomfort, Woods often was unsure what each new day would bring.

Then there was his visit to Washington, D.C., where President Donald Trump presented Woods the Presidential Medal of Freedom in a White House ceremony in the Rose Garden on May 6, 2019. It is the highest honor a president can bestow on a civilian.

Trump referred to Woods as a "true legend" and "an extraordinary athlete who has transformed golf and achieved new levels of dominance."

Trump, an avid golfer himself, also went off script, saying, "He's a great person. He's a great guy. Tiger Woods is a global symbol of American excellence, devotion, and drive."

Trump had called Woods from Air Force One the day after his victory to congratulate him and tell him that he would be invited to the White House, the fourth golfer to receive the medal.

"This has been an unbelievable experience, and to have the support that I've had for all these years," said Woods, who acknowledged the family and friends who attended. "You've seen the good and the bad, the highs and the lows, and I would not be in this position without all of your help. This is an honor."

The PGA Championship was a little more than a week later, at a venue where Woods won the 2002 U.S. Open—Bethpage Black on Long Island. He'd also tied for sixth there at the 2009 U.S. Open, so there was hope that his familiarity with and success on the course, combined with his overall strong play at the Masters, might mean another week of contention.

But it was clear this wasn't the same Woods. Cooler temperatures didn't help. A Wednesday illness that kept him from the golf course added to the angst. Then he hit just 3 fairways in the opening round, shooting 2-over-par 72 to trail leader and eventual winner Brooks Koepka by nine shots.

A 73 the following day meant a rare missed cut in a major championship for Woods. Somewhat out of character, Woods seemed relatively at peace with the idea of missing the weekend of a major championship. Normally he'd have been steaming, but Woods was clearly still relishing the Masters victory while recognizing—at least internally—that he was simply not up to the task yet.

"Well, it's a nice problem to have," Woods said. "You know, I've enjoyed being the Masters champion again and the PGA was a quick turnaround, and unfortunately I just didn't play well. I didn't do all the little things I need to do correctly to post good scores and put myself in position to shoot good scores."

It was the first time in his career that Woods missed a cut at a major after winning the previous one. Of course, in winning his first fourteen majors from 1997 to 2008, Woods missed just a single cut in major championships—at the 2006 U.S. Open.

Woods beat Koepka by a shot at the Masters but was clearly lacking the same firepower at Bethpage. A month off with no competition and a light practice schedule led to a lack of sharpness that doomed him to a weekend off.

"You miss fairways, it'll catch up with you," said Joe LaCava. "It wasn't like he was hitting it everywhere. But on this course, six feet off the fairway and you're screwed. And obviously his feel was off on the greens.

"He didn't say anything about being hurt, but he came out of that 9-iron [approach] on 14 and the sand wedge on the last hole. Which is very unlike him. I don't think he's hurting, but those are shots where he had nice yardages on both. That's not typical Tiger."

It was just the nineteenth missed cut of his professional career on the PGA Tour (and twentieth worldwide). For perspective, Koepka, then 29, had missed eighteen to that point. It was also Woods' ninth missed cut in a major.

THIS IS HOW MUCH OF THE SUMMER PLAYED OUT FOR WOODS. He had flashes of brilliance, but not often enough. At times, he looked off. He tied for ninth at the Memorial, a tournament he had won five times. In his return to Pebble Beach, where he won the 2000 U.S. Open, Woods tied for 21st, and was never really in the tournament.

He did play his last 12 holes in 6 under par after a slow start, offering some hope for a resurgence. But then he was not going to play golf again until The Open due to a scheduled family vacation. He didn't announce it, but Woods was headed to Thailand to visit the homeland of his mother, Tida. That didn't help his preparation for The Open at Royal Portrush, where he again missed the cut.

Woods skipped the World Golf Championship event the following week in Memphis and returned at the FedEx Cup playoffs, where he withdrew following a first-round 75 at the Northern Trust tournament, citing an oblique strain.

The following week, at the BMW Championship played at Medinah—where Woods had twice won the PGA Championship, in 1999 and 2006—he was being careful about his injuries during the pro-am, at times walking along without hitting shots.

And this is where it was fair to wonder if Woods' Masters victory was a last great accomplishment. He had put so much into the 2018 return and played more than anyone expected. The lead-up to the Masters saw him play well but without contending over the final holes.

Much like Jack Nicklaus, who "caught lightning in a bottle"

when capturing the 1986 Masters and holding off an all-star cast to win his eighteenth major at age 46, Woods might have very well done something similar. At 43, he still had the guts and guile to compete, and on that stage where he was so comfortable and familiar, he produced when it mattered to accomplish a historic feat in a way that was so in keeping with his stardom.

But after the Masters, Woods never looked the same in those tournaments through the end of the season. The BMW Championship is where it seemed most apparent. Withdrawing the week prior? Barely hitting any shots during the pro-am? Moving around with discomfort?

He finished a distant tied for 37th in the no-cut event that had just seventy players. Woods was nearly out of the tournament from the start. A year after his epic victory at the Tour Championship, he did not even qualify for the thirty-player tournament—despite having won the Masters and having had all that early-season success.

A specific contributor to his lackluster play soon became clear and gave even more reason to question his ever winning again. A few days after the Tour Championship, Woods announced he had an arthroscopic procedure on his left knee but still expected to return to play a PGA Tour event in Japan outside of Tokyo in late October.

On Twitter, Woods released a statement from Dr. Vernon Cooley, who said, "I expect Tiger to make a full recovery. We did what was needed, and also examined the entire knee. There were no additional problems."

It was the same knee that Woods had reconstructive ACL surgery on following his 2008 U.S. Open victory. It was believed to be the fifth procedure on his left knee dating to 1994, when he was an amateur.

Cooley was part of an orthopedic clinic in Park City, Utah,

along with Dr. Thomas Rosenberg, who performed the 2008 surgery.

"I'd like to thank Dr. Cooley and his team," Woods said in his statement. "I'm walking now and hope to resume practice in the next few weeks. I look forward to traveling and playing in Japan in October."

A JOURNEY TO THE OTHER SIDE OF THE WORLD FOR TIGER Woods was yet another reminder of how he leads a different life from the rest of us and that trips such as this one involve far more than playing golf.

Woods arrived in Japan on the Friday prior to tournament week. It was ostensibly to get acclimated to a 13-hour time change, as well as to get in some work at a golf course he had never seen before: a Monday Japan Skins event and then the ZOZO Championship—his first competitive golf in nine weeks.

But due to a recent typhoon that hit Japan, Accordia Golf Narashino Country Club was closed over that weekend because of wet conditions. All Woods could do was hit balls Saturday on the driving range with LaCava, who was not even permitted to walk the course to chart yardages and walk off greens.

The only golf Woods got in Sunday was part of a clinic he gave at a Nike-sponsored event in Tokyo—likely part of the reason he decided to sign up for the first-ever PGA Tour event in Japan. Mixing business in and around his golf schedule has been part of Woods' existence ever since he signed a multimillion-dollar deal with Nike in 1996 before hitting a shot as a pro.

It all made the task of preparing to play tournament golf that much more challenging for Woods, whose well-chronicled back woes were always in play, with the added issue of his having to overcome that knee procedure.

That's why expectations were tempered. Woods showed so little after winning the Masters, missing the cut at two major championships, then needing repairs on his knee. The idea of him winning seemed preposterous, and it was barely even considered.

More than ever, it was natural to wonder how he would look.

"It's always been that way whenever I've had one of these layoffs," Woods said after playing in the Monday Skins event. "It was nice to get out there and compete, to get back in the flow of things. My range of motion, my strength, is there again. I just have to work my way back and hope I find a feel for the round quickly."

There was a time when long breaks hardly impacted Woods. He'd take weeks off and come back and win again. He'd show up at Torrey Pines following a lengthy break and perform like he'd been playing and practicing all along.

His physical woes made that extremely difficult now. The demands that come with being Tiger Woods—father, golf course designer, endorser, foundation head, golfer—added more distractions. And twenty-plus years into his pro career, Woods was simply at a point where he could not give his peers such a head start and be competitive.

He returned to that arena that Monday for the Skins game with Japan's Hideki Matsuyama, Rory McIlroy, and Jason Day and looked . . . well, not very good. But there was no anger, no frustration. Woods spent the day smiling and needling McIlroy, Matsuyama, and Day. He did on-course interviews, stood for photographs and generally looked and seemed healthy.

And that was the most positive aspect to Woods' return. He acknowledged that the knee surgery he had in August was something he meant to do a year prior but put off after winning the Tour Championship. After capturing the Masters, his knee slowly got worse, to the point that it was difficult for him to squat down and read putts.

He said the knee pain and uneasy walking led to other issues with his back. It was viewed as an explanation for Woods looking out of sorts for most of the summer. Why the back stiffness and unsteady gait led to some unseemly scores, especially for a Masters champion. And maybe it is why he seemed so at ease early that week, knowing that things were on the right path.

But on the path to victory?

It didn't seem possible. Nobody but the most positive of Tiger optimists was seriously thinking about Woods winning for the eighty-second time in his PGA Tour career and matching a record set by Sam Snead—whose last tournament victory came in 1965. I wrote that week for ESPN that "Woods should be in no hurry to perform" following his nine-week break and all but dismissed any chance of a good performance. And a win? I saw little to no chance.

There was some chatter about whether he would pick himself for his own U.S. Presidents Cup team that was due to play an international squad in Australia in December. There was time to show improvement before then, but this didn't seem to be the place where it would all come together. Not after surgery. And not after another lengthy layoff.

"I'm one of the guys who need a [captain's] pick," Woods said, smiling. He was the captain who would make that decision two weeks later, with another month to prepare for the Hero World Challenge, followed by the Presidents Cup.

"I'll be in Australia whether I'm playing or not," he said.

Then he opened the ZOZO Championship with a 64. Few saw a victory coming, but a low score like that was seemingly out of the question. Especially after he opened the tournament with three straight bogeys.

Yep, Woods went to all that trouble, including the Nike clinic and the Skins game and the work to get his skills in some semblance of shape, and bogeyed the first three holes. This looked like a disaster in the making, but amazingly Woods made birdies on nine of the remaining fifteen holes to make up for the slow start.

Despite those early-round issues, he hit 15 greens in regulation for the day. The legendary iron play returned. It was "only" good enough for a tie with Gary Woodland, but nobody is going to find too many faults with a 64.

"This is how I've been hitting it at home, so that wasn't a real big surprise," Woods said. "It's a matter of, with a scorecard in your hand, you've got to post a number now. You're not playing for autos and hammers [in gambling games] like we normally do at home. It's actually time to grind out a score.

"It was ugly early, and it was nice to be able to flip it and really get it going. Now I'm in a position where we're going to have a long, long weekend of golf that I hopefully can keep going."

IT WAS A TYPHOON OF ALL THINGS THAT INTERRUPTED WOODS' unlikely brush with history. As the rain hammered down on Friday after Woods began the tournament with that unlikely 64, the torrent postponing play and causing considerable upheaval in the region, Woods and several others ventured to a Narita movie theater to catch *Joker*.

Woods called the film "dark," and he knows all about that word: from the scandal of a decade prior to the numerous back surgeries and pain medication issues and struggles to ever assemble a golf game again.

Now he had earned himself a share of the first-round lead—and had to wait through the most unusual of weather delays, which led to an eerie Saturday of golf.

And there were a few instances where Woods had to catch himself. There was no point tipping his cap, no reason to acknowledge the crowd. Because there wasn't one.

Other than a few officials, media, and members of Accordia Golf Narashino Country Club, Woods and the rest of the field played in virtual peace. It was a shame, really, because Woods would have given the masses plenty to cheer about on a day when spectators were not permitted due to safety concerns.

Birdies on the final two holes meant a 6-under-par 64 and a two-shot lead over Woodland, putting Woods 36 holes away from tying Snead's record.

"I wasn't sure I'd be able to score as well as I have," Woods said. "It normally takes some time to do that. But the conditions are soft and I've been able to strike my irons really well to this point."

Woods had not played a competitive round of golf since August 18. His season ended in disappointing fashion, with him unable to qualify for the Tour Championship, despite winning the Masters. For most of the summer, Woods struggled with his fitness. Coming back from all that meant lowered expectations, and Woods only began working on his game about a month prior.

And he shoots 64–64?

That epitomizes Woods' career, but really? Now?

The results through two rounds were excellent. Woods hit 12 greens in regulation after hitting 15 in the opening round, and although he didn't give himself as many birdie looks, he nonetheless made seven birdies and limited his mistakes to a single bogey.

Torrential rain that produced dangerous conditions Friday in the Chiba area dumped more than six inches on the Narashino course and caused PGA Tour officials to alter the par-4 10th hole, playing it from just 140 yards so the tee could be moved up to avoid water—but still classifying it as a par-4.

The rest of the course was in amazingly good shape considering the onslaught, but tournament officials elected to play it safe, keeping the twenty thousand spectators expected to attend off the property to better manage course conditions and prevent injuries.

"I've only played like this one other time, and it was at Congressional [in 2012], my tournament [AT&T National]," said Woods of the third round, which was played with no spectators due to a vicious storm that hit the area. "A couple of putts, I wanted to put my hand up [to acknowledge applause] and said, 'Don't put your hand up. There's no one clapping. Just move on about your business.'"

Woods did just that, but not before dealing with his own storm-related mishap that saw him, girlfriend Erica Herman, and several other PGA Tour players get caught for nearly 90 minutes in Narita without transportation due to roads being closed.

They killed the time by going to see *Joker*, but as conditions progressively got worse, and with nowhere to go, Woods, along with Jordan Spieth, Justin Thomas, Bubba Watson, and Ryan Palmer, headed to . . . Domino's Pizza.

"One was dark, one was happy," said Woods, who ended up signing a few autographs for fans who recognized him on the nearly desolate streets.

Once the weather turned nice, Woods showed no effects and immediately birdied the first hole.

He saved the best for last as he stuck an iron shot close for an easy birdie at the 17th and then hit a laser 5-wood to the par-5 18th, setting up a two-putt birdie for his second 64 of the tournament. He finished two strokes ahead of U.S. Open champion Woodland and three ahead of Keegan Bradley and Matsuyama.

Woods had seven birdies and a single bogey to finish at 128, 12 under par. Woodland shot 66 to finish two strokes back, with Bradley (63) and Matsuyama (67) three shots back.

Due to the unique circumstances, the tournament decided to

pair everyone in threesomes for the final two rounds, with the hope of getting as much done on Sunday as possible and likely knowing it would spill into a Monday morning finish.

While there was still a long way to go, the idea of Woods winning again suddenly seemed more than possible. Those of us who gave him no chance at the start of the week were reminded yet again that you doubt Tiger at your own peril. He was doing something nobody thought possible.

Sunday saw a lot of golf. Woods ended up playing twenty-nine holes, a considerable amount for a guy with a bad back and a repaired knee. And what had appeared to be an easy stroll to that eighty-second win got a bit more interesting as Matsuyama birdied his last two holes before darkness halted play.

Just a few minutes earlier, Woods had led the tournament by five strokes. And now the lead was down to three against the one player in the field that the Japanese fans might want to see win more than they did Tiger.

"I just tried to increase it," Woods said. "I figured if I stayed where I was at, I was not going to have the lead. I had to make some birdies. The golf course was soft, pretty benign. I felt like I had to keep making birdies, and for the most part I did."

Woods played eleven holes of the fourth round before darkness halted play. He made three birdies and a bogey to get to 18 under par and completed fifty-four holes at 16 under.

Matsuyama was also 2 under for his round through thirteen holes. As the only player in the field who could rival Woods' popularity, he was doing his best to make it interesting.

Woodland and Sungjae Im were the next closest players, and they were six shots back of Woods.

Woods had never failed to win a PGA Tour event when leading by at least three strokes heading into the final round. He made six birdies and two bogeys during the third round.

After a 45-minute break, he went back out for the start of the fourth.

He had just chipped up close for a par on the 11th hole when play was stopped. Matsuyama had just birdied the 12th hole.

"Starting off with the 12th hole is not easy," Woods said. "One of the hardest par-fours on the golf course. It's 490 yards. It's going to be cool tomorrow morning, so the hole is going to play really long. It's important I get off to a good start . . . I've got to do my job starting out."

Woods was looking to match Snead, who was given credit for his record-setting 82 total at the 1965 Greensboro Open, where he also became the oldest player in PGA Tour history to win, at age 52.

Woods, 43, had some pretty good history on his side.

He had converted a 54-hole lead 54 out of 58 times on the PGA Tour, including 43 of 45 times when he was the outright leader. The only times he failed to follow through with a victory were at the 1996 Quad City Classic and the 2009 PGA Championship.

It still didn't figure to be easy. Matsuyama, who had five PGA Tour victories to that point—and who would win the 2021 Masters—along with twelve in his native Japan, is a massive figure in his country. He was ranked 27th in the world at the time, having climbed as high as No. 2 in 2017.

The temperature was considerably cooler when play resumed Monday morning, and Woods appeared to be a bit stiff, certainly compared with the fluid movement he had shown throughout the tournament thus far.

He bogeyed the tough par-4 12th and the lead dropped to two, but he got it back with a nice birdie putt at the 14th after watching Matsuyama miss from 3 feet on the hole in front of him. When Matsuyama birdied the 16th, Woods again led by just two. But a miss from 15 feet at the 17th by Matsuyama meant a two-shot cushion with two holes to play. Woods birdied the 18th for the final margin of victory.

For the week, Woods led the field in birdies with 27, and hit 55 of 72 greens while taking 111 putts, averaging 27.8 per round. A putting tip from his friend Rob McNamara—to move his hands farther forward—proved to be a big help. "He just kept reminding me, because I tend to forget things like that."

The victory came nearly twenty-three years to the day that he captured his first tour title, at the 1996 Las Vegas Invitational. Woods had been a pro for a matter of weeks and beat Davis Love III in a playoff.

While much had been made of Woods' pursuit of Jack Nicklaus' major championship record of eighteen, it would have been impossible to foresee way back then that he'd approach Snead's number.

"I probably thought about it when I got north of fifty, but then unfortunately I went through some rough patches with my back and didn't play for a number of years, so that record seemed like it was out of reach," he said. "Having had my fourth back procedure and being able to come back and play at a decently high level again, it put the number back in the conversation again.

"Lo and behold, here we are tied."

During the awards ceremony on the eighteenth green, Woods said, "I know what it's like to have this game taken away from you."

If it is odd to consider another career-defining victory coming in Asia that saw Woods tie Snead's record while most American sports fans were taking in the NFL back home, it is certainly fair to wonder how any of it happened at all.

For all the positivity that his Masters victory engendered, it was short-lived. By the time he was missing the cut at The Open, all those good vibes were washed away along the shores of Northern Ireland.

Too many times, Woods had showed up for a golf tournament and didn't look right. And the more that happened, the more you wondered if the earth-shattering victory at Augusta National had swallowed up every last bit of energy he had mustered in an effort to win another major championship.

"It was a combination of things," McNamara says. "The knee led to him start to slide and swing differently. And then it affected his back, and then a little bit his neck, and then his oblique. It was sort of a chain reaction of events, because he wasn't working properly in the golf swing. Then couple that with some bad weather, and it just wasn't going to happen."

The knee. Who knew? Woods never once let on that anything was amiss. But as he disclosed at the ZOZO Championship, he needed to have an arthroscopic procedure to clean out cartilage. And he put it off.

Instead of doing it a year prior, he waited. And it finally caught up with him over the summer, when he missed two cuts and withdrew from another event in just six tournament appearances. On August 20, 2019, he had what was described as routine surgery. A week later—so as not to interfere with the Tour Championship and the FedEx Cup—he announced it.

"The knee didn't allow me to rotate," Woods said. "And because of that it put more stress on my lower back and my hip. As the year went on, it deteriorated a bit, and I struggled. Now I'm able to clear a little bit better, I feel better."

When the tournament began, Woods hit his opening tee shot in the water—and proceeded to make three straight bogeys. And then it changed. Woods made nine birdies to shoot 64. He made seven more in the second round—after the typhoon diversion—to shoot another 64. A 66 in the third round gave him a three-shot lead, a position from which he had not failed in twenty-four previous opportunities.

Due to the typhoon and the delay of play, Woods finished the tournament on Monday in Japan—allowing TV viewers to see it Sunday night in the United States—holding off Matsuyama to match a fifty-four-year-old record.

"Well, it's a big number," Woods said. "It's about consistency and doing it for a long period of time. Sam did it into his 50s and I'm in my early to mid-40s. So it's about being consistent and doing it for a very long period of time. I've been very fortunate to have had the career I've had so far.

"To have won this tournament in Japan, it's just so ironic, because I've always been a global player. I've always played all around the world, and to tie the record outside the United States is pretty cool."

Woods had now won PGA Tour events in seven countries: the United States, Canada, Scotland, England, Ireland, Spain, and Japan. (He's also won other titles in the United Arab Emirates, Australia, Germany, and Thailand.)

The victory came in Woods' first start of the 2019–20 season at the first-ever PGA Tour event to be contested in Japan. And despite his summer physical woes, Woods had posted three PGA Tour victories in his last fourteen starts. The win moved him to No. 6 in the world—a remarkable rise given that he was outside of the top thousand in late 2017.

That Woods managed to pull it off was just as extraordinary—in its own way—as winning the Tour Championship and capturing the Masters for his fifteenth major title.

Those tournaments are bigger and carry far more weight in the game, but Woods was trending toward those triumphs. He showed plenty of form going into each tournament, and it lessened the surprise at the time that he won either event.

A week before the Japan victory, nobody knew what kind of game he had, least of all himself. His odds at Caesars were 40–1.

"His ball-striking was a joke," says Woodland, who played the final thirty-six holes with Woods. "I pride myself on being a pretty good ball striker, but his distance control was something I've never seen. His misses are all in the right spots. He didn't hit the ball left for two days. When you have a one-way miss you can be aggressive. And then his speed control with his putting.

"He looked like the best player in the world. It was impressive to watch, pretty special."

Woods later picked himself for his own U.S. Presidents Cup team, which was to be preceded by the Hero World Challenge. He had some time again to decompress and work his way back into form before those events. (He finished fourth at the Hero and went 3–0 as captain in a U.S. victory in Australia.)

None of that seemed possible prior to the ZOZO Championship, which was supposed to be another struggle but turned out to be a remarkable triumph, yet another example of his drive.

"It's satisfying to dig my way out of it and figure out a way," Woods said. "There were some hard times trying to figure it out, but I've come back with different games over the years, moving patterns, and this one's been obviously the most challenging.

"Then having another procedure a couple months ago and again coming back and winning an event, not easy to do."

Not at all.

16

THE SEPTUPLE

On what should have been the night of the Champions Dinner at Augusta National Golf Club, Tiger Woods paid homage to the occasion by sending out a photo via his Twitter account showing him at a table in his South Florida home with his family, donned in the green jacket and the Masters clubhouse trophy in full view.

The food spread looked incredible, and Woods had a huge smile on his face. He was making the best of a terrible situation.

"Masters Champions Dinner quarantine style. Nothing better than being with family," Woods wrote.

With him was his girlfriend, Erica Herman, along with his children, Sam and Charlie.

The Champions Dinner is a tradition that began at Augusta National in 1952 at the suggestion of Ben Hogan. Only past Masters champions and the club chairman, now Fred Ridley, attend the gathering.

The dinner is hosted by the defending champion, who picks the menu for the evening (although the attendees are allowed to order whatever they want off the club's menu). Woods had chosen the menu from 2006, the last time he won the Masters: steak and fajitas along with sushi and sashimi. He'd also considered milkshakes—which was part of the menu in 1998, the first time he'd had the honor.

It was at that same dinner in 2017 that Woods thought his career was over due to his recurring back pain.

Now times were different. The world—not just golf—had come to a standstill in April 2020. A few weeks earlier, when it was learned that golf and numerous other activities were on hold due to the coronavirus pandemic, the Masters came out with its decision to postpone the tournament.

It was understandable, if not unprecedented. The Masters, which began in 1934, had been played every year without fail starting in 1945, after being halted due to World War II.

The tournament was eventually rescheduled for November, meaning the first-ever fall Masters. It was a cool idea, especially under the circumstances. Brown leaves instead of blooming azaleas. A newly green overseeded course with ryegrass, laid down just a few months prior—as is always the case in the fall at Augusta National.

Given the dire circumstances, it would be a welcome diversion. Considerable speculation centered on how the course would look at a time when the outside world never got to see it. And many wondered if it would play as well.

ESPN's *College GameDay*, which typically travels around the country on college football Saturdays to a stadium hosting a big game, set up shop on Augusta National's Par-3 Course. It was a surprising and welcome addition made possible by the powers that be at Augusta. Ridley was on set, and stumped for his college team, the Florida Gators.

For Woods, it meant a delayed defense of his epic Masters title. And while the idea of playing the Masters in the fall was cool, the notion that Woods would make magic again during football season seemed remote.

Woods never got well for the entirety of the interrupted year. He tied for ninth in his first start of 2020 at the Farmers Insurance Open, then finished 68th and seemed to be hurting at the Genesis Invitational. Cool temperatures were never good for his back, and the Poa Annua greens at Riviera Country Club were never good for Woods' putting stroke. It would be his final event prior to the start of the pandemic in mid-March.

When golf resumed in June, Woods did not resume with it. He waited some six weeks to make his first start, at the Memorial, which had been rescheduled for July. He tied for fortieth. At the PGA Championship, played at San Francisco's Harding Park, where Woods went 5–0 at the 2009 Presidents Cup, he tied for thirty-seventh.

In the six tournaments Woods played following the resumption of play, he had no finish better than the PGA, and he missed the cut at the U.S. Open at Winged Foot Golf Club.

All of these tournaments were void of fans due to pandemic restrictions, and that undoubtedly was a hindrance to Woods, as it was to many players, who noted how much they missed the buzz of crowds, the boost it gave them.

Certainly Woods thrived in the more boisterous settings. As much as he loved the solitude he so dearly sought in his personal life, the throngs of spectators who followed him and cheered him on for decades undoubtedly were a rush that could not be duplicated.

He would never use it as an excuse. After all, any top player missed the crowds. It was just one more aspect that made the situation so unusual.

The Masters was going to be Woods' last start of 2020, and he opened with a 68, matching his best first-round score ever at Augusta National.

As expected, the leaves had turned brown and the fall foliage was stunning. Augusta National, with that overseeded rye turf that had only come in full form a month prior, looked terrific.

And when the gates opened on that Thursday morning, Jack Nicklaus and Gary Player hit the traditional ceremonial tee shot, and the tournament began—in semi-silence.

Only members and their guests and a few assorted friends and family were on the grounds. Everyone wore masks as they traversed the course, which didn't have gallery ropes—because they weren't needed.

And while it was great to have golf at Augusta National and was exceedingly rare to be able to see the course in all its glory, with unimpeded views of the rounds, that wonder lasted all of about a day.

By the second round, some of the luster was gone. There were no roars emanating from Amen Corner, no stampede through the merchandise pavilion—it was closed.

Yes, the Masters was being played, and that was great. But the reality of our collective situation was real. The pandemic raged on, with no end in sight. A vaccine was months off. Nobody knew for sure how things would play out as the holidays approached. And the grandeur of Augusta National, with all of its green glory and rousing reverberations through the trees, was gone.

WHEN WOODS TEED OFF BEFORE A GATHERING OF AROUND A hundred people—including NFL commissioner Roger Goodell and former quarterback Peyton Manning, both Augusta National members—the sun was out and the air warm.

Getting used to a spectator-less environment is something that Woods is unlikely ever to adjust to; as he noted several times, players in the group had to ask television personnel where their golf balls had landed.

Woods feeds off the adrenaline the crowd provides, and it was extremely awkward to be playing a place he knows so well amid such peaceful surroundings. The nerves were there, the usual tournament jitters. But Woods was not alone in suggesting that all those spectators brought a vibe that could not be replaced.

By the time the third round came to an end, Woods had not yet come to terms with the idea that the green jacket he'd been carrying around for the previous eighteen months would be staying at Augusta National after he left the grounds the next day.

But it was in the back of his mind all week, knowing that as his title defense loomed at the Masters, the possibility that the signature item associated with winning this major championship might long stay put in his locker.

Never one to give up, Woods still had an outside chance as the third round began. But his even-par 72—after playing eight holes to complete the second round on Saturday morning—knocked him out of contention, a four-shot deficit turning into nine shots as he was simply unable to make much happen.

Woods said that attending and speaking at the Champions Dinner was an emotional experience for him, knowing the difficulty of defending his title after a year of lackluster performances.

"I have not thought about tomorrow yet," said Woods, who managed just two birdies and two bogeys after beginning the round in touch with the leaders. "I was focused on trying to get myself in contention going into tomorrow . . . We'll see how emotional it'll be after tomorrow's round."

Woods was trying his best, and his trademark never-quit attitude was still apparent, but he was destined to be putting the green jacket on someone else after another early tee time on Sunday. With rounds of 68–71–72, he was 5 under par and eleven shots back of third-round leader Dustin Johnson, tied for 21st place.

BY THE TIME HE REACHED THE 12TH HOLE DURING THE FINAL round, Woods was well out of contention. At the 2019 Masters, some seventeen months earlier, at this same spot on the course, he all but took command of the tournament. While competitors Brooks Koepka and Ian Poulter ahead of him had found the water that fronts the green, so too had Francesco Molinari and Tony Finau in Woods' group.

Back then, Woods had calmly struck a 9-iron that he hit a bit left of center, aiming over the bunker that fronts the green, giving himself a long birdie putt but safe from the water the others had found.

On this day, he could not avoid that same fate.

The stakes were far less, of course, but Woods still shockingly came up short with his tee shot at the 12th, with what occurred over the ensuing minutes difficult to comprehend.

Fooled by the wind, his 8-iron shot hit on the front of the green but spun back into the water. (Imagine if that had happened a year earlier.)

Then, after a penalty drop, and playing from behind Rae's Creek and 70 yards from the pin, Woods hit another shot that hit on the green and came back into the water.

After another drop, his fifth shot went over the green into the back right bunker.

Facing an awkward stance for his sixth shot, Woods bladed the ball out of the sand and saw it skitter across the green and into the water.

He took a penalty drop in the sand and got his eighth shot onto the green, then two-putted for a 10.

Three balls in Rae's Creek. Seven actual shots. And the only double-digit score on any hole in Woods' career.

A septuple-bogey 10.

His previous worst score was a 9 that he made on the third hole at Muirfield Village Golf Club during the 1997 Memorial Tournament—twenty-three years prior.

Woods' previous highest score at the Masters was an 8, twice, both on par-5s—the 15th hole of the second round in 2013 (which included a two-stroke penalty due to the infamous drop in the fairway) and the eighth hole of the first round in 1999.

"I committed to the wrong wind," he said. "The wind was off the right for the first two guys, and then when I stepped up there, it switched to howling off the left. And the flag on 11 was howling off the left. I didn't commit to the wind, and I also got ahead of it and pushed it, too. Because I thought the wind would come more off the right and it was off the left. And that just started the problem from there.

"From there, I hit a lot more shots and had a lot more experiences there in Rae's Creek."

In eighty-nine previous Masters rounds, Woods had made worse than a bogey at the 12th just three times—two double bogeys and a triple.

"He made three there last year; that's all I care about," said caddie Joe LaCava, taking the big-picture view.

AT THE TIME, WOODS WAS 9 OVER PAR FOR HIS ROUND AND IN danger of shooting his worst score ever at Augusta National. And this was the point in time when mere mortals simply play it out. For Woods, this was to be his last tournament of a long, frustrating 2020. Did his final score really matter?

It had been eons since the tie for ninth in January at the Farmers Insurance Open. The pandemic was frustrating for everyone, but Woods was never the same golfer. There were back issues, as was not learned until two months later in mid-January when Woods announced he'd had another microdiscectomy (his fourth, along with the spinal fusion) just before Christmas.

That helped explain a few things, if not directly then certainly by connecting a few observations. A microdiscectomy is meant to relieve pressure on a disk, and since Woods had previously undergone a fusion to take care of the lowest part of the spine, it is reasonable to believe that this was farther up the spine.

Anecdotally, it simply appeared that Woods was not healthy. Some of the shots he hit, the scores he shot, suggested he was having difficulty with his back, if not all the time, at least in spurts. His back was typically put under the most duress for shots with the shorter clubs, the ones where he had to bend over more from the waist.

So putting, chipping, even short-iron shots . . . none of it was sharp. And it helped put into focus why his game was not as good. The microdiscectomy was performed just more than a month after the Masters, so it was possible he had already decided to have it done or at least knew he was headed for another offseason of medical decisions.

And now he was going to grind out the last six holes at the spectator-less Masters? Few would have cared at this point. Six more holes, take in the scenery, get to the clubhouse, say a few words to the media, handle the green jacket duties with the winner, and head home to Florida.

Not Woods. He played those final six holes like the tournament was on the line. Perhaps this was a subtle example of his drive, that instead of cruising in Woods stepped on the gas for one last push.

It won't be found in the record books anywhere, but Woods' finish was a small, simple reminder of his resiliency, his determination. Why bother? That just wasn't Tiger Woods' manner. He rarely, if ever, quit on a round, and he wasn't going to do it here.

Woods stepped to the 13th tee and blasted a tee shot into the fairway and proceeded to birdie the par-5 hole. After a par at the 14th, he birdied the final four holes, including the 17th and 18th, only his second and third birdies he made all week on par-4s.

Looking like he might shoot 80 or worse, Woods finished with a 76, one better than his then-worst score of 77, shot during the third round of the 1995 Masters, when he was 19 years old and playing the event for the first time.

Woods showed enormous pride in finishing off the round as he did. He wanted no slaps on the back, nor did he revel in it. Ultimately it moved him up only a few places in the final standings, but to him, that always mattered.

"That's part of our sport," he said. "This sport is awfully lonely sometimes. You have to fight it. No one is going to bring you off the mound or call in a sub. You have to fight through it. That's what makes this game so unique and so difficult mentally. We've all been there, unfortunately. I've been there, and you just have to figure out the next shot, and I was able to do that coming home."

Woods shot scores of 68–71–72 and 76 to finish in a tie for 38th, one spot off his best in seven starts since returning from the pandemic shutdown.

"It definitely struck me," says Scottie Scheffler, who played with Woods in that final round and would go on to win the Masters two years later. "That was my first time really spending time with Tiger. I had never played with him before. He struggled the first twelve holes. He didn't have his best stuff. And then he made that big number on 12 and kind of flipped the switch.

"He hit some of the best iron shots I think I've ever seen, still to this day. It was really cool for me to see him just kind of flip the switch. He hit one really nice shot into 13 and all of a sudden it's 'game on.' I knew he was frustrated. I didn't know him well enough at the time to kind of rib him about it.

"I was actually joking with him [at a tournament in 2022] about that round. And he was like, 'Yeah that really pissed me off.' No.

12. That's one of those special things that makes Tiger Tiger. A lot of guys would have thrown in the towel there for sure."

During his fifth Masters victory, Woods had hit one of his most iconic shots to the par-3 16th, an 8-iron that hit on the right side of the green and trickled ever so slowly toward the pin as the roar of the crowd grew louder and louder. It eventually stopped 3 feet past the hole, and when Woods knocked in the birdie putt, he led the 2019 Masters by two strokes.

Now, there was nothing at stake but pride when he got to the 16th tee.

"The shot he hit into 16 was probably the best iron shot I've ever seen," Scheffler says. "The wind was blowing hard. Pin was on top right. Greens were soft. He hit this no-spinning cut 7-iron. No matter what direction the wind was going to go, I felt he was going to hit that ball to a foot. It was just so purely struck. Not a lot of spin. Fading toward the pin. It was pretty amazing."

Shane Lowry also played with Woods during that final round. The Irishman had won The Open at Royal Portrush in 2019 and could say he won a major title in the same year as Woods. Now, they were hopelessly out of contention, but Woods' finish taught him something. The way his drive did not cease stuck with Lowry.

"I've talked to other people about this," Lowry says. "When I see him now and then, he mentions it. It still gets to him that he did that. He was so mad that day, and then he played the last six holes like Tiger Woods.

"We played week in and week out on tour, we go out on Sundays lying in 50th or 60th spot, and you see lads giving up. I don't give up. I don't think I've ever given up. Always try to shoot the best score I possibly can. I think I learned even more about it that day from him. He made a 10 and went to like 50th in the tournament and was obviously really pissed off. And then he went and tried his nuts off for the last six holes. When the greatest of all time to do it doesn't give up, the rest of us should follow suit."

Woods' comeback crossed Lowry's mind when playing the Dunhill Links Championship in October of 2022. It was a chilly, fall Scottish day, and the pro-am-style event contested over three courses saw foul weather for round two. Playing the Kingsbarn course a few miles up the road from St. Andrews, players faced gusty winds, rain, and cold temperatures. It was the kind of day when nobody wanted to be on a golf course.

Lowry found himself 7 over par through eight holes. "I was standing on the ninth tee going I could actually shoot the worst score I've ever shot today," Lowry says.

And then he thought of that Woods comeback at Augusta.

"Stuff like that keeps me going," he says. "I was one under for my last six holes to break eighty. And I was actually quite proud of myself. You take stuff like that. We're proud golfers. You look at your score after a round and you want it to be good. Tiger provided a great lesson."

Woods' own tournament in the Bahamas was canceled due to the pandemic. He played in a 36-hole exhibition called the PNC Championship with son Charlie in late December, the story for one of the rare times not about him. His golf was fine, but it was clear he was not at his best. The surgery a few days later—not disclosed for almost a month—was confirmation.

It wasn't long after that that speculation began concerning whether or not Woods would be able to return for the Masters. He looked terrible in a television interview from the Genesis Invitational and gave no definitive answer as to his ability to play at Augusta National.

Two days later, it didn't matter. Woods was involved in the horrific car crash that could have taken his life. Initial reports were dire, and weeks and months of operations and rehabilitation ensued.

And for a long time, it seemed quite possible that the last golf we would ever see Woods play occurred over the closing holes at the 2020 Masters, a remarkable tiny sample that as much as any other of his exploits perfectly encapsulated his drive.

17

The Crash

The video lasted all of three seconds, but packed into that short glimpse of Tiger Woods swinging a golf club could have been a thousand questions followed by a thousand more words.

Posted to Woods' Twitter account, it had nearly eight million views.

All to see a golfer wearing black cargo shorts, a white shirt with tight sleeves, and a white trucker cap. Importantly, there was a black compression sock meant to improve blood flow that ran from inside his shorts to his ankle.

Behind him was a device meant to measure distance and ball speed, to his side a basket of golf balls and a perfect divot pattern from where he had been hitting wedge shots.

It was the first time anyone had seen Woods upright, on a golf course, swinging a club, since his horrific car crash earlier that year in 2021. "Making Progress" was the caption.

And this video, posted the Sunday following Thanksgiving in 2021, offered hope to all those entranced and watching it repeatedly. He was pushing the boundaries again, showing another example of his drive.

Reality presented far less cause for optimism.

Woods hitting shots at all was remarkable—and the measuring device behind him was a nice, serious touch. He was nine months removed from the crash that made worldwide headlines and that for a time had many wondering if he would survive.

That high-speed crash occurred on the morning of February 23, 2021, when Woods was on his way to shooting a documentary series of celebrity lessons as part of an endorsement deal he had with Discovery and *Golf Digest*.

A day earlier, he had appeared at the same Rolling Hills Country Club course in Rancho Palos Verdes, California, and appeared with actors David Spade and Jada Pinkett Smith and former NBA star Dwyane Wade, giving lessons that eerily—and with Woods' permission—were released later in the year.

This was all rather routine stuff for Woods. Over the years, he would have participated in countless video shoots for various endorsers and partners. Photos. Meet-and-greets. Video. It was all part of the deal for one of sports' most marketable stars.

Although Woods was still not feeling great due to recent back surgery—his fourth microdiscectomy had occurred just two months prior to Christmas—he still took part, but limited what he was doing with a golf club.

As was almost always the case with these things, Woods was not mailing it in. He was fully engaged and by all accounts in a good mood.

He had arrived in the area on the weekend as part of his hosting duties at the Genesis Invitational, where in 2017 he became the tournament host of the long-running event in Los Angeles, played at Riviera Country Club.

Due to the back procedure, Woods was unable to play the tournament, but he made a Sunday appearance in the CBS-TV broadcast booth, where he appeared uncomfortable, his face puffy. CBS's Jim Nantz asked if "we'll be seeing you in six weeks' time," a reference to the Masters and the question that was on everyone's mind. "God, I hope so. I gotta get there first," Woods said. "This is the only back I've got. I don't have much wiggle room left here."

Woods was not back to hitting full shots yet, an ominous sign, and his bloated appearance also raised all kinds of conjecture.

Two days later, none of that mattered. Woods' courtesy car lay in ruins, his golf career in shambles, his life in danger.

According to a twenty-two-page report released by the Los Angeles County Sheriff's Department, Woods was driving alone on a winding road on his way to the course just after 7 a.m., traveling at more than 82 mph in a 45-mph speed zone. It was unclear if he'd attempted to negotiate a curve in the road.

Woods drove straight into a median, struck a curb, knocked down a wooden sign, and drove into the opposite lanes before hitting a tree and rolling over in the Genesis GV80 SUV provided by the tournament.

The vehicle was a mangled mess, and many credited its size and durability with helping save Woods' life. It was also noted how fortunate he was not to have engaged oncoming traffic or pedestrians during a typically busy time of day.

Woods suffered broken bones in his right leg and injuries to his right foot and ankle. But those words don't begin to describe the damage. Woods endured multiple surgeries in the coming days and weeks. He later said he was "lucky to have this leg," suggesting that amputation was considered.

Numerous doctors and experts not associated with Woods' care weighed in on the various possibilities, including how compromised his right leg and ankle would be, given the severity of the injuries. And there seemed to be some solid anecdotal acknowledgment of that as Woods emerged in public and attempted to play golf again.

But back then, golf was on nobody's mind. Police interviewed

Woods at the hospital following the crash, and the report said he mistakenly believed he was in Florida. An empty pharmaceutical bottle was found in a backpack at the scene with no label or indication of what was inside it. Woods' blood pressure was "too low to administer any type of pain medication" shortly after the crash, likely due to shock.

Woods was not issued a citation, because there were no independent witnesses and no officers who observed the collision sequence, according to Sheriff Alex Villanueva. The sheriff also said his department did not try to examine Woods' blood for evidence of medication because there was not strong enough reason for it.

During his first news conference following the crash on November 30, 2021 at the Hero World Challenge in the Bahamas, someone questioned Woods on what he remembered about it.

"Yeah, all those answers have been answered in the investigation, so you can read about all that there in the post report," Woods said.

Clearly, that was not true. The police report provided no answers as to what Woods remembered or how he felt or even what medication he had taken. And the direct questions about the crash ceased after that single one. And were not asked in a public setting during the months afterward.

Why? Well, having been there for a majority of his news conferences over the years, there is fantasy and reality. Fantasy is thinking that you can keep peppering Woods with the questions until you get an answer that is acceptable.

Reality is that there is so much managed time where questioning is concerned. All who read the police report are aware that Woods was not tested for drugs, nor was there any finding of major wrongdoing. Why would he answer anything beyond that? And if you keep going down that path of questioning, you run the risk of the rest of the news conference going adrift or even being cut off.

And there were numerous other questions that reporters wanted to cover and that fans or observers wanted answered.

Asked about his more difficult moments afterward, Woods said:

"I think just laying there, laying still," he said. "I was in the hospital for only three weeks. I was in a hospital bed for three months. That in itself is difficult. Being assisted everywhere I go, not being able to move anywhere. As I said, just looking forward to just getting outside. Eventually I got to a point where they could wheelchair me outside safely and I could feel the sun; that was like a milestone. It's little things like that that added up.

"And then eventually when I started [using crutches] around the house, I never—I built a really nice house, but I didn't realize how big it was until you start putting crutches on. Yeah, there were times where I had to take breaks, but I tell you what, though, there's a point in time where my triceps got pretty jacked, so that was a lot of fun.

"As a whole, it's been tough at times, yes, some dark moments, but then again, as I was making progress through it, too, I could see some light, and that was giving me hope. I'm able to participate more with my kids and their activities and more just in life in general. I'm on . . . as I said, I'm on the positive side."

The report had been issued on the day prior to the 2021 Masters, where Woods' absence was noted with relief and sadness. He was alive. But there was so much unknown, and such a long road to recovery ahead. Rickie Fowler, who was not in the Masters, visited him during the tournament.

"He's not lacking any fire in there right now," Fowler said of his visit with Woods. "Never has. For what he's dealing with. J.T. [Justin Thomas] had been over there a handful of times before I got to go over and see him. Rory stopped by. And that was one thing J.T. told me. He went over pretty much right after [Woods] got back from L.A. [where he was hospitalized], and J.T. told me, honestly, he was a lot better than I expected. So that was good to hear.

"Then to get over there and see him getting around, and now you guys have seen some of the pictures that he's posted and he's out and about a little bit. Because early on it was more so he had to keep his leg up for inflammation, couldn't be walking around on crutches that much, although I'm sure he wanted to, because he didn't want to just be laid up.

"So it was good to see him. Hung out and spent some time with Charlie, and Sam was there for a little bit before she had to go to soccer practice. I'm just . . . I think his main focus and concern is getting back to being a dad, go play golf with Charlie, push him around, and be able to run around with Sam. But his golf clubs are right there in the living room and he can stare at them all he wants."

That fall Masters, played five months earlier, was looming as perhaps his last competitive rounds. In late April, Woods posted a photo of himself in his backyard, on crutches, wearing a cast and a boot. For months afterward, there were no public updates on his health.

THE SHORT VIDEO WOODS POSTED JUST AFTER THANKSGIVING was the first meaningful communication from him in months. A few days later, he'd be in the Bahamas for his annual Hero World Challenge tournament, where he made his first public comments.

He was both optimistic and realistic about his professional golf future.

"I'm lucky to be alive and also have a limb," Woods said at the Albany Golf Club, site of so many of these updates over the years.

"This one's been much more difficult," Woods said, referencing the various injury comebacks in his career. "The knee stuff was one thing. That's one level. Then the back. With this right leg . . . it's hard to explain how difficult it is. Being immobile for three months. Just to lay there. I was just looking forward to getting outside. That was a goal of mine. Especially for a person who lived his entire life outside, that was a goal.

"I transitioned from a wheelchair to crutches and now nothing. It's been a lot of hard work." And he admitted: "There's a long way to go. As far as playing at the tour level, I don't know when that's going to happen. Now, I'll play a round here or there, a little hit and giggle; I can do something like that. The USGA suggested Play It Forward [the tees]. I really like that idea now. I don't like the tees on the back. I like Play It Forward. Come on, let's move it up, let's move it up.

"To see some of my shots fall out of the sky a lot shorter than they used to is a little eye-opening, but at least I'm able to do it again. That's something that for a while there it didn't look like I was going to."

Woods was vague about when he'd be able to begin walking again and how much golf he had played but acknowledged he had played "some holes."

He also noted that his comeback from spinal fusion surgery in 2017 to win the 2018 Tour Championship, the 2019 Masters, and his eighty-second victory at the 2019 ZOZO Championship made it easier to accept his fate.

"I got that last major and I ticked off two more events along the way," he said. "I don't foresee this leg ever being what it used to be, hence I'll never have the back what it used to be, and the clock's ticking. I'm getting older; I'm not getting any younger. All that combined means a full schedule and a full practice schedule and the recovery that would take to do that . . . No, I don't have any desire to do that.

"But to ramp it up for a few events a year and as I alluded to what Mr. [Ben] Hogan did, and he did a pretty good job of it, and there's no reason that I can't do that and feel ready. I may not be tournament-sharp in a sense that I haven't played tournaments, but I think if you practice correctly and you do it correctly, that I've come off surgeries before. So I know the recipe for it; I've just got to get to a point where I feel comfortable enough where I can do that again."

Hogan, who won sixty-four PGA Tour events and nine major championships, was involved in his own serious auto accident in 1949, when he and his wife, Valerie, where driving to Texas from a tournament in Phoenix. They were hit by a Greyhound bus, and he suffered significant injuries, including to his legs.

Following the accident, Hogan never played more than nine tournaments in a year, the most coming in 1950. In 1951, he played just four times, winning twice—the Masters and the U.S. Open. In 1953, he played just six times, winning five, including all three major championships he played.

All those accomplishments led to the Golf Writers Association of America naming an award in Hogan's honor and giving it annually to a player who overcame medical or injury issues. It is the award Woods received on the night before the start to the 2019 Masters due to his amazing return from back surgery.

A comeback from this would be just as arduous, if not more so. And Hogan was younger than Woods when he suffered his injuries. Woods would turn 46 on December 30.

"I have a long way in the rehab process of this leg, and it's not the fun stuff of the rehab," Woods said. "It's just reps and breaking up scar tissue and things that really hurt. So that part of it's not going to be fun, but the challenge of it is. I enjoy the challenge of getting in there and trying to push it to the next level; sometimes it's two steps forward, one step back, but you've got to go through it. I enjoy that part of it and maybe one day it will be good enough where I can get out here and I can compete against these best players in the world again."

As he sat in the interview room that day, Woods acknowledged that he was experiencing pain in his back and his leg. That was part of what he needed to overcome, he said.

While noncommittal about any schedule or a return, Woods was asked specifically about the 2022 Open at St. Andrews, a place where he had won twice.

"I would love to be able to play that Open Championship, there's no doubt about it," he said of the tournament, which was not scheduled until the following July. "Physically, I hope I can. I've got to get there first. Tournament's not going to go anywhere, but I need to get there."

When asked about his looming 46th birthday, Woods joked it would mean that in four more years "I'm in a cart," referencing the practice of PGA Tour Champions when they reach the age of 50. "This year's been a year I would like to turn the page on," he said.

JUSTIN THOMAS ENJOYS THE ABUSE THAT COMES HIS WAY FROM Woods, most of it good-natured, nearly all of it delivered with a sharp edge. Despite the eighteen-year difference in age, the two are close, and have been since Woods began to embrace the younger generation of golf stars that began showing up in his absence.

That's why the Genesis Invitational in February of 2022 was both somber and celebratory for Thomas. It was a reminder both of the horrific car crash that could have taken Woods' life and of the notable recovery he had made to that point.

Woods was all smiles at Riviera Country Club, where his TGR Foundation runs the tournament and he is the host. And despite the long recovery that figured to keep him from competing for some time, the fifteen-time major champion looked and sounded good—a stark contrast from a year earlier.

Woods still had his keen wit, and he used it on Thomas, suggesting via text message on the Friday afternoon of the 2021 Genesis that perhaps they might meet for dinner—knowing full well that Thomas, steaming, had missed the 36-hole cut and was already on his way out of town.

"He does so much crap like that to me," said Thomas, unable to keep track of all the various times that Woods had needled him.

But this one hit home. It was among the last times they communicated before the horrific car crash.

"I can't believe it's been a year," Thomas said. "It feels like it's been longer than that. So it's great seeing him here. I know he loves it—catching up with all of us and all the other guys. Yeah, anytime you get to have him around, especially with all he's been through the last year, it's definitely great for everybody."

Woods was upbeat but realistic about his future. There remained plenty to overcome. In addition to the broken bones in his right leg and injuries to his right foot and ankle, he'd had a rod inserted into the tibia to stabilize the fractures, with screws and pins inserted into his foot and ankle. There was also trauma to the muscle and soft tissue of the leg, requiring surgery to relieve pressure due to swelling.

"It's altered," Woods said during that February 2022 news conference at Riviera. "My right leg does not look like my left, put it that way."

Woods was initially treated for his injuries at Harbor-UCLA Medical Center, the trauma center located closest to the accident site. Three days later, he was transferred to Cedars-Sinai Medical Center in Los Angeles, where he stayed for a few weeks until returning to his South Florida home.

A year later, many questions remained, including why Woods'

blood was not tested to determine if he had taken any medication that could have caused drowsiness or even sleep.

"People said, 'Oh, they should have drawn blood or done this or done that,'" Villanueva said. "Without the signs of impairment we don't get to the point where we can actually authorize a search warrant and determine the probable cause to get that and execute that search warrant, so that did not happen. And this is not preferential treatment. That would occur in any collision of this type."

In the time after the crash, golf understandably was not on anyone's mind. Woods' accident was at the forefront; one of the most famous athletes of his generation saw his well-being as his ultimate concern. If it wasn't evident already from the horrific photos of his smashed car, the release of the final police report made clear how lucky Woods was to have survived. His ability to resume normal activity and achieve quality-of-life goals seemed far more important than anything to do with a golf career.

Southern California native Max Homa had particularly vivid memories, because it was he who won the Genesis Invitational just days before the crash, having accepted the tournament trophy from Woods. Winning a tournament was big enough. Having Tiger hand you the trophy and pose for photos was on another level, the stuff of dreams. Like many of his generation, Homa revered Woods.

"Not to seem like super corny, but I think golf is probably the only sport I could think of where you end up competing against your idols and heroes," Homa said. "I was six years old when I first heard of Tiger Woods and . . . I'm still playing against him, I'm still around him. I think that's rare."

The glow of victory at an iconic venue and his interaction with Woods still enveloping him, Homa went to the next event in Florida, and while players were practicing or arriving at the Concession Golf Club in Bradenton, Homa's phone blew up.

Like others, he was learning of the news that had occurred three time zones away.

"It was eerie," Homa said. "It was the exact same feeling I felt like with the Kobe Bryant news [when former NBA star Bryant was killed in a helicopter crash in January of 2020], which was about a year prior, which was just super bizarre. This one was definitely closer to home, but it's just like—not to get too deep—but just the mortality of your entertainment heroes, I guess.

"Everyone grew up at least watching a show or something, where playing for me is sports and you just think that person's just always going to be there, there's just no thought of why they wouldn't be. Maybe they won't be playing anymore, but they'll be there.

"When that went away with the Kobe thing, it was super bizarre. And Tiger, like I said, is much closer to home. It was very weird. I mean, obviously it isn't about me, but I was thinking about the fact that that was the first time we like hung out kind of, like I had the coolest moment of my life and he was a part of it, and then the next day I thought he might not be here anymore.

"That was just a weird concept to wrap my mind around. Again, it's the least important part of it, but that's just where my head went. It was very eerie."

MANY WONDERED WHY WOODS WAS DRIVING AT ALL, WHY HE didn't hire someone to do the task, why someone didn't pick him up, why one of his friends or his agent or someone else wasn't behind the wheel that morning.

That simply was not Tiger. As famous as he is, Woods often drove himself, whether it was at home or to a tournament site with his caddie sitting in the passenger seat. This was his habit, and it certainly was striking to see a person of his stature and fame driving, alone, to a public venue or golf course.

The memory of such seemingly mundane matters was vivid as news of the crash circulated and details emerged. Something that had been considered neat about Tiger—a celebrity who didn't want a driver—now seemed sad. Perhaps events would have played out differently if someone whose job it was to get people from one place to another had been driving.

The Discovery people even caught some grief over this, and were questioned about it, but you can be sure if such a driving service had been offered, Tiger would have declined. That is how he operated.

After the viral video post and the brief news conference in the Bahamas, Woods actually played in a 36-hole exhibition a few weeks later with son Charlie. The duo finished second to John Daly and his son, John Jr., and put on quite the birdie display during the final round. But Woods was using a cart, and it was obvious at times that the struggle to walk was real. The idea of doing it in the context of 72-hole tournament play appeared daunting.

As good as Woods' swing looked, and as much hope as it gave to a comeback, it was clear it would not be anytime soon. Or so it seemed.

"I can still play, but I'm in a cart," Woods said at Riviera in February of 2022. "Being a weekend warrior is easy, that's not that hard. Hit your ball, hop in a cart, ride, barely step out of the cart, grab your club, and hit the next one. And the longest walk you have is probably from, what, the cart to the green and back.

"I can do that, that's not that hard, but walking a golf course, that's a totally different deal. Then walking out here for days on end, long days. Don't forget when my back was bad, when we had rain delays and had to reactivate everything and go back out there again. I've still got that issue, too. I've got a long way to go. Did it give me hope? Yes, it did, because I went through a very difficult year last year."

As was his wont, Woods would not disclose a timetable. Jim Nantz tried to get Woods to say if he would play in the Par 3 Contest on the eve of the Masters (a 1,060-yard 9-hole course) and Woods did his best to shut it down. He would not commit to any tournament goals, but that did not stop the rest of us from speculating.

The Masters and its undulating Augusta hills would seem highly unlikely. Woods would be there for the Champions Dinner, being hosted by Hideki Matsuyama. Perhaps he would stick around for the Wednesday Par 3 Contest, although that is not really his style.

Then where? Southern Hills for the PGA? The Country Club for the U.S. Open? Maybe those courses are more forgiving, but they are still difficult major championship venues. Would he really be able to take on the rigors of such activity while getting his game in shape for a major championship venue?

The Old Course at St. Andrews was a popular pick for a return—it is relatively flat and not particularly difficult. It became the target everyone pointed to for a possible official tournament. Nobody would care if Woods shot 90, so happy would they be to see him in Scotland, waving to the cheering masses from the Swilcan Bridge or from any of the famous spots along the course.

That seemed the most likely and realistic place. But if not at the Home of Golf, where? The conventional thinking was his Hero event in the Bahamas.

"You'll see me on the PGA Tour," Woods said. "I just don't know when."

That Woods was even offering that up a year removed from the crash speaks to his remarkable recovery and resiliency. Whether he ever played golf again at a high level would be discussed and debated at length before a tee would go in the ground at his first event back.

Then, it was more about reflecting on where he was and what he'd endured to get to that point.

"I'm very lucky, very lucky," Woods said. "As a lot of you guys know, I didn't know if I was going to have the right leg or not. So to be able to have my right leg still here, it's huge. I still have a lot of issues with it, but it's mine, and I'm very thankful for that. Thankful for all the surgeons and doctors and nurses, for all the countless surgeries that we went through and countless rehabs—and the PT sessions are brutal—but it's still mine, and I'm very thankful for that."

Little did any of us know that he was plotting a return far sooner than could possibly be imagined.

DURING WOODS' NEWS CONFERENCE AT RIVIERA, EVERYTHING he said about returning to competitive golf was about lowering expectations. But it appears he was not believing what he was saying.

Woods made a point to downplay a return. The talk was the future, the distant future. The Open at St. Andrews seemed a nice goal, but it was five months away and who really knew?

Nobody was seriously discussing any of the other majors, and certainly not the Masters and Augusta National, with its hilly terrain and quite possibly the most strenuous walk in the game. Woods, even at this news conference, showed a limp as he moved in and out of the room, and the idea of him navigating the undulating landscape in Georgia simply seemed too much, too soon.

The year's first major championship was still seven weeks away, and that hardly seemed enough time to get body and mind ready for not only a difficult physical challenge but the rigors of tournament golf and getting a game in shape.

Woods clearly had other ideas.

And yet as the spring of 2022 played out, Woods drifted into the background. His recovery seemed secondary. While he was diligently putting in the work at home and going far beyond what anyone dreamed possible, driving to return at the unlikeliest of places, the game was turned upside down.

The very week of his tournament outside of Los Angeles, the new LIV Golf rival league became a huge story.

Phil Mickelson, Woods' longtime adversary who had made strong, disparaging comments about the PGA Tour a few weeks prior in a *Golf Digest* interview, made more headlines with the release of an excerpt from a biography of him written by Alan Shipnuck.

Mickelson acknowledged that the Saudi Arabian backers of LIV Golf were "scary motherfuckers to get involved with," because of the country's poor human rights record, its treatment of women and gay people, and the killing in 2018 of *Washington Post* journalist Jamal Khashoggi, who had been critical of the Saudi government.

"Knowing all of this, why would I even consider it?" Mickelson said. "Because this is a once-in-a-lifetime opportunity to shape how the PGA Tour operates.

"They've been able to get by with manipulative, coercive, strong-arm tactics and we, the players, had no recourse. As nice a guy as [PGA Tour commissioner Jay Monahan] comes across as, unless you have leverage, he won't do what's right. And the Saudi money has finally given us that leverage. I'm not sure I even want [the new league] to succeed, but just the idea of it is allowing us to get things done with the [PGA] Tour."

Those bombshell comments became the talk of golf. Soon, players who had been leaning toward signing with LIV Golf recoiled. Several spoke in favor of the PGA Tour. Players such as Dustin Johnson and Bryson DeChambeau—who later *did* leave for LIV Golf—pledged their support for the PGA Tour.

Rory McIlroy decried Mickelson's comments, saying, "I thought they were naive, selfish, egotistical, ignorant—a lot of words to describe that interaction he had with Shipnuck. It was just very surprising and disappointing, sad. I'm sure he's sitting at home sort of rethinking his position and where he goes from here."

Though McIlroy said he believed that LIV Golf was "dead in the water," the story completely overshadowed what occurred on the golf course, where Chile's Joaquin Niemann won the tournament. (Niemann would later join LIV Golf.)

At the end of February, Mickelson announced a leave from the game in the wake of all the negative publicity. (He would miss the Masters for the first time since 1994. He skipped his title defense at the PGA Championship.)

A few weeks later, at the Players Championship, Monahan was asked several questions about LIV Golf and proclaimed that the Tour was moving on. A week later, LIV Golf announced it was going to stage eight tournaments in 2022.

All the while, Woods was out of sight, out of mind. Nobody seriously considered he'd be back at the Masters. He would later make his feelings known, talking strongly in favor of the PGA Tour and the legacy he created there. But that was down the road. At this point, with the Masters looming, there was little indication he was even ramping up to attempt to play—let alone make a dramatic comeback.

18

THE MASTERS (AGAIN)

On the Tuesday prior to the 2022 Masters week, the golf world was shaken again, but it had nothing to do with LIV Golf or the never-ending chatter that surrounded it. After weeks of acrimony and upheaval and controversy, the first major championship loomed, and suddenly there was the unreal news that Tiger Woods might be trying to compete in the tournament.

There had been a few unsubstantiated reports that had him hitting balls at the Medalist, the South Florida club where he plays, but nothing solid. Club members are typically respectful of Woods' privacy, and the idea seemed far-fetched anyway. After his words at the end of 2021 and again at the Genesis Invitational, which suggested he was a long way off—not to mention the considerable obstacles he would face—was Woods really trying to play the Masters?

The idea gained far more credibility when internet sleuths and social media accounts reported Woods' private plane heading from the executive airport in Stuart, Florida, toward Augusta, Georgia. Then a source on the ground at Augusta National told me for a *Sports Illustrated* story that Woods was there that day, along with Charlie, to play a practice round.

First, consider how neat was the idea of Woods getting to play with his son at such a special place. "It was cool for me as a parent to watch him enjoy it," Woods said later. The source relayed that he saw Charlie hitting balls on the range with that unmistakable mimic of his dad's moves. Justin Thomas was there, too.

In his few public comments, Woods had made it clear that he would never play a full schedule again, that he could see a limited amount of events in which he prepared for major championships and a few other tournaments. And that the process was a long one due to the significant injuries he suffered.

The trip to Augusta National was clearly to see how Woods would handle walking the hilly course. And since he did not have to disclose if he intended to compete until the week of the tournament, Woods could test his ability to play via practice rounds and work at home before making a final decision.

And that is basically how it played out.

Woods made a Sunday announcement that his participation would be a "game-time" decision, and then he arrived at Augusta National that afternoon to play nine holes.

When the gates opened to massive Monday practice-round viewing, Woods was there again, this time with Fred Couples and Thomas to play nine holes amid a scene that had the look of a regular tournament day.

Every step was viewed with the keenest of interest, and it understandably appeared that Woods was not moving around the hills of Augusta National as smoothly and as effortlessly as we once might have remembered.

But when it came to hitting the golf ball, there was not much to fault.

Couples was celebrating the thirtieth anniversary of his 1992 Masters victory. Joe LaCava, who caddied for Couples during that win, was now on Woods' bag.

And Couples could have not been more effusive in his praise for Woods.

"To hit it like that, now it's just the walking part," Couples said. "If he can walk around here in seventy-two holes, he'll contend. He's too good. He's too good."

The relatively short period of time since the crash was on everyone's mind. Although Woods moved around easily enough, it was clear that he was favoring his right foot, as if he had a blister. Obviously, it was considerably more than that.

As we saw more of Woods over the months and into 2023, that limp was simply part of what was expected. But in April of 2022, much of the world had not seen him other than when he rode a golf cart the previous December at the PNC Championship. To see him struggle took a little getting used to.

The hills of Augusta—walking both up and down them—did not make the task any easier.

Couples spent a good while marveling at Woods' participation in the tournament. The two stay in close contact, but Couples didn't get the sense that Woods was ready to return until just prior to the Masters, when the fifteen-time major champion said, "I've got to start back sometime."

After arriving early that afternoon, Woods practiced for an hour before heading to the first tee. A massive first-day crowd on hand after two years of there being virtually no spectators due to the coronavirus pandemic.

Woods was cheered on nearly every tee, and hit plenty of good shots, including reaching the par-5 eighth in two. He hit five of 7 fairways and five of 9 greens and spent considerable time chipping and putting to various hole locations. The fact that we kept notes on the details of an otherwise meaningless practice round is evidence of the interest and enormity of this comeback.

"What impresses me the most is he was bombing it for one,"

Couples said. "If you want to talk golf, he was bombing it. I know J.T. is not the longest hitter on the Tour, but I know he's damn long. He was with him flushing it. I guess he played nine yesterday, but as a friend and the way he looked, he's very impressive."

Couples added: "He's doing all this to play in this, which is impressive in itself, because I'm telling you—you guys walk, you follow players—it's brutal to walk, and to go through what he's gone through, whatever it is, fourteen months ago, to be playing today? I hope everything keeps going Tuesday and Wednesday, and I'm sure he's going to tee it up Thursday."

When Woods played the back nine a day earlier, he ran into first-time Masters participant Cameron Davis, who won the Rocket Mortgage Classic the year prior to qualify for the Masters. Davis said Woods caught up to him and they played the last few holes together.

"Still a little slow going up a couple of hills on 17 and 18. I mean, I was as well," Davis said. "He's been through a lot more than I have. He's striking it well. He's hitting it far enough to play the holes the way you need to play them. I don't see any reason why he wouldn't be able to put rounds together out here.

"It was cool to see. He's hitting the shots that you know you should hit, but it's just executing them. He wasn't doing anything special, but he was playing well. Everything was looking pretty solid. It will be great to see him out here if he decides to tee it up on Thursday."

By this point it seemed inevitable. Woods was going about his late-career routine of preparing for a major championship, playing just nine-hole practice rounds or none at all, as a way to conserve energy while preparing on the range.

It was a sound strategy, as he would have to weigh the balance of too much walking to prepare with not enough walking to be ready to compete.

WHILE NOTHING WAS REALLY NORMAL FOR WOODS AS HE EMbarked on his first official competitive round since November of 2020 at the Masters, some things were business as usual.

Tiger might have been happy to be there, and he expressed his gratitude multiple times. But once inside the ropes, the old competitive fire that marked his career was more than apparent. Woods wasn't going to simply smell the azaleas and wave to the spectators.

On a few occasions his frustrations could be picked up by microphones, the blistering four-letter missives that he's sometimes been known to utter in disgust on a golf course audible for all to hear. That provided the best clue that he was back.

But after playing that first round, Woods acknowledged the enormity of the accomplishment, shooting a 1-under-par 71 in which the numbers on a scorecard could not begin to tell the story.

The fact that Woods was playing at all was impressive enough. That he was able to break par was on a legendary level. There was no overstating the accomplishments of the day. Not in terms of technical issues, such as ball-striking or length of tee shots or the quality of his short game. No, this was more about finishing a round on one of the game's most exacting courses and standing before the assembled media to talk about it.

This, in a different way, was a victory.

"If you would have seen how my leg looked to where it's at now . . . the pictures. Some of the guys know," he said. "They've seen the pictures, and they've come over to the house and they've seen it. To see where I've been . . . to get from there to here, it was no easy task.

"I've said this before: We haven't taken a day off since I got out of bed after those three months," Woods added, while thanking his team, which included two specialists who were part of the gallery that day. "Granted, some days are easier than others. Some days we push it pretty hard, and other days we don't. But we're always doing something.

"So it's a commitment to getting back and a commitment to getting back to a level that I feel I can still do it. I did something positive today."

Woods was opening up more and allowing the world to understand his struggle, if even just a little bit. While he would never pound his chest over one round of golf, it was clear he was stoked. This was a big day, no matter how the rest of the tournament played out. And he had every right to be proud.

He hit eight of 14 fairways and just nine of 18 greens, and there could not have been anything more fitting than for Woods to go through his round like it was old times. He made nice par saves on the first and ninth holes, and had an impressive up-and-down at the 18th. And his first birdie post-crash came at the par-3 6th, where he stiffed his approach shot to loud, boisterous cheering just a few feet away.

His biggest regret was the way he played the par-5 eighth hole, where he was just 50 yards from the green in two shots but walked off with a bogey-6. "Lack of concentration," he said. "Lack of commitment. Then blocked a putt. So just three bad shots in a row."

But Woods was hardly going to beat himself up about it. Not on this day. Not at this time. It might have been the way he had thought and the reason he was so good, but this was different. Far different. A crash that could have taken his life, nearly took his leg . . . and competing so soon in one of the game's biggest tournaments?

It was impressive, and every bit in keeping with a career that saw him overcome and persevere.

"To play this golf course and do what I did today—to hit the shots in the right spots—I know where to hit to a lot of these pins and I miss the correct spots and give myself good angles. I did that all day, and I was able to make a few putts and end up in the red [under par] like I am now."

Woods was higher on the leaderboard than defending champion Hideki Matsuyama, Shane Lowry, Adam Scott, Kevin Kisner, and others. When he completed his round, he was just three shots back of the leader at the time, Cam Smith.

But the hard part was yet to come. An extensive process of rest and rehabilitation would follow the round. Just to get ready for the next day was going to require an early wake-up call that included a litany of fitness protocols involving both his leg and his back. Without providing much detail, Woods told of needing ice baths to reduce the swelling.

As for the process of playing golf, there were going to be issues, as played out over the summer and into 2023. Woods had no trouble hitting the shots. It was getting to them that was the problem.

"No, it did not get easier, let's put it that way," he said. "I can swing a club. The walking's not easy, and it's difficult. As I said, with all the hard work, my leg, it's going to be difficult for the rest of my life. That's just the way it is, but I'm able to do it.

"That's something I'm very lucky to have, this opportunity to be able to play, and not only that, to play in the Masters and to have this type of reception. I mean, the place was electric. I hadn't played like this since '19 when I won, because in '20 we had COVID and we had no one here, and I didn't play last year. So to have the patrons fully out and to have that type of energy out there was something to feel."

Fans saw it and felt it. So did media and the other players.

"He struggled walking the whole way around, you could see it," says Louis Oosthuizen, who played the first round of the Masters with Woods. "It was going to be tough. But you never write the guy off. It was pretty amazing that he came back and played. You never know with him. Certainly coming back from all of that to make the cut and do all of that was really, really impressive. Obviously he knows what he is capable of. It might look funny to us, but he is able to figure out what works for him.

"All of the things he's pulled off in his career, all of the things he's done, I don't think you're going to find anyone as mentally strong as him. The guy has done everything basically, and he still comes back from so much and shows he can do it."

Woods displayed even more resolve in the second round, when he simply was far from his best.

How else do you explain battling back from a poor start, powering through the pain he must have felt in his right foot, to make the cut with plenty of shots to spare, and looking forward to a weekend at the Masters?

"He made the cut on one leg," LaCava said. "That's pretty good."

It was the twenty-second time in a row that Woods made the cut at the Masters, as he overcame bogeys on four of his first five holes to shoot 2-over-par 74 on a difficult day that included cool temperatures and swirling winds.

While he was nine shots behind leader Scottie Scheffler, Woods noted he was just four shots out of second place.

"I'm proud of the fact that my whole team got me into this position," Woods said. "We worked hard to get me here to where I had an opportunity and then not to have, as I said, any setbacks this week, and we haven't. Kept progressing.

"Along the way I kept getting my feels and hitting shots. I was able to practice and get my touch, practice on my short game, hit a lot of putts, which was great. Start seeing break again. I've been in Florida. I haven't played the [PGA] Tour in forever, so we don't see break.

"Start seeing ten feet of break, you've got to get used to it to the eye, and I haven't played a lot of competitive golf. So it's taken a little bit to get used to it, but I finally got my eye back."

As the first few holes unfolded, things didn't look good. Woods found a fairway bunker off both the first and second tees. He couldn't save par at the first, couldn't make birdie at the second. The wind got him at both the third and fourth holes. A wayward drive led to another bogey at the fifth.

Woods made what appeared to be a routine birdie at the eighth, a good par save at the ninth. And then he hit his shot of the tournament at the par-4 10th, a 5-iron from 218 yards that he drilled to 2 feet for a kick-in birdie.

"That 5-iron on 10 was kind of like the old days," LaCava said. "It's all good. It was fun."

Joaquin Niemann, who played with Woods and was in contention at 1 under par, was impressed. "I think he hit it way better than yesterday," Niemann said. "He looked great. He's [hit some] amazing tee shots, some amazing iron shots. On ten today he was amazing. So, yeah, he's still got it."

It might not have always looked that way, but perspective was again in order. It was Woods' first official event in seventeen months. It was just two rounds of golf, and not only did he manage to make the cut but he put himself in a nice position.

Sadly, more poor weather awaited. In his prime, Woods would have relished such a day. Not so much anymore, but he tried to keep up a good front.

"Tomorrow is going to be tough," he said. "It's going to be windy. It's going to be cool. It's going to be the Masters that I think the Masters Committee has been looking forward to for a number of years. We haven't had it like this.

"It's going to be exciting, and it's going to be fun for all of us."

WOODS WAS RELISHING THE CHALLENGE, BUT SATURDAY'S weather was too much for even him. There was no way it was fun. Spectators showed up in all manner of cold-weather gear, bundled up in sweaters and ski caps. Woods played in a long-sleeved white sweater with a blue-collared shirt beneath, sometimes using a sleeveless vest.

It was not a day you'd otherwise play golf.

The steps were measured. Woods was conscious of which foot went first as he emerged from the scoring area following the third round and again when having to get up onto a podium for a brief interview with reporters.

He was careful to put the left foot first, bearing all of his weight, an understandable reflex on a day in which it was clear that Woods was far from his best physically.

And after signing for a 78—his highest score at Augusta National in ninety-three rounds over twenty-four years—and doing a few minutes' worth of interviews, he took his time getting to the clubhouse.

A scene such as this seemed inevitable, given the speedy timetable of Woods' return. But don't forget his fused spine and all the back issues he endured. That, too, played a role on a brutal weather day when the temperature never climbed out of the 50s and the windchill made it colder.

"It's not as limber and loose as it normally is, that's for sure," Woods said afterward.

As tough as it was on Woods to walk, it was also not a stretch to suggest that a good bit of his problems were due to his back. When Woods' lower back is bothering him, it plays out more in his short game. The clubs used for chipping and putting and even short-iron shots into greens cause him to bend over more. The instinct is to lessen the pain, which can lead to different techniques and postures.

Perhaps that had something to do with four three-putt greens and a four-putt. In his entire PGA Tour career, Woods never had more than 4 greens in a round in which he took three putts or more. He had thirty-six putts total. And he played his last three holes in 4 over par, including a double bogey at the 18th.

Woods did not blame his back for the poor putting.

"I mean, it's just like I hit a thousand putts out there on the greens today," he said. "Obviously it's affected the score. You take those away and I have normal two-putts, I'd be even par for the day. I did what I needed to do ball-striking-wise, but I did absolutely the exact opposite on the greens.

"I just could not get a feel for getting comfortable with the ball. Posture, feel, my right hand, my release, I just couldn't find it. Trying different things, trying to find it, trying to get something, taking practice strokes and just trying to feel the swing and the putter head, trying to get anything, and nothing seemed to work."

And then Woods was self-deprecating.

"Even as many putts as I had, you'd think I'd have figured it out somewhere along the line, but it just didn't happen," he said.

Woods hit 11 of 18 greens in regulation, his best of the tournament. He hit 11 of 14 fairways, also his best. He made birdies at the 2nd, 12th, and 13th holes, but also had two double bogeys, including a four-putt green at the fifth hole.

It was a day with just nine scores under par and a scoring average over 74.5.

"It hasn't changed," Woods said of the physical challenge. "Today was a challenge with the conditions. The conditions were tough today. They were tough yesterday starting out, but at least we got a little bit of a lull at the end. It's just been blustery all day. You add in the temperature difference, it was cold starting out; the ball wasn't going very far.

"I thought it was tough. Some of the other guys may not say that, but for me I had a tough time."

Woods dropped into a tie for 41st place. His worst finish in twenty-one previous appearances as a pro was 40th in 2012. Playing seventy-two holes was never going to be easy, and it was made worse by the cold weather day.

"I'm sure his leg is hurting," said Kevin Kisner, who played the third round with Woods. "I mean, I'm hurting, and I'm healthy, so I hope he can get back out there and play a couple more events with us here soon."

SPECTATORS LINED THE ROPES AS WOODS MADE THE JOURNEY from the eighteenth green to the Augusta National scoring area adjacent to the clubhouse, a scene reminiscent of his 2019 victory at the Masters.

Then, he was walking on air following perhaps the greatest win of his career. On this Sunday, he was hobbling, both literally and figuratively, after shooting a second straight 78, only his signature on the scorecard left to make it official.

Bubba Watson was there to greet him first, telling Woods, "I'm proud of you." The sentiment was similar to that of those who cheered for Woods as he made his way to the clubhouse after a surreal week that saw him return in such surprising, and relatively successful, fashion.

Also there was his mom, Tida; his girlfriend, Erica; his kids, Sam and Charlie; his friend Rob McNamara; and several people who work for him or his foundation.

In the end, Woods produced his worst 72-hole score at the Masters, 301, 13 over par; and he finished in his worst position, tied for 47th (aside from the one time he missed the cut as an amateur). And his Saturday and Sunday scores of 78 were the worst in ninety-four Masters rounds to that point.

No matter. This was but part of a remarkable process, one that had him looking forward to future tournaments, including The Open and perhaps the PGA Championship a month later.

"I won't be playing a full schedule ever again, so it'll be just the big events," Woods said. "I don't know if I'll play Southern Hills [site of the PGA Championship] or not. But I'm looking forward to St. Andrews. That is something near and dear to my heart. I've won two Opens there. It's the home of golf, and it's my favorite course in the world. I will be there for that one.

"But anything between that I don't know. I will be there. There's no doubt. Like this week, try and get ready for Southern Hills and see what this body can do."

Woods managed just a single birdie and struggled with putting and chipping. It was understandable given his long layoff and lack of competition. He hit ten of 18 greens but needed thirty-four putts to rank last in the field among those who made the cut.

Afterward, Woods was not too focused on the details, but more on the big picture. In noticeable discomfort as he was finishing his round, Woods acknowledged he would need a few days to recover before getting back to work. He left open the possibility of the PGA Championship, but everyone knew there would be no warm-up event.

And that was okay. For a man who had eighty-two PGA Tour titles and fifteen major championships, competing at Augusta that week was a different kind of victory.

"For not winning an event, yes. Yes, without a doubt," he said. "To go from where I was to get to this point, I've had an incredible team that has helped me and incredible support.

"Then to come here on these grounds and have the patrons—I played in a COVID year [2020], and then I didn't play last year. The 2019 victory was the last time for me that I experienced having patrons like this, and it's exciting. It's inspiring. It's fun to hear the roars, to hear the holes in ones.

"We had just an amazing day today, and now the wind is starting to pick up, it's starting to swirl a little bit," Woods said as the leaders were starting their rounds. "I think it's going to be fun to watch."

As it turned out, Woods would play in just two more tournaments in 2022, completing neither of them.

19

The Golden Bear

A few yards away from the Augusta National Clubhouse, Jack Nicklaus is amid a flurry of weeklong activity, in his accommodations overlooking the grounds, the first tee of the golf course a mere pitch shot away.

A six-time winner of the Masters, Nicklaus was invited to join the club in 2001 and stays in myriad cabins on the property whenever he visits. This time he's mere steps from spectators enjoying an afternoon lunch under umbrellas on the day prior to the 2023 Masters.

Nicklaus' wife of sixty-three years, Barbara, is visiting with Susan North, the wife of two-time U.S. Open champion Andy North, a longtime Nicklaus friend. At one point, Nicklaus' son, Steve, pops his head in to say hello, trying to decipher eating plans.

The following morning, Nicklaus, who turned 84 in January of 2024, would take part in the ceremonial opening tee shot alongside Gary Player and Tom Watson. Nicklaus, who played his last Masters in 2005 at age 65, has taken part in this tournament tradition since 2010 when he joined the only other former Masters champion to become a member, Arnold Palmer.

The big-screen TV is showing various sports highlights as

Nicklaus' longtime assistant, Scott Tolley, arrives with a visitor who is there to discuss Jack's legacy—and that of Tiger Woods.

There might be no topic Nicklaus has discussed more over the past thirty or so years, or with so much patience and depth. Wearing shorts, loafers, and a long-sleeved T-shirt, Nicklaus is self-deprecating and accommodating as he sits down to talk Tiger, recalling stories from his own career, the Masters, and some of his conversations with Woods.

Just the night before, they had spent some time together at the annual Champions Dinner in the Augusta National clubhouse.

And without wasting much time, the Golden Bear's big-picture view of Woods' career comes without reservation.

"Early on, Tiger's ability was just so good that he didn't even think about it," Nicklaus says. "Then he had some adversity. And he didn't really have any adversity until he had the issues with his wife and that situation. Then his back started getting to him, and before that he won the U.S. Open on one leg, basically.

"I know this last one [the car crash] was bad. He almost acts like he relishes the adversity to overcome it. And this was a big one. It's very tough. I sit next to Tiger every year at the Masters dinner. And he said his game is fantastic. 'Every part of my game is right where it should be. Except I can't walk. How long I'll be able to do it until it affects my game I don't know.' That's sad to me. He's so good. He's still well within his prime."

SO MANY COMPARISONS BETWEEN WOODS AND NICKLAUS HAVE been made over the years. It started way back when Woods had a list of Nicklaus' accomplishments to use as his own benchmark for achievement.

"I don't know what he put up, but I know he had a list on his wall," Nicklaus says. "When he was young, he beat the devil out of me."

Woods' goals were for a long time believed to include surpassing Nicklaus' record of eighteen major championships.

And why not? It became clear early on that Woods would be knocking off majors unlike anyone since Nicklaus. Woods completed the career Grand Slam—winning all four major championships at least once—in 2000 at age 24. And for a majority of his time before injuries started to thwart him, Woods was on a pace that eclipsed that of Nicklaus, who won his first at age 22 at the 1962 U.S. Open and his last at the age of 46 at the 1986 Masters. Nicklaus and Woods are the only players in golf history to capture each of the major championships at least three times.

But Woods later disclosed that winning nineteen majors was not part of his childhood goals. At least not as far as that list was concerned. In a 2015 *Time* interview, he spelled it out.

"Here's the major misconception that people have gotten all wrong," Woods said. "It was what was posted on my wall, about Jack's records. It was not the majors, OK? . . . It was the first time he broke 40, the first time he broke 80, the first golf tournament he ever won, first time he ever won the state amateur, first time he won the U.S. Amateur, and the first time he won the U.S. Open. And that was it. That was the list. It was all age-related. To me, that was important. This guy's the best out there and the best of all time. If I can beat each age that he did it, then I have a chance at being the best."

Woods did beat nearly all of Nicklaus' age records (although he never won the California Amateur), and his was a prominent name in the game well before he turned professional.

Nicklaus won the U.S. Amateur at age 19 in 1959, and again in 1961. Woods won it three straight times, the first at age 18. And that was after winning three straight U.S. Juniors. He captured an NCAA title in there, too. (Nicklaus won the 1961 NCAA title.)

At the 1996 Masters, a year after he made his debut in the tournament as an amateur and while still attending school at Stanford, Woods sought a practice round with Nicklaus and Palmer, who was amazed to see Woods pull out an iron at the par-5 13th hole where he had popped up his drive. Palmer believed Woods was going to lay up.

"Oh, Arnie," Jack said. "He's not." Woods rifled the shot over the creek and onto the green.

Later that day, in a pre-tournament news conference, Nicklaus could not have been more positive in his praise for Woods, saying he should win as many Masters as Palmer and him combined—which would be ten.

"That was a comment that people took literally," Nicklaus says. "The comment was basically saying the guy was really good. His chances of doing something were limitless."

IT IS FUN TO DEBATE: WHO HAD THE BETTER CAREER? YOU COULD go back and forth on this all day and never really get the right answer. You could argue for either side—and not necessarily be right or wrong.

Jack won eighteen majors, Tiger has fifteen. But Woods has won eighty-two PGA Tour events to the seventy-three posted by Nicklaus.

Nicklaus had an amazing nineteen runner-up finishes in majors and nine third-place finishes, while Woods had just seven seconds and four thirds. But Woods won a U.S. Open by 15 strokes, a Masters by 12, and an Open by 8, numbers the Golden Bear could not touch.

Then again . . . Nicklaus had seventy-three top-10s in majors and an incredible thirty-five out of forty in the decade of the 1970s. Woods had forty-one top-10s.

It is nearly impossible to compare players across eras, but attempts to do so nonetheless are made.

Nicklaus had a slew of Hall of Fame rivals whom he not only beat but who beat him: Nicklaus twice finished runner-up to Lee Trevino in majors, as he did to Tom Watson. One of his seconds was to Palmer at the 1960 U.S. Open, when Nicklaus was an amateur and played the final two rounds with Ben Hogan; he also finished second to Gary Player, Johnny Miller, and Seve Ballesteros.

Woods did not have the same top-level challengers, but he still had a slew of Hall of Famers in his era, including Phil Mickelson, Ernie Els, Vijay Singh, Mark O'Meara, and Retief Goosen.

He also finished second to some players who seemingly came out of nowhere, such as Rich Beem, Michael Campbell, Trevor Immelman, and Y. E. Yang. This suggests that Tiger almost certainly faced deeper fields than Nicklaus, a premise that Jack acknowledges.

"When I started out there were probably twenty or so guys who could win in any given week, of whom you'd really look at maybe five," Nicklaus said in the 2005 updated version of his book *Golf My Way*. "Today there are probably a hundred or so possible winners of any PGA Tour event, without about twenty you'd favor. It's simply a matter of more players playing better."

Or as the late Phil Rodgers—who worked with Nicklaus on his short game ahead of his two-major 1980 season—said in a 2002 *Golf Digest* interview: "Especially in the '60s, you'd see a lot of majors where at the end there would be only five or six guys within ten strokes. Maybe three or four guys would have a chance to win on the weekend. Today, at a major, you see twenty guys finish within ten strokes. One of the reasons Jack was able to finish second and third so often is he didn't have to contend with that kind of depth."

TO GET WHERE NICKLAUS DID IN HIS CAREER, HE HAD TO POSsess some of the same inner drive as Woods. It can't all be done on talent. There is something inside that made them each work hard and continue to push despite their immense abilities. "Resiliency" and "determination" are words thrown around a good bit, but they apply.

"I never really thought about it. I don't think Tiger did either," Nicklaus says. "When I first came on Tour, my ability was there. I had to develop beyond that to win. But I was doing that by playing. It was never an issue to me. I didn't show up thinking I was going to win. I showed up figuring I needed to work at it, but I was putting myself in a position to win. It was never in my mind that I wasn't going to.

"Winning breeds winning, at least I've always felt that way. You've got to win the first time to get over that barrier. I had three seconds prior to the [1962] U.S. Open. Then I beat Arnold in the playoff [at Oakmont for his first career victory as a pro]. Had I not beaten Arnold in that playoff, I don't know if I would have started to doubt whether I could win or not. But once I won the playoff, there wasn't a doubt in my mind then about my ability to go play and win."

You could easily say the same things about Woods. Like Nicklaus, he came to the pro game with considerable fanfare for all he accomplished as an amateur. And he had success quickly, winning his fifth pro start at the Las Vegas Invitational. When he won the 1997 Masters, it was his first major as a pro.

While Woods said he never looked at Nicklaus' record as a goal, he certainly had benchmarks to attain. Nicklaus, on the other hand, said he never really thought much about it. While he put extreme focus on the major championships, building his schedule around them and doing all he could to be prepared for them, the world was not as fixated on the numbers.

Nicklaus has often cited the example of the 1970 Open Championship at St. Andrews. It was there he won his second Open and first at the Old Course, the home of golf.

Afterward, Bob Green, the Associated Press golf writer, advised him of his standing in the all-time count of major championships.

"I walked in the press room, I'll never forget that, and Bob Green said, 'Jack, that's ten major championships. You've only got three more to tie Bobby Jones.'

"Honest to gosh truth, I never counted them. And nobody had ever mentioned it before."

The win over Doug Sanders in a playoff was Nicklaus' eighth professional major, but Green viewed it as his 10th overall because he was counting Jack's two U.S. Amateur victories. That was common at that time.

Jones had thirteen majors if you count his five U.S. Amateurs and one British Amateur. As a lifelong amateur, he never played in the PGA Championship. And his Masters appearances came after he had retired from competitive golf. Jones won the U.S. Open four times and The Open three times. On the all-time major list, he is credited with seven majors.

(An interesting aside: as Nicklaus was bearing down on his 1986 Masters victory at age 48, CBS-TV's Pat Summerall referenced it as his twentieth major title, which included the two U.S. Amateurs. Sometime after that, the amateurs were dropped as part of his major total. Woods would have eighteen if you included his three U.S. Amateurs.)

That suggests there was little fanfare whatsoever when Nicklaus surpassed the eleven major championships held by Walter Hagen, who is third on the all-time list behind Nicklaus and Woods.

For Woods, such comparisons were endless. When he captured

his third straight major in 2000 at the PGA Championship, that tied him with Byron Nelson and Seve Ballesteros. When he got his sixth by completing the "Tiger Slam" in 2001 at the Masters, he matched Nick Faldo and Lee Trevino.

His 2002 Masters victory meant tying Palmer, the U.S. Open win that year meant tying Tom Watson, the 2005 Masters put him alongside Gary Player and Ben Hogan. Every major was measured against who had done it before, with the big prize being Nicklaus down the road.

We'll never know how Yang's 2009 PGA victory—the first time Woods did not convert a major after holding the 54-hole lead—or the marital scandal of later that year or the numerous injuries that caused him to miss fourteen major championships from 2014 through 2021 impacted his final numbers.

"I feel sorry for Tiger from that standpoint," Nicklaus said in 2005 as he was about to play his final Open. "They started counting [for] him before he won one. So I had a head start on the number as far as worrying about pressure and that kind of thing. But that's when that happened."

Nicklaus tied Hagen with eleven pro majors and Jones with thirteen overall at the 1972 U.S. Open. He surpassed them both with his next major title at the 1973 PGA Championship and went on to win six more.

NICKLAUS NEVER HAD INJURY ISSUES. HE PLAYED A REMARKable 146 consecutive major championships starting with the 1962 Masters through the 1998 U.S. Open—from age 22 to 58. The only time he ever withdrew after starting was at the 1983 Masters.

Along the way, Nicklaus put together what was then the second-best made-cut streak in PGA Tour history, going from the 1970 Sahara Invitational until the 1976 World Open without missing a cut. He made 105 in a row, which was second to the record of 113 set by Nelson.

Woods surpassed both those marks, making 142 in a row from the 1998 Buick Invitational until missing the cut at Nelson's tournament in 2005. The next best after Nicklaus is 86 in a row by Hale Irwin.

Once again, Nicklaus was making history and not fully aware of it.

"When I missed, it was the first time anyone ever mentioned it," Nicklaus says. "When I came on Tour, you didn't make money every tournament when you made the cut. There might be seventy make the cut and only fifty made money. I made money in every tournament I played, as well as making the cut. Which I thought was pretty good. I did have several fiftieth-place finishes."

Among the qualities that helped Woods make so many cuts in a row was that "he could overcome and never give up and never mail it in," says his former coach Hank Haney.

The same is true of Nicklaus—except for one instance that he still remembers clearly.

"I'm embarrassed to mention it," Nicklaus says. "There was a tournament where I really didn't care if I made [the cut]. It was Pecan Valley at the PGA Championship in 1968. I got to the last hole. It was hot. Miserable. I was playing terrible. I had about a 7- or 8-foot putt to make the cut. If I missed it I knew I'd miss [the cut]. And for the first time I could ever recall, I didn't care whether I made it or not.

"I was embarrassed afterward when I got done. 'Really, you're out here to compete. How many people in the world would love to make the cut in the PGA Championship?' And I didn't care. Missed it. I was embarrassed that I didn't care. Never let that happen again.

"I did it one time in my life and it embarrassed me and taught me a lesson to never do that again."

TIGER AND JACK ARE SEPARATED BY THIRTY-SIX YEARS. WHEN Nicklaus won the 1986 Masters, Woods was 10. Although he was already famous in his own right, the idea that he'd ever be challenging Nicklaus' records had yet to gain hold.

Given Nicklaus' longevity, they did end up competing in the same major championship twenty-two times. And Nicklaus actually finished ahead of Woods in four of those tournaments.

"I clipped him a couple of times," Nicklaus says, chuckling.

Three of them—the 1995 Masters, the 1996 Masters, and the 1996 U.S. Open—occurred when Woods was still an amateur.

But the 1998 Masters was one of the more remarkable events for someone who did not win the tournament.

Nicklaus was 58.

Woods, 22, was the defending Masters champion.

Earlier that week, Nicklaus had been honored with a plaque near the 16th tee as he was competing in his 40th Masters. Nobody dreamed he'd be contending on Sunday, and he eventually tied for 6th.

After opening the tournament with rounds of 73–72–70, he started the final round by birdieing four of the first seven holes. He played with Ernie Els, then the No. 1–ranked player in the world. They were a group behind that of Woods and Davis Love III.

"It was special," Els says. "I remember Tiger, he was playing in front of us, and we crossed paths and he said to me, 'Are you having a good time?' I joked I needed ear plugs because it was as loud as I've ever heard it.

"Jack was just winking at me the whole day. Every time he made a putt he winked at me. You knew he was fifty-eight, but the way he was playing and putting . . . and nobody knows those greens better than he does. You bet he thought he could win."

Woods tied for 8th. "We got a great view all day, and every hole [Nicklaus] was getting standing ovations," Woods says. "At every tee, every green. Down in Amen Corner, the echoes are so much louder and so cool. It was just so great that day, the atmosphere."

Nicklaus' run eventually ended and he finished four shots behind winner Mark O'Meara, who birdied the final hole to edge Couples and David Duval. He finished ahead of Woods, Els, Justin Leonard, and Love—the major champions of the previous year.

Two months later, Nicklaus played in the U.S. Open at the Olympic Club after the USGA gave him a special exemption and he tied for 43rd. But he decided to end his streak of majors after that, his left hip becoming bothersome enough that he did not want to compete in The Open at Royal Birkdale. He later had surgery.

"I've reflected on [the streak] for a lot of years," Nicklaus said then. "My sole thing has been to not embarrass myself. I think I've been playing on borrowed time for the last couple or three years. I don't want to stretch any further. I think I stretched it far enough when I was healthy.

"When I played at the U.S. Open, I played nine holes in the two weeks before the tournament. I couldn't play. I played pretty well at the U.S. Open. I made a stance change that allowed me to get it around the golf course.

"I've always prided myself on being able to prepare. There's no excuse to not be prepared. But I didn't think I could do that. If I couldn't do that, I really don't deserve to play."

Of course, virtually nobody would have been bothered if he decided to play anyway, so great was the desire to see the legend compete. Even if he was at less than his best, few minded that Nicklaus was no longer Nicklaus.

Just as few have a problem with Woods attempting to play at the later stages of his career when not at his best. But it goes against every instinct both he and Nicklaus possess, given their pride and competitiveness.

AFTER HIS MAJOR STREAK ENDED, NICKLAUS MADE JUST ONE more cut in the big tournaments. In 2000, he decided to end his run at the U.S. Open, played at Pebble Beach. That's where Woods won by fifteen shots to capture his third major title.

Later that summer, for the only time in a major, Nicklaus and Woods were grouped together at the PGA Championship, played at Valhalla in Louisville. Woods was on the cusp of history, attempting to win a third straight major for the first time since Ben Hogan did it in 1953.

It is a feat that the greats of the game, including Nicklaus, never accomplished. Vijay Singh, who won that year's Masters, was the third player in the group.

Coming to the final hole of the second round, Nicklaus nearly holed his third shot for an eagle, one he needed to make the 36-hole cut. He missed by one, and Woods went on to win that tournament, too, outlasting Bob May in a dramatic playoff.

"I was sixty years old at the time—no way I could compete against him," Nicklaus says. "But he was phenomenal."

If there was a difference in their games at their primes, Nicklaus pointed to Woods' short game.

"I think it won a lot of tournaments for him," Nicklaus says. "Because of my back, I couldn't practice my short game. I couldn't stay out there long enough to do it. My back would start killing me. And Tiger was not a big kid when he was younger like I was. I was probably around 175 pounds when I was 13 years old. That's a pretty good-sized kid. Tiger was a scrawny little kid. He had to rely on his short game to do it.

"I thought his dad did a very good job of preparing him. He

didn't go for the modern equipment as fast as he could. He had him learn how to play shots rather than distance. He developed a short game that could stand up against everybody. He had that, which I didn't have. I was a good putter by instinct. He was a good putter because he practiced it. That was totally different.

"Maybe I was a better hitter of the golf ball in my prime than him. I was a better driver. Tiger was long, but he missed half the world [fairways] half the time. We both were good middle iron players. I think I was a better driver and his short game was better. Some areas he was better than I and some I was better than him."

IT IS PERHAPS NOTHING MORE THAN AN AMAZING COINCIDENCE, but the tournaments in which Nicklaus played the majors for the last time were all won by Woods.

The 2000 U.S. Open and PGA were the first two. Then Nicklaus decided to make the 2005 Masters his forty-fifth and final official tournament at Augusta National. Awkwardly, due to weather conditions that necessitated a two-tee start, Nicklaus finished his final round on the 9th green on Friday afternoon.

Woods was on his way to a dramatic win, his first major title since the 2002 U.S. Open. He needed a sudden-death playoff victory over Chris DiMarco to do it, having bogeyed the final two holes in regulation.

And then came that summer at St. Andrews, the home of golf. There was tremendous fanfare as Nicklaus was set to bid farewell to the majors and official tournament golf. He was grouped with Watson and Luke Donald, and it was clear as the final round was unfolding that Nicklaus was not going to make the cut.

As Nicklaus finished up on the home hole, Woods was headed to the first tee, which sits only yards away from the 18th green. It was a glorious scene, with spectators spilling out of balconies and perched on rooftops, cheering the Golden Bear one last time. He made a birdie, too, saying afterward, "The hole would have moved wherever I hit it," a last great act of an amazing career.

Woods was on his way to another victory, his second major title of the year and tenth overall.

He would get his own emotional walk across the Swilcan Bridge to teary-eyed cheering at the home hole seventeen years later—under much different circumstances.

20

The Swilcan Bridge

Tiger Woods stifled a tear as he carefully navigated his way across the Swilcan Bridge, a 700-plus-year-old structure that links the final tee box to the final fairway to the final hole at the Home of Golf.

Woods powered his way over the centuries-old concrete while removing his cap to wave to thousands of spectators who had lined both sides of the wide swath of ground that makes up the first and 18th fairways at the Old Course in St. Andrews, Scotland, during the second round of the one hundred fiftieth Open.

That very bridge has come to signify the place where the greats of golf wave goodbye.

Arnold Palmer did it in 1995—and Woods was there to watch him hit his opening tee shot of that final round. Jack Nicklaus did it in 2005—and Woods was also there to see him tee off in a tournament that Tiger would win for the second time. Tom Watson, Lee Trevino, Nick Faldo . . . all took a bow as they bid farewell to golf's oldest championship.

Not Tiger. He kept right on going, carefully navigating that slippery bridge so as to not compromise his right lower leg, which was throbbing. The pain was real, but Woods never showed a hint of discomfort, as if he was going to make this a journey of triumph rather than one of despair.

There could have been a million thoughts racing through his mind, from the time he first set foot on the ground as an amateur in 1995 to his historic win in 2000 to a tenth major title in 2005 to the difficulty of 2010 to the immense struggles of 2015. Woods was playing in his sixth Open at St. Andrews, and he was unsure if there would be a seventh.

Woods knows his golf history, and so he made it a point not to stop on that bridge. He was not sure if his time had come to an end at St. Andrews—the date of the next Open Championship to be played there had yet to be announced—but he made it clear later he wasn't done with golf.

And yet . . . just in case.

Spectators in the double-tiered grandstand behind the green rose and applauded. Those located to the right of the fairway and green were 10 deep. Players starting their rounds on the first hole, including Rory McIlroy, stopped to tip their caps.

The ancient buildings that border the hole teemed with people, too. They waved from windows and rooftops. The newly renovated Rusacks hotel had an upper-level bar that was packed with cheering people. The building where the long-ago purveyor of the Old Course, Tom Morris Sr., lived and worked had no room for anyone not watching the scene unfold.

For more than two minutes, Woods had this huge, expansive stage, waving in all directions as the cheering continued. His playing partners, Max Homa and Matt Fitzpatrick, and all the caddies dropped back to give him the space he deserved. And if there had not been more golf to be played just after 3 p.m. on this sunny, Scottish day, they would have kept right on.

Having managed to secure a spot to the right of the green, I had a clear view of Woods as he plotted out his final strokes. Over the years, I've been lucky enough to have such vantage points, witness to the greatest golfer of my generation, perhaps ever. This was Tiger's eighty-fourth major as a professional golfer, and I was there to witness eighty of them, never missing one of his fifteen victories, there for all but one of his U.S. starts (thwarted only by COVID-19 restrictions at the 2020 U.S. Open).

It is a nice perch, which has allowed me to become a Tiger specialist and be among one of the few who have been fortunate enough to get a modicum of access. In the days leading up to this Open, we chatted briefly during a practice round on the Old Course, and he shared his concern over the plight of the future of U.S. Ryder Cup captains, given the upstart LIV Golf endeavor, which was in its early stages but dominating headlines. The rival tour saw players who might be part of the Ryder Cup conversation defecting to the new endeavor, with huge guaranteed contracts, but putting their PGA Tour and Ryder Cup futures in peril.

When I suggested to Woods that, given his stature, he simply become the permanent U.S. Ryder Cup captain (a joke but not necessarily a bad idea), he dropped a quick expletive in my direction, smiled, and continued on.

Five days later, he was going to miss the 36-hole cut by a considerable amount, but this was obviously a big moment. Just as with Nicklaus seventeen years earlier, it was obvious that this was more than a legend finishing up a round of golf.

As he was about to stand over the putt, I began recording on my phone. Woods had 4 feet left for a birdie, and somehow missed, the ball catching the edge of the hole. (In 2005, at age 65, Nicklaus made a 15-footer for birdie, his final stroke in a major championship.)

There were groans, but after tapping in for a final par, Woods heard the cheering again. For nearly a minute and a half, the noise never stopped, as he walked off the green, shook hands with the other players, the rules officials, and the caddies, and hugged his own caddie, Joe LaCava. Then he turned toward the Royal & Ancient Clubhouse (R&A), and the ovation didn't stop until he disappeared.

Billy Foster, the veteran caddie from England who has worked for the likes of Seve Ballesteros and Lee Westwood and numerous others in a decades-long career, was working for reigning U.S. Open champion Fitzpatrick. He knows Woods going way back, having once even caddied for him during a Presidents Cup.

Foster had a difficult time keeping it together as it played out.

"I caddied for Darren Clarke at the K Club in 2006, six weeks after his wife had died," says Foster, recalling the Ryder Cup played outside of Dublin and the 2011 Open champion. "And he won all three of his matches. It was an emotional thing watching Darren cry. The magnitude of the situation—winning the Ryder Cup, twenty thousand people around the 16th green, after his wife died. It was unbelievably emotional.

"Tiger walking up the last at St. Andrews is the second-most emotional thing I've experienced in forty years. It was that immense."

It was not the ending for which anyone—Woods among them—had hoped. He traveled to Scotland with designs on a better showing, of maybe even contending, despite the horrific car crash that left him hospitalized for weeks and required several surgeries to his lower right leg. His playing there seemed so unlikely just months prior.

And yet, while downplaying it publicly, Woods had pledged to be there. Well before anyone thought it was possible, in late 2021, Woods made it clear to his friend Justin Thomas that St. Andrews and The Open were circled on his calendar.

"Quite often," says Thomas, whom Woods has often said is like a little brother to him. "Yeah, he reminded me many times that he planned on beating me here at this tournament for quite a while."

It didn't matter that Woods shot scores of 78–75 to miss the cut. Not only did he make it to The Open, it was his third tournament of the year, and something most observers did not see coming.

"He was never going to be the Tiger we knew in the early 2000s," Foster says. "He's evolved into something different. It's a never-say-die attitude. His mantra is the strongest mind that there has ever been in the game. He's basically been playing with a handicap. He's lucky to be walking. And the great determination he showed to try and compete with these lads and made a couple of cuts has been nothing but inspiration and incredible."

Homa, who seventeen months earlier had stood with Woods at Riviera and accepted the Genesis Invitational tournament trophy in his presence, had never played with him prior to those two rounds at St. Andrews.

"The walk up 18 was as surreal as it gets," Homa says. "It was a real cool experience. A good learning experience as well. A huge crowd and a big, big stage.

"It was really impressive. Even when it was obvious he was not going to make the cut. He still grinds. All the stories you heard about him being a guy who never gives up—it was very, very apparent. He was still working his tail off.

"I was going to miss the cut unless I made eagle [at the last hole]. I did get to kind of watch. It was cool. We were behind him and we saw after he was pretty emotional. So we got the hell out of the way. It was very obvious it was that kind of moment."

DAVID FEHERTY, IN WHAT TURNED OUT TO BE HIS LAST BROADcast for NBC and Golf Channel, saw in person what many others saw on TV. "He just didn't have the wheels," Feherty says. "He had a lot of guts. You could see the way he was walking toward the end—there was discomfort for sure."

Feherty has been around Woods as much as just about anyone in the broadcast world.

Before leaving to be part of the LIV Golf broadcast team in 2022, Feherty had worked at NBC for six years and for eighteen years prior to that at CBS Sports. In the early days, Feherty was an on-course reporter, and often followed Woods' group. The two had a solid rapport, to the point that Feherty could work in his humor on Woods without fear of retribution.

And he learned early on just how dedicated Woods was to being as good as possible.

"He always had that about him," Feherty says. "You could see it in a microcosm the way he was on the golf course. I was with him from the very beginning. When I became a broadcaster, he turned pro. I was attached to his group and I think I saw him win more than fifty times.

"The way he would fix himself on a golf course was unlike anything I ever saw. If he got off to a bad start, he had a great finish. Every fucking time. It was uncanny the way he could do it. We're seeing that in a wider sense now. I don't think he's playing if he didn't think he could win. I think he can. The only mistakes I ever made about Tiger Woods were when I underestimated him. I thought he can't come back from that. Well, he fucking can, it turns out."

Feherty has numerous stories to draw on from his time following Woods, but one that stands out occurred at the 2000 NEC Championship in Akron, Ohio. Due to a thunderstorm delay, the final round finished in near darkness around 8:30 p.m.

The week prior, Woods had won his third consecutive major title, defeating Bob May in a playoff at the PGA Championship.

Now he was competing in a World Golf Championship event

at Firestone Country Club in Akron, and in nearly any other circumstance, Woods would not have even attempted the shot he had from the fairway on the final hole. It was too dark to play. But Woods held an 11-stroke lead.

With an 8-iron from 168 yards, Woods hit a shot that landed just past the flagstick and spun back to just 2 feet. The fans who gathered behind the 18th green could barely see the ball in the air, but roared with approval, holding up burning lighters.

The win was Woods' eighth of the season.

"He hit a shot in the dark at Firestone," Feherty said. "All I could see was his teeth afterwards. His ability to lead and keep pushing on was unlike anything I ever saw. When he got in front, five, six, seven, eight shots . . . That's really hard to improve upon. Do I risk making double bogey by hitting this shot? He did. It's the reason why he won by so many.

"Ernie Els was No. 2 [in the world] for a long time. He'd hit shots and I'd be with him frequently too. And then Tiger would hit a shot, and Ernie would look at it and think, 'Fuck, I haven't got that. But I have to try.' And they'd try. Either him or Phil [Mickelson] or Vijay [Singh]. Or whoever it was.

"They'd make bogey and he'd make birdie and the gap got wider. He wins a U.S. Open by fifteen [in 2000]. The last person who won by fifteen was Old Tom Morris, and he was playing [a golf ball] with badgers' testicles stuffed with seagull feathers. It's uncanny. He wins a Masters by twelve [in 1997]. Those are remarkable wins because of the way he kept his foot on the gas. Others would be content to win by four or five."

Feherty spoke a truth that was evident but not often said: Most players didn't have the arsenal of shots that Woods possessed. Some of that has changed as time has passed.

"I see Rory McIlroy hitting those shots," Feherty says. "Justin Thomas. Dustin Johnson. There's a half a dozen players who can almost hit the shots. But some of the shots I saw Tiger hit . . . with his foot halfway up a Christmas tree at Castle Pines. Cutting an eight-iron out over the water into the 12th green. He called me out so often. I was an expert until Tiger Woods fucking showed up. I could tell you . . . I played the game at the highest level [as a pro on the European Tour]. I knew what the players at the highest level could do from any given situation. It was my job to predict that: 'Well, he's got to punch it out sideways here.'

"First time he ever did it to me was at the Western Open at Cog Hill in Chicago [1997]. Very first time I went out to watch him on the golf course. I knew he was a good amateur and all the rest. He hit it into the trees on the right of the ninth hole. I walked over. [Broadcaster Gary] McCord had the call at the hole. Fluff [Mike Cowan, Woods' caddie at the time] was there. Tiger was walking up from the tee. He's got a lie that is not conceivable. He's got a root in front of him where he can't drive it low underneath the trees. He's got about 230 yards to the hole, he's got to come out sideways. I come back out in the fairway and McCord says, 'What's he got?' I say, 'He's going to have to punch it out sideways. He'll have a couple hundred yards left for his third shot.'

"So he gets in there and he hits a shot where I was in the way. He's aiming it right at me. I know where to stand. He cuts a 3-iron over my head, rockets it out there, cuts about forty yards, runs up ten or fifteen feet from the hole. McCord says, 'That must have been lying better than you thought.'

"No, it fucking wasn't! It's like a crime scene investigation. I go over there toward the divot. He was looking back at me and said, 'You called that one, didn't you?' I said, 'I don't know what you are but there weren't two of them on Noah's Ark.' Those are the very first words I ever said to him. He got a kick out of that."

THERE WERE MANY TIMES WHERE ANALYST BRANDEL CHAMBLEE was highly critical of Woods. He was particularly tough on him in 2013, when Woods uncharacteristically had a series of rules violations.

A two-stroke penalty for taking an improper drop from what he thought was an embedded lie in Abu Dhabi caused him to miss the cut. He had the infamous improper drop at the Masters that was only discovered by a television viewer, with a two-shot penalty being assessed the next day—but without a scorecard disqualification.

There was what was viewed as a dubious drop after his finding the water during the final round of the Players Championship, a situation that was signed off on by a fellow competitor but deemed proper by the rules officials on his way to a victory. And there was an incident at the BMW Championship where slow-motion video saw Woods' ball move as he attempted to move debris. Woods believed it "oscillated," but he was still assessed a two-shot penalty.

Chamblee, in his role as a Golf Channel analyst, raised questions about these incidents, and he wasn't shy about it. He claimed Woods was "being cavalier with the rules."

In 2015, Woods was hurting. The 2014 microdiscectomy never quite took. Woods started his year in Phoenix and suddenly couldn't chip. One of the game's best short-game players looked lost. He chunked and skulled and bladed so many shots around the greens it was alarming.

A week later, just 11 holes into the opening round of the event at Torrey Pines, Woods withdrew. A lengthy delay prior to the round caused his back to stiffen. He said afterward that he could not get his "glutes to activate." It was also clear his chipping problems were not alleviated.

Woods took a nine-week break from the game, and many pundits, including Chamblee, believed he'd never get over those chipping woes. Same for his former coach, Hank Haney. Such issues are difficult to overcome, especially for a 40-plus golfer dealing with back pain, which makes it difficult to practice.

"You could probably find fifty clips of me saying he'd never overcome it," Chamblee says. "People love to throw it in my face. But I always said that I've never seen anybody do it. I didn't think he'd come back from it.

"Tiger has proven to have the strongest mind in the history of golf. I would say I hope I'm wrong. That if anybody can come back from it, Tiger can. Tiger maintains it was his back issues and taking medication. And there's no doubt that contributed. I know for a fact he would have hit thousands and thousands upon thousands of shots in his backyard trying to address that problem. And he didn't solve it. He kept coming back with the issues. At some point he had to think he's never going to solve it. It had to creep into his mind.

"Lo and behold, here he is back at the Hero [World Challenge in the Bahamas in 2017]. His back was fine and the chipping is fine. Maybe it was just the back. And that would explain him overcoming it. But the mental scar tissue he had . . . I've never seen anyone get past it."

It was during that Hero tournament, Woods' first since the spinal fusion surgery, that Chamblee was convinced.

"The first swing he made, his ball speed was around a hundred eighty miles an hour," he says. "So physically, with one swing of the club, I knew he was fine. But to me, the larger issue wasn't evident until the sixth or eighth hole of the second day. He was chipping into the grain and short-sided [meaning there was little room on the green between him and the flagstick].

"[Golf Channel announcer] Steve Sands is telling a story as Tiger is hitting the chip. And as he's telling the story, it might have been the most important shot that Tiger Woods ever hit. It was a little-bitty pitch into the grain. He had done nothing but chunk and blade and fat those for two and a half years when we had seen him.

"He hit a beautiful pitch that was spinning and stopped right by the hole. With two shots, I knew it was game on. So while it was amazing that he won a major championship in 2019 for the first time in eleven years, the possibility was put into my head after the Hero in 2017."

WOODS ESSENTIALLY HAD FOUR COACHES IN HIS CAREER. HE began working with Butch Harmon as a 16-year-old amateur phenom. It was a relationship that lasted through the first six years of Woods' pro career, with eight major championships.

They parted under somewhat odd circumstances following the 2002 PGA Championship. Woods had won the first two majors that year, but apparently got antsy. There was never any formal breakup.

"He never told me why," says Harmon, who has coached a bevy of world-class players, including Greg Norman and Phil Mickelson. "He never said. Now, I heard from some people that he thought I got too much credit for how well he was doing. But he never said anything to me. And we've had a great relationship after that."

Harmon helped mold Woods into a professional golfer, and after the 1997 Masters victory he helped him make changes to his swing that would better suit him for the long haul.

"One of the great things about Tiger was he always wanted to learn, he always asked questions about the greats of the game," Harmon says. "He would ask me about my dad [Claude Harmon Sr., who won the 1948 Masters] and Ben Hogan, and you don't get that a lot. One of the greatest thrills my dad ever had and he said it was walking up the last [fairway] at Augusta with a five-shot lead.

"So there I am in '97 behind the 18th green and I've got sunglasses on with Tiger's mom and dad, and tears are streaming down my face. And here he's got a bigger lead than that. It's hard to top that, hard to get any better than that."

Woods more or less went without a coach for more than a year, although it became clear in 2004 that he was working with Haney. There were significant changes made, mostly, Woods said, to relieve stress from his left knee. The Harmon way and the Haney way were considerably different, and it's a tribute to Woods that he figured out a way to change and be just as successful.

Under Haney, Woods won another six major championships and a total of thirty-one PGA Tour events before their relationship ended in 2010.

"I don't think anybody can approach him in any area," Haney says. "Skill, talent, and mind. Pick any area. Pick resiliency. Pick talent. Pick any element, and nobody comes close. Not even in the vicinity. 'Rory is that, Rory is that.' Please. He's not even close to what Tiger was. None of them. Phil Mickelson was an incredible player. It's unbelievable how good he was. One of the top-ten all time. But he was never number one [in the world] for a minute. Yes, he beat Tiger a few times. But their record isn't even close. Not even in the same stratosphere. That doesn't mean Mickelson isn't great.

"It's a combination of everything. It's human nature that we want simple answers to complicated questions. His greatness is a complicated question. There are so many things that make up greatness. All of them contribute to it. It's everything that made up that greatness. Incredible. Mind-boggling, really.

"I guess I'm biased on the deal. In my mind, I think Tiger is the greatest athlete ever. I know he'd be on a lot of people's short list. It's hard not to put Michael Jordan there or [Wayne] Gretzky. They played with other people on a team. Somebody has to pass the puck to Gretzky. With Tiger, it was all himself. I just feel like he's the greatest. Not just the greatest in golf, but in my mind he's among the greatest athletes."

For all their success together, Haney never was appreciated to the level he felt he deserved. The scrutiny on Woods' game intensified under his guidance, far more than it ever did under Harmon's. Woods had a lean year in 2004 when Haney started working with him, and there was relief in 2005 when Woods won two major championships. Throughout their time together, there always seemed to be some tension. Haney never quite knew if he was being blamed for Tiger's deficiencies, and yet it is hard to deny the record, the consistency.

It finally came to an end in the spring of 2010. Haney actually did the firing, deciding he no longer wanted the job. After Woods came back from the marital scandal, the impatience to find his game was apparent. Despite an incredible performance at the 2010 Masters, Woods struggled for most of that year, and Haney could sense the impending implosion. They parted ways soon after the Players Championship in May.

Woods' game took a severe turn that summer. Even though he contended at the Masters and the U.S. Open, tying for fourth at each tournament, he regressed. Putting was a problem. He wasn't a factor in The Open at St. Andrews, where he had won the previous two times.

Always searching, Woods had liked the work Sean Foley did with some players he knew, such as Hunter Mahan and Justin Rose. Foley was near his then-home in Orlando. They ended up working together for four years.

Woods never won a major with Foley, but he was at one of his lowest points in 2010 when Foley began the process of getting him back to the top. It's also when the injuries came up again. Achilles and knee injuries surfaced following the 2011 Masters, causing him to miss the U.S. Open and The Open. When he came back in August, his game was a mess, and Woods missed the cut at the PGA Championship.

Somehow, Woods kept fighting to put things together. He won his own tournament, then called the Chevron Challenge, in December of 2011. When he won the Arnold Palmer Invitational in March of 2012, it was Woods' first official win since December of 2009—just before the scandal broke—and his first PGA Tour victory since the BMW Championship in September of 2009.

Woods won three times that year and another five times in 2013, not only capturing two World Golf Championship events but the Players Championship as well. After falling outside of the top 50 in the world, he returned to No. 1.

"It was a fantastic time," Foley says. "It was challenging. It was challenging getting used to that amount of attention. There really are no rules when it comes down to it. I signed up for it . . . I'm not sure if Tiger used what was out there as fuel to come back and prove [himself] to everyone. I'd say probably yes. I think it was difficult when he came back at the start.

"On Wednesday, you guys would interview him, and it would normally be about the tournament he had just won. Now it's about affairs and divorce and it's gone from golf to TMZ. It's just impossible when you're someone like Tiger. Constantly reminded of what you did six months ago. Then it gets to the point where he hasn't won in fifteen weeks and seventeen weeks and then twenty weeks.

"No matter how strong you are or how well you cope with it, you can't unhear what you hear."

Foley was there at the start of Woods' back troubles in 2014, when he had his first microdiscectomy, causing him to miss the Masters for the first time. The rest of the year was mostly a waste, and it's clear in retrospect that Woods needed to give the procedure more time.

Later that year, Woods and Foley parted amicably, as Woods felt a need to work with someone—Chris Como—who was better suited to deal with back issues.

"One of the worst things you can do is bend over at the waist and turn really fast in both directions," Foley says of golfers and bad backs. "It amasses over time. He's not unique when it comes to back pain and back issues on the PGA Tour. He just had this capacity to cope and deal with it and get through it."

TIGER'S BACK PROBABLY WASN'T DOING HIM ANY FAVORS AT ST. Andrews, either. All of the focus was on his right leg and the laboring stride as the day progressed. But the truth is, he still had back problems, too, and they impacted his golf game in a different way.

Woods had no trouble hitting the golf ball. It was getting to it that was the problem. Throw in the soreness in his lower back that was bound to be apparent more than not, and the recipe for indifferent golf was real.

All of it made his 2022 return more remarkable. And explains why there was so much emotion on that Friday afternoon in the old Scottish town.

"That's when I started to realize, hey, that's when I started thinking about the next time it comes around here I might not be around," Woods said.

"As I walked further along the fairway, I saw Rory [McIlroy, playing the first hole] right there. He gave me the tip of the cap. It was pretty cool—the nods I was getting from guys as they were going out and I was coming in, just the respect; that was pretty neat. And from a players' fraternity level, it's neat to see that and feel that.

"And then as I got into the shot—or closer to the green, more into the hole—the ovation got louder and . . . you could feel the warmth and you could feel the people from both sides. Felt like the whole tournament was right there.

"And they all had appreciated what I've done here for the years I've played—I've won two championships here—my British Open success and all my times I've enjoyed here in Scotland and playing, I felt like it just came to a head right there as I was walking to my golf ball."

Fitzpatrick, who had won the U.S. Open a month earlier at The Country Club in Brookline, Massachusetts, where Woods was unable to play, took it all in while trying to concentrate on his own golf.

"It was amazing. It gave me goosebumps," Fitzpatrick said. "Just looking around, seeing everyone stood up and giving him a standing ovation coming down eighteen. Yeah, it was incredible. It's something that will live with me forever, for sure. It's thoroughly deserved, and I think towards the end of it, you could see he was a little bit emotional as well. It was a big deal."

That Woods ended up lipping out his birdie putt on the 18th didn't matter, but epitomized the week. Though his scores were nowhere near making the cut, nobody was going to quibble with the details.

Woods put considerable effort into returning for the tournament. If there was a goal he had while lying in that hospital bed or confined to his home or even getting around on crutches, it was to be at St. Andrews for the 150th Open.

Perhaps it was too soon.

"I'm a little ticked that I'm not playing on the weekend," Woods said. "I certainly did not play good enough to be around. I wish I would have played better. I wish I had a little bit better break at the first hole yesterday and maybe started off a little better. But that's just kind of how it all went from there. Just never really kind of materialized.

"I fought hard. And unfortunately I just could never turn it around. I struggled with the green speeds again today. And I could never hit putts hard enough. I was leaving them short again. So consequently I didn't make enough birdies."

Woods suggested The Open might not return to St. Andrews until 2030, which would be news to the rest of the golf world. The R&A had only announced sites through the 2025 Open at Royal Portrush. Perhaps it will want to get back on its traditional five-year cycle, which would mean 2027, when Woods will be 51.

Then again, it is quite possible Woods knew something. He was made an honorary member of the R&A that week, and maybe he had been briefed on plans behind the scenes during the week.

More immediately, Woods said he is not retiring and would be playing in future Opens.

"But I don't know if I will be physically able to play back here again when it comes back around," he said. "I'll be able to play future British Opens, yes, but eight years' time, I doubt if I'll be competitive at this level.

"It's a struggle just playing the three events I played this year. That in itself was something I'm very proud of—I was able to play these three events, considering what has transpired. Hopefully we do more hard work and give myself some more chances next year to play a few more events."

It was clear that Woods needed more competitive rounds in order to be prepared for the biggest events. But the injuries made that difficult. The quandary: putting too much stress on his leg versus not doing enough to be prepared. His short game, especially his putting, appeared particularly beneath his standards.

Woods was set to play in the Hero World Challenge later in the year but withdrew on the Monday of tournament week due to plantar fasciitis that was indirectly related to his injuries; in an effort to get ready for the Hero, Woods did too much. It was yet another setback.

He did compete in a one-day made-for-TV event along with McIlroy, Thomas, and Jordan Spieth, and then again with his son Charlie in the 36-hole PNC Championship, an exhibition in which he was allowed to ride a cart.

The number of quality shots he made during those two events was yet another reminder that the skills were still there. The ability to traverse the real estate between the shots, unfortunately, was not.

"I understand being more battle-hardened, but it's hard just to walk and play eighteen holes," Woods said. "People have no idea what I have to go through and the hours of the work on the body, pre and post, each and every single day to do what I just did.

"That's what people don't understand. They don't see. And then you think about playing more events on top of that, it's hard enough just to do what I did."

Woods takes ice baths to reduce swelling in his leg. He also has a physical trainer who travels with him.

The next goal became trying to get ready for his foundation's event, the Genesis Invitational, the same tournament that is near where the crash occurred in 2021.

FOR THE FIRST TIME SINCE THE 2022 MASTERS, WOODS COMpleted a 72-hole golf tournament. The achievement was not insignificant, even if we analyzed his flaws. He finished under par, the walking was far better than it had been, and his swing looked excellent.

Woods finished the Genesis Invitational on February 19, 2023, with a 2-over-par 73 at Riviera Country Club to complete 72 holes at 283, 1 under par and in a tie for 45th—showing some of the signs of wear and tear that are inevitable given the difficulties with his right foot and ankle.

"It was progress, but obviously I didn't win," Woods said. "My streak continues here at Riv."

Woods was being self-deprecating, noting that he's never won the tournament formerly known as the Los Angeles Open, where he played in a pro event for the first time as an amateur at age 16 in 1992. It was his fifteenth appearance and fourteenth at Riviera, the most of any event he's played without a victory.

Not that anyone really expected that. Woods was competing for the first time in an official event since The Open in July. And though lamenting a lot of missed opportunities on the greens, he looked far better, putting together two under-par scores.

"I felt like the first couple days I left certainly a lot of shots out there with some putts, especially Friday when I was blocking everything," he said, referring to pushing putts to the right. "Yesterday was better. Still wish I could have gotten within a touch of the leaders, but today they're running away with it. Even with a good round yesterday I wouldn't have been in touch today.

"[But] it means a lot. It's progress, headed in the right direction, yes. It certainly was a little bit more difficult than I probably let on. My team has been fantastic in getting my body recovered day to day and getting me ready to play each and every day. That's the hard part that I can't simulate at home. Even if I played four days at home, it's not the same as adrenaline, it's not the same as the system being ramped up like that, the intensity, just the focus that it takes to play at this level. No matter how much—I'm very good at simulating that at home, but it's just not the same as being out here and doing it."

Woods had five bogeys and three birdies in the final round, hitting eight of 14 fairways but only nine of 18 greens. He failed to get up and down for par four times when he missed a green, and his short game let him down several times.

He was still impressive, however. Especially when you consider it was almost two years to the day that he was involved in the car crash that led to multiple surgeries and more than a year off from golf.

"I think it's unbelievable he's doing what he's doing," said Kramer Hickok, who played with Woods during the final round. "I saw him leaving the clubhouse last night, and he was limping pretty good. The work just to get up walking is a lot . . . being able to walk up and down these hills and hitting golf shots. It's insane. Just to be out here and playing again shows his heart and determination.

"But he's still got so much game. I wouldn't be surprised if he wins again this year."

That, of course, would not happen. There was thought given to playing the PGA Tour's flagship tournament, the Players Championship, but Woods passed, with the Masters his next opportunity.

"Like I told you guys last year, I'm not going to play any more than probably the majors and maybe a couple more," he said. "That's it, that's all my body will allow me to do. My back the way it is, all the surgeries I had on my back, my leg the way it is, I just can't. That's just going to be my future.

"So my intent last year was to play in all four majors; I got three of the four. Hopefully this year I can get all four and maybe sprinkle in a few here and there. But that's it for the rest of my career. I know that and I understand that. That's just my reality."

As it turned out, there would be just one major. After some concerns he might not play, Woods did play at Augusta National, but was again dealt the bad luck of a poor-weather weekend.

The conditions were miserable on Saturday morning and got progressively more so as time passed. Woods slogged along on the back nine of Augusta National, perhaps one of his most cherished courses, in the conclusion to the second round.

Bogeys on the last two holes seemingly doomed his fate to a first missed cut as a pro at the Masters, but the weather being so poor, others, such as his buddy Thomas, also struggled coming in, meaning Woods would survive.

"Well, I already made it to the weekend," Woods deadpanned in the rain afterward.

His point was that he wanted two more rounds—although that didn't quite work out either, whether or not he truly believed that was a debate that might last until the rain finally stopped.

Of course, Woods wanted to play on. That is the epitome of his being. The man has shown throughout the course of his Hall of Fame career that he does not quit. He didn't win those fifteen majors and eighty-two PGA Tour events by giving up. And there's that record 142 consecutive cuts made on the PGA Tour as a sign of the ultimate in perseverance.

There are numerous other examples, perhaps highlighted best by his comeback from spinal fusion surgery in 2017 that led to a Masters victory and fifth green jacket in 2019. Or maybe the crowning moment was when he played on a stress fracture and torn ACL on his way to the 2008 U.S. Open.

Even his comeback at the Masters in 2022, just twelve months after the car crash that could have taken his right leg, was impressive for reasons beyond his winning a golf tournament.

And there he was again, still dealing with the issues associated with his damaged foot and ankle, trying to play golf in 50-degree weather on a soaked golf course that could present the most strenuous walk in the game.

As it played out, Woods ended up making a Masters cut for a

twenty-third consecutive year. It tied a record held by Fred Couples and Gary Player, but is not the kind of milestone that Woods cares that much about. For him, it's about winning. But this was a victory nonetheless.

"I've always loved this golf course, and I love playing this event," Woods said before he learned his fate regarding the cut. "Obviously I've missed a couple with some injuries. But I've always wanted to play here. I've loved it.

"I hope I get a chance to play this weekend. . . . I wish I get a chance to play two more rounds."

He didn't.

It didn't help that the conditions were miserable. Heat is Tiger's friend, and the temperature had dropped 30 degrees from the Thursday-Friday balminess, when Woods could sweat profusely through his rounds and not be bothered by it.

Now the temperature was in the low 50s and felt colder. The wind gusted at times. The rain was steady.

To give you an idea: Both Thomas and Jon Rahm needed to hit fairway woods into the 18th hole, their drives leaving them more than 220 yards to the green. They would normally hit short-iron shots. Both bogeyed. So did Woods, which should really not have been a surprise.

It was unfortunate that Woods had to deal with poor weather or cold temperatures in his limited golf time.

A year prior at the Masters had brought brutally cold and windy temperatures. After making the cut, he shot his worst scores at the tournament—a pair of 78s.

He grinded to make the cut at Southern Hills for the PGA Championship, then was faced with another cold Saturday and withdrew after the round with complications due to his injuries.

This time, Woods made it through another cut at the Masters. The last time he missed he was a sophomore in college in 1996. It was Woods' second Masters as an amateur. Doug Ford, who was born in 1922, played in that Masters, won by Nick Faldo.

Woods began his record-tying streak a year later, winning the Masters by 12 and changing the golf landscape forever.

That win was monumental. His "victory" on that Saturday in 2023 was by a considerably smaller margin, but consequential nonetheless. And then it all went awry with the start of the third round. Woods teed off on the 10th and by the time he got to the 17th fairway, the conditions were so horrible that play was suspended, eventually for the day.

Video surfaced of Woods limping to his bag under an umbrella held by LaCava. He could not have looked more miserable. And the following morning, prior to the resumption of play, Woods announced he was withdrawing. He cited a recurrence of plantar fasciitis. It didn't much matter—trying to play in that weather was a waste of time. Woods was hurting. And it soon became apparent that the issues were worse than thought.

As it turned out, that Saturday morning media scrum when Woods explained why he wanted to make the cut was the last time he spoke publicly at an official golf tournament. Rahm went on to victory without Woods in attendance.

A little more than a week later, Woods announced via social media that he had surgery—a subtalar fusion on his ankle and foot to address arthritis that stemmed from a previous talus fracture.

Various experts reported that recovery from such a procedure takes three months, which meant the time frame was unlikely to allow him to compete in any more major championships in 2023. The Open, played at Royal Liverpool, where he won his last Claret Jug in 2006, was all but certain to be off the calendar, which was later confirmed.

The procedure was done specifically for pain relief, and while it was suggested that Woods might sacrifice some mobility in his lower leg, he was also likely to have more stability.

All of which cast further doubt on his future as a golfer.

WOODS WILL UNDOUBTEDLY BE REMEMBERED MOST FOR HIS sheer volume of gaudy numbers. The eighty-two PGA Tour victories. The fifteen major championships. The 142 consecutive cuts. The ten five-victories-or-more seasons. The ten PGA Tour Player of the Year honors. The nine Vardon Trophies for low scoring average.

Much if not all of that will never be touched. It's hard to see anyone in today's era getting to half of Woods' PGA Tour victory total. Mickelson, with forty-five wins, is the only player in Woods' time to do it. And it's equally difficult to envision anyone getting to half of Woods' majors total. Mickelson has six. Brooks Koepka got to five with his 2023 PGA Championship win, while Rory McIlroy has been stuck on four since 2014.

With all of that, it is still fair to wonder how much better his career might have been without some considerable obstacles in his path.

The reckless behavior that cost him his marriage in 2010 and the subsequent fall from grace and constant ridicule took a toll. Woods went more than two years without winning when he was seemingly at the height of his powers. Even Tiger was not immune to the public pressure that came with such a scandal, and the mental toll it took is impossible to measure.

The injuries most certainly took a huge chunk out of his ability to add to his career totals. Woods missed two major championships in 2009, two more in 2011, two in 2014, and eight in 2016–17. In 2018, he finished sixth at The Open and second at the PGA Championship, then won the Masters the following year. But all of 2021 was wiped out due to the car crash.

How much more might there have been from Woods had there not been so many injuries?

Woods faced more off-course scrutiny in 2023, when the breakup with his girlfriend, Erica Herman, was revealed in court records due to her seeking monetary compensation and the right to discuss it publicly despite a non-disclosure agreement she'd signed. She later dropped a lawsuit seeking $30 million in damages.

While the behind-the-scenes troubles are unclear, what's not is the fact that Herman was with Woods for a good bit of the time he dealt with all of the back problems. They began dating in 2016 when he was not playing, and she was a big part of the scene when he returned to competition in late 2017 after the spinal fusion surgery.

Herman was visible at nearly every tournament Woods played as part of his comeback in 2018, and often would note the struggles he faced that the public could not see. She was there for the historic Tour Championship win, the Masters victory, the win in Japan. And by all accounts, Herman was good with Woods' kids.

As much as anyone in those later years, Herman lived the pain and suffering with Woods, and could probably tell a few stories about the difficulty of the journey.

For as long as Woods' achievements are discussed, the time lost due to injury will always be among the greatest "what-ifs."

And then you wonder how much better—or worse—he might have fared if he had not changed his swing so many times. Doing so under Harmon the first time was controversial, but so, too, was leaving him. Haney had great success with Woods, but Tiger's swing was considerably different from what it was under Harmon. Another change took place with Foley, and after a brief time with Como, Woods went without a teacher.

It is a tribute to him that he managed to excel under all those coaches and took on the task of revamping or reimagining his game time and again. His drive to improve was part of each of those decisions to change course.

To do so again is going to require some patience—and maybe what would have once been considered an absurd notion. The idea of Tiger playing senior golf would have been preposterous ten years ago. You'd get laughed out of a room for seriously suggesting it, and Woods would have all but scoffed at the notion if it had been presented to him privately, while likely being deferential publicly.

There was no way you could see him doing it. He wouldn't need the money, of which there is far less in senior golf anyway. He almost certainly would have looked down on the idea of 54-hole events and riding a golf cart and not competing against the best. The PGA Tour Champions, originally called the Senior PGA Tour, requires you to be at least 50 years old to compete.

But Woods has dropped hints.

He's joked about getting to "ride a buggy" when he turns 50 and playing alongside some of his longtime peers. While staunchly opposed to riding a cart in competition—it is possible Woods could get approval to do so under the Americans with Disabilities Act—he seems fine with the idea on the Champions Tour, where use of carts is routine.

It leads to a rather dream-like scenario for a time approximately after Woods turns 50. The dilemma concerning walking too much to prepare to play golf and practicing too little to be competitive remains real, no matter how often he plans to play in the future.

So the PGA Tour Champions offers Woods the best of both worlds. He can use a golf cart, which will allow him to sharpen his game and be better prepared when he shows up for the major championships, where he will have to walk but can do so having dialed in his game at the seniors events without stressing his leg.

The circumstances were different, but Nicklaus did this during his senior career, and had some limited success in major championships after turning 50, twice finishing in the top 10.

Admittedly, this is a bit of a reach, but with Woods you never know. He's spent his entire career doing things nobody thought were possible. He won by margins big and small, amassed the game's biggest trophies as well as the minor ones, and kept pushing when all evidence suggested he either shouldn't or couldn't.

The victories, the trophies, the records will always be there for us to discuss and debate. They define a career of excellence, one that can seriously be considered the greatest of all time (with all due respect to Nicklaus).

But it was about more than just talent. If his abilities were superior to others, Woods still felt the need to build on them, to improve, to never get complacent. And so he didn't.

To accumulate the résumé he did in twenty-plus years of professional golf, there had to be an inner fortitude that pushed him, an attitude that did not allow him to settle for what likely would have been good enough.

We saw it in ways that were monumental, such as his 2008 U.S. Open victory with two fractured bones in his leg, as well as the 2019 Masters, where he won just two years after major back surgery. Accomplishments such as his 142 straight made cuts were perhaps more subtle, but the underlying theme was the same: Woods had a drive to succeed that was unmatched.

Perhaps that same drive will push him to stay in the competitive arena a bit longer. There are more Masters and Opens to be played. And if he wants one last walk across the Swilcan Bridge to a proper and popular send-off, that would be cool, too.

Ranking Tiger Woods' Major Victories

They all count the same, and every one is historic in its own right. Winning one major championship can make a career. Capturing fifteen of the game's biggest trophies is rare air, shared only by Jack Nicklaus, who won eighteen in his legendary career. The trick here was to put each of Tiger Woods' major victories into some sort of order. Not easy. And not final. This list can certainly be debated, which is part of the fun.

THE MASTERS, APRIL 14, 2019
(81st PGA Tour win, 15th major title)

Determining No. 1 might be about recency bias, but given the length of time between majors and the injury issues he faced, this tops them all. Woods was no longer the superpower 21-year-old, nor the guy everyone feared. He was almost two years removed from serious spinal fusion surgery, and believed his career was likely over; quality of life trumped competitive golf. And yet he won his first Masters in fourteen years. His first major championship in eleven years. He beat back players nearly twenty years younger, including Brooks Koepka and Xander Schauffele. And he came from behind to win a major for the first time. The celebration afterward, with Tiger hugging his kids as he had hugged his father in nearly the exact same spot behind the 18th green after winning in 1997 . . . it just doesn't get any better. It was an unreal scene, and an incredible victory.

THE MASTERS, APRIL 13, 1997
(4th PGA Tour win, 1st major title)

The first major remains some of Tiger's finest work. Woods was just 21. He went to Augusta National with tremendous fanfare. And then, playing the first round with defending champion Nick Faldo, he went out in 40 strokes to seemingly throw away his chances. He then came back in 30, shot 70, took the second-round lead, and never looked back. He trounced Colin Montgomerie in a third-round pairing that saw him increase his lead to nine shots, setting up a Sunday coronation that the world tuned in to in droves, despite the inevitable outcome. And he set or tied twenty-seven tournament records, including youngest champion and lowest 72-hole score of 270, 18 under par—since tied by Jordan Spieth. He won by 12 shots over Tom Kite.

U.S. OPEN, JUNE 18, 2000
(20th PGA Tour win, 3rd major title)

In one of the game's all-time remarkable performances, Woods won by 15 shots and was the only player to shoot under par at Pebble Beach. Even a triple bogey during the third round could not stop Woods. Not only did he annihilate the field, but he beat the course—and the game. And he left a world of golfers deflated, including runner-up Ernie Els.

THE OPEN, JULY 21, 2000
(21st PGA Tour victory, 4th major title)

Picking up where he left off a month earlier at the U.S. Open, Woods again posted a large-margin major championship win, completing the career Grand Slam at the Home of Golf and winning by eight shots over Ernie Els and Thomas Bjorn. Woods was never in a bunker over 72 holes at the Old Course in St. Andrews, in a performance that would be heralded with far more fanfare had he not won by 15 a month earlier at Pebble Beach.

U.S. OPEN, JUNE 16, 2008
(65th PGA Tour win, 14th major title)

This could easily be No. 1. Woods had no business winning this tournament, given his physical state and—frankly—the number of mistakes he made at Torrey Pines. Woods, we later learned, was playing with two fractured bones in his left leg. He had not played a tournament since the Masters due to a knee procedure. And three times, he double-bogeyed the first hole. After all that, he needed to make a 12-footer for birdie on the 72nd hole, the last man on the course, the only one with a chance to tie Rocco Mediate. The putt dropped, and the Southern California earth shook. Woods then defeated Mediate in an 18-hole playoff that needed an extra hole. A few days later, Woods had his ACL repaired and didn't play for the rest of the year. His 2008 tally: four wins in six starts, with a tie for fifth his worst showing.

THE MASTERS, APRIL 8, 2001
(27th PGA Tour win, 6th major title)

Woods had nearly eight months to think about the unthinkable—winning four consecutive majors, something never done in the modern game and only accomplished once prior, in 1930 by amateur Bobby Jones, who won the British Amateur, U.S. Amateur, The Open, and the U.S. Open. Woods trailed by five strokes after a first-round 70, but a second-round 66 pulled him into a tie with Phil Mickelson, just two strokes back. Woods led by one over Mickelson heading to the final round. David Duval briefly tied Woods with a birdie at the 15th hole, but gave it back with a bogey at 16 and Woods birdied the 18th for a two-shot win—his fourth consecutive major and sixth overall. It was also his 27th PGA Tour victory.

PGA CHAMPIONSHIP, AUGUST 20, 2000
(22nd PGA Tour win, 5th major title)

Woods had to work hard for a third consecutive major championship, outlasting Bob May in a thrilling final-day duel that went to a three-hole aggregate playoff at Valhalla. May—once a Southern California phenom who never won on the PGA Tour—shot 66 to Woods' 67 before Woods finally prevailed, producing that iconic scene in the playoff where he walked in a birdie putt and pointed at it as the ball dropped into the cup. Woods became the first player since Ben Hogan in 1953 to win three major championships in the same year.

THE OPEN, JULY 23, 2006
(49th PGA Tour win, 11th major title)

A rare emotional display followed Woods' victory at Royal Liverpool, where he won his first major title since the death of his father, Earl, two months prior. Playing the baked-out Hoylake course, Woods famously hit just one driver during the tournament, electing to use irons off of tees and to rely on a precision approach game. For the second time in consecutive years, Woods had to hold off Chris DiMarco in a major and won by two shots for his eleventh major championship title—tying him with Walter Hagen for second all-time behind Jack Nicklaus.

THE OPEN, JULY 17, 2005
(44th PGA Tour win, 10th major title)

Woods won his second major of the year and his second Open at the Home of Golf, opening with rounds of 66–67 at the Old Course in St. Andrews. Woods led by just two after three rounds but cruised to a five-stroke victory over Colin Montgomerie to capture his tenth major. Jack Nicklaus played his final major championship and Woods completed a unique slam of sorts—he won each of the four majors in which Nicklaus played for the last time (2000 U.S. Open and PGA; 2005 Masters and Open).

THE MASTERS, APRIL 14, 2002
(31st PGA Tour win, 7th major title)

Woods became just the third player and first since Nick Faldo in 1990 to defend his Masters title. A third-round 66 moved him into a tie with Retief Goosen, two shots ahead of 2000 Masters champion Vijay Singh and four ahead of Ernie Els, Phil Mickelson, and Sergio Garcia. Woods shot a final-round 71 and was never really threatened as Goosen fell back with a 74 and nobody else challenged.

U.S. OPEN, JUNE 16, 2002
(32nd PGA Tour win, 8th major title)

Woods grabbed the first-round lead at brutal Bethpage Black and, despite shooting higher scores each day, won by three strokes over Phil Mickelson. In the process, Woods became the first player since Jack Nicklaus in 1972 to win the Masters and U.S. Open in the same year, a feat that has occurred just seven times, with Jordan Spieth being the last to do so, in 2015.

PGA CHAMPIONSHIP, AUGUST 15, 1999
(11th PGA Tour win, 2nd major title)

Woods was feeling the pressure of not having won a major since his 1997 Masters triumph. Ten majors had passed, and there were questions about Woods' ability to rack up a slew of major titles. And he'd won just once in 1998. Woods got a big scare from 19-year-old Sergio Garcia down the stretch at Medinah before prevailing by a shot with a final-round 72. The overall total makes this victory seem more mundane, but it was huge at the time, given the hype and lack of majors after his first at the '97 Masters.

THE MASTERS, APRIL 10, 2005
(43rd PGA Tour win, 9th major title)

Woods had gone nearly three years between major wins when he prevailed at Augusta National in a playoff with Chris DiMarco. And he was coming off a bleak year that saw him win just once after making changes under new instructor Hank Haney. His victory came in dramatic fashion, as he had the remarkable chip-in for birdie from behind the 16th green, then gave it away with consecutive bogeys to drop into a tie with DiMarco. Woods birdied the first extra hole for his ninth major title.

PGA CHAMPIONSHIP, AUGUST 12, 2007
(59th PGA Tour win, 13th major title)

In sweltering conditions that topped 100 degrees throughout the tournament at Southern Hills in Tulsa, Oklahoma, Woods nearly became the first player to shoot 62 in a major championship, narrowly missing a birdie putt in the second round on the 18th and settling for 63. He went on to win by two shots over Woody Austin for his thirteenth major title.

PGA CHAMPIONSHIP, AUGUST 20, 2006
(51st PGA Tour win, 12th major title)

What had been an otherwise dreary year with the death of his father and his first missed cut in a major championship as a pro became exceptional in a matter of weeks, as Woods followed his victory at The Open with another at the PGA Championship. He forged a third-round tie with Luke Donald at Medinah, then shot a final-round 68 to win by five strokes over Shaun Micheel for his twelfth major title, tying Billy Casper with fifty-one wins.

ACKNOWLEDGMENTS

The morning of April 14, 2019, was considerably different from most final-round Sundays at the Masters. The tension and excitement were prevalent, to be sure. But there was far less time for it to build.

Most years, the wait for the leaders to tee off in the afternoon allowed for a lengthy period to ponder all manner of possibilities. For those in contention, a restless night might be followed by a good bit of nervous energy to control prior to putting the tee in the ground on Augusta National's first hole.

But due to the threat of inclement weather in the afternoon, Augusta National officials made the unusual decision to alter the schedule and move tee times up in an attempt to avoid the impending storm.

So instead of a 2:33 p.m. tee time—as eventual winner Jon Rahm had in 2023 alongside runner-up Brooks Koepka—Tiger Woods faced an early-morning wake-up call. He would be teeing off at the 2019 Masters alongside Francesco Molinari and Tony Finau at 9:20 a.m.

At a time when Masters patrons would normally be strolling onto the grounds to locate a prime location for afternoon viewing, all of the competitors would already be on the course, having been grouped in threes and sent off the first and 10th tees.

Woods, who had spent a good bit of the past six years dealing with painful and debilitating back issues, faced a pre-dawn litany of stretching and rehabilitation with the physical therapists who tended to him, helping him get ready to play. It made his plight that Sunday all the more daunting.

Meanwhile, in the lavish Augusta National press building that sat at the end of the driving range, there was already an early-morning buzz. The fourth and final round had begun early and the Masters would be crowning its champion in a manner of hours rather than as the sun was setting.

And there was obviously some added spice. Woods was in contention to win a major championship, something many had long taken for granted but in recent times was rare. It had been eleven years since his last major triumph at the 2008 U.S. Open and fourteen years since that incredible chip-in from behind the 16th green led to a fourth Masters.

Could Tiger really pull this off?

There's the old sportswriter axiom, "No Cheering in the Press Box," a phrase taken from a book written by *Chicago Tribune* baseball writer Jerome Holtzman that was published in 1974. While the book was a collection of tales among the greats in the business at the time, that title became something of a mantra: you don't root for the team you are covering.

Or in the case of golf, the players you are covering.

Of course, every writer rooted for the story, and one involving Woods trying to win a major championship after all he had endured was as compelling as it gets. Having Tiger in contention at any tournament, but especially a major championship, always created great interest. And was rarely lacking in drama.

It was similar to when Tom Watson, at age 59, lost in a playoff to Stewart Cink at The Open in 2009. He'd been the oldest major champion by miles. Undoubtedly, Jack Nicklaus' 1986 Masters victory fits that description. Everyone there that day knew the enormity of the Golden Bear winning his 18th major title at age 46—six years after last winning a major.

Tiger's victory that Sunday, a 15th major title and fifth Masters, is the basis for this book. What he overcame to win anything, let alone a major, will long be part of his legacy, which upon further exploration, goes well beyond his enormous skills. His "drive"—hence the title—is apparent in ways not often explored.

And so Woods is an obvious starting point. You don't tell a story like this without such a compelling figure, one whose career is filled with so many highlights but also a fair share of roadblocks.

Woods, at times, has had an uneasy relationship with the media. It's far more understandable when you see what he endures on a daily basis at a golf tournament, his popularity so overwhelming, the tugs and pulls apparent in the most basic of circumstances.

As the years passed, Woods softened some. Nobody answered more post-round questions in a career than Tiger, it's not even close. Nicklaus might challenge for the "honor" but Jack enjoyed the banter. Tiger mostly endured it, and yet he still did it.

The number of times he declined over a period of a couple of decades is a tiny percentage of the times he stood at the microphone, good score or bad, and took the questions. The fact that he did that, and let some of us glean insight through various other interview opportunities over the years, is highly appreciated.

Through all these years, there have been numerous other people in Tiger's orbit who have been immensely helpful, such as his caddies Steve Williams and Joe LaCava. Williams wasn't so friendly during his time on Tiger's bag—he was the golf world's greatest enforcer—but became an excellent source of info after their relationship ended, understanding his role in history and that of the man he caddied for during 13 major championships.

LaCava has been a favorite of all in the game for three-plus decades. He's seen it all, and there's a reason Tiger has been so fond of him. Joe was incredibly loyal when Woods' future was often in doubt. He waited through all the downtime, turning down other opportunities. He was rewarded with one of the greatest strolls ever at that 2019 Masters. And his insight and cooperation have been invaluable.

Through the years, Tiger had three lengthy tenures with coaches, Butch Harmon, Hank Haney, and Sean Foley. Harmon (here's hoping he gets a much-deserved induction into the World Golf Hall of Fame) remains an incredible resource on Tiger some twenty years after last coaching him. Haney offered considerable insight for this book and it is fact that Tiger had his most consistent stretch of golf while working with him. Foley had the unenviable task of having to deal with a glut of Tiger's injuries and always did his best—and still does—to answer all the questions.

As he continued to deal with injuries and made yet another comeback, Woods decided to go without a coach. His longtime friend and executive at his company, Rob McNamara, became a constant companion. A fine player in his own right, McNamara became Tiger's "eyes and ears," and while not a coach in the true sense of the word, he helped fill that role. Along the way, he offered his own insight, careful to not breach his friendship with Woods but also taking pity on those of us who needed some guidance. McNamara is undoubtedly an underrated asset who was part of Woods' resurgence.

And there are more. Mark Steinberg, Woods' longtime agent, has seemingly forever put up with innocuous queries, handling the numerous requests amicably. Woods' former public relations guru, Glenn Greenspan, also dealt with his share of annoying phone calls, emails, and texts.

Woods' mini-empire spreads even further with his foundation, the dream of his late father, Earl, but one that has evolved into a powerhouse that has seen hundreds of kids further their education through various programs. Thanks to past CEOs Greg McLaughlin and Rick Singer, as well as current vice president, Mike Antolini, who, among other things, is in charge of the golf tournaments run by the foundation.

I leaned heavily on two writing titans, Gene Wojciechowski and Ian O'Connor, who each have shelves full of books they've written. Their support and guidance cannot be repaid.

Michael Bamberger and Rick Reilly, prolific authors and golf lovers, also provided enormous counsel. As did John Strege, whose 1997 book *Tiger* remains an incredible read all these years later, and Jaime Diaz, perhaps the foremost authority on Tiger dating to his earliest days.

A special thanks to two of my former colleagues at ESPN who to this day remain great friends, Jason Sobel and Michael Collins. They've been along for a good part of the Tiger journey. Same for longtime colleagues Scott Michaux, Ron Green Jr., Rex Hoggard, Jay Coffin, Geoff Shackelford, and Ryan Lavner. And the dean of all golf writers, Doug Ferguson of the Associated Press.

Nobody traipsed more fairways and roughs with me than Steve DiMeglio, who needed twice the number of steps to keep up but was always there for *USA Today/Golfweek*.

And there is the golf team at *Sports Illustrated*. Thanks to former editor Joy Russo, as well as golf editors Jeff Ritter and John Schwarb, who gave me time to work on this book and never got mad when I was late with an assignment. Also thanks to my writing colleagues Alex Miceli, Gabby Herzig, and Michael Rosenberg.

There have been no shortage of books written on Tiger over the years, several of which I relied on for background and reporting, including *Tiger Woods* by Jeff Benedict and Armen Keteyian; *Tiger* by John Strege; *The Big Miss* by Hank Haney; *The Second Life of Tiger Woods* by Michael Bamberger; and my own book *Tiger and Phil: Golf's Most Fascinating Rivalry*.

Thanks as well to fact-checking and editing gurus Ben Everill and Julie Bennett.

Unless otherwise noted, the material in this book is the result of my own interviews and reporting, and having covered all 15 of Woods' major titles as well as more than 50 of his 82 PGA Tour victories. If the word "says" is used with a quotation, it has come from my own interviews for the book with recent reflections; when quotes were given in a group setting, from a post-round media session or news conference or from some time ago, the past tense "said" is used.

Facts and figures, such as statistics, were gleaned from various sources, including the PGA Tour, the Official World Golf Ranking, the DP World Tour (formerly the European Tour), The Masters.com, the United States Golf Association, the PGA of America, and the R&A.

Finally, thanks to my editor at St. Martin's Press, Pete Wolverton, who has now put up with me through two books, as well as his assistant, Claire Cheek, who rescued me from numerous obstacles. And a big thanks to my agent, Susan Canavan from the Waxman Agency, who guided me through another project.

INDEX

Accenture Match Play
Championship, 54
ACL (anterior cruciate
ligament), surgery, 1,
39–40, 88
Albany (golf development in
the Bahamas), 84–85
amateur golfer, TW as, 17
"Amen Corner," 150, 155
Andy Williams event, 43
Appleby, Stuart, 45
Arnold Palmer Invitational,
53, 54–57, 118
Asian-born golfers, 59
AT&T National, 58, 193
Augusta National Golf Club,
17–18, 62–63, 229, 241
Black members at, 145–146
Butler Cabin, 178–179
Champions Dinner, 5, 83,
94, 152, 200–201
the course, 154–161, 226
footballer members, 203
TW honors at, 145
Australia, 62, 190
Azinger, Paul, 23

back problems, 4, 73, 74, 82,
87, 90, 95–99, 100–108,
238
Bahamas, 84–85
Ballesteros, Seve, 17
balls, 86, 263
Barclays tournament, 90
Bay Hill Club, 54
Begay, Notah, 95–96
Ben Hogan Award, 148, 219
TW's acceptance speech,
148–151
Bethpage Black course, 58,
184–185, 290
betting, 19–20
birdies, making spares,
194–195
Blacks, admissions to golf
clubs, 145–146
Blair, Zac, 75–78
BMW Championship, 61

bogey, septuple, 205
Bonnalie, Geno, 138
Boros, Guy, 18
Bowskill, Jon, 8
Bradley, Keegan, 178, 193
break, seeing, 236–237
Bridgestone, 86
broken bones, 10
Brown v. Board of Education, 146
Bryant, Kobe, 223
Buick Invitational, 30, 53
Buick Open, 58
Burgoon, Bronson, 135–138
Burke, Jackie, 179
Burns, Sam, 139
Byron Nelson Championship, 33

CA Championship at Doral, 54
California Amateur, 245
car crash of February 2021, 3, 10, 15, 210–226
  police report, 214–215, 222
  treatment of injuries, 221, 226
car crash of November 2009, 62
car off-road accident of May 2017, 108–109
  police reports, 108
carts
  TW in, 220–221
  TW's opinion of, 224, 282
Casey, Paul, 117
Chamblee, Brandel, 75, 99, 265–266
Champions Dinner. *See* Augusta National
Championship at Doral, 54
championships, TW's goal, 145
charity golf tournament, 85
chipping yips, 73, 75, 90, 265–266
Choi, K. J., 67
Cink, Stewart, 36–37, 41
Clarke, Darren, 260
coaches, 267–270, 281–282
College GameDay, 201
comebacks
  2016, 85, 94
  2018, 124–125
  2020, 231–233
  2022, 271
Como, Chris, 92, 97, 271, 281
Cook, Austin, 140
Cooley, Vernon, 187–188
Copperhead course, 114, 117
coronavirus pandemic, 201–202
Couples, Fred, 14, 17, 65, 166, 230–232

cuts
  making money on, 31
  missed, 82, 185–186
cut streak
  events without, 27
  TW's, 26–37

Dahmen, Joel, 86, 138–139
Davis, Cameron, 232
Day, Jason, 5, 30, 169–170, 189
DeChambeau, Bryson, 163, 167, 170, 227
DiMarco, Chris, 176, 255, 289, 290–291
DiMeglio, Steve, 82, 85
Discovery, 223
divorce, 146
drive of TW, 2, 11
driving, Woods habit of, 223–224
drugs
  medical, 108–109
  TW denies use, 64
Dubai Desert Classic, 53, 93, 98–99

each and every shot means something, 4
East Lake Golf Club, Atlanta, 126
80s, scores in, 76–78
Elder, Lee, 24, 146
Els, Ernie, 32–33, 53, 78
endorsements, 86–87
ESPN, 62, 85, 190, 201
European Tour, 4
events, "no cut," 27
extramarital affairs, 64

Fahy, Damian, 100–101
Faldo, Nick, 7, 19, 20–21, 257
falls, 90, 110–111
fans
  chanting and uproar of, 177, 259
  engaging with, 117
  missing because of epidemic, 202
  TW's need for, 203–205
Farmers Insurance Open, 41, 43, 93, 115, 164, 202, 206
FedEx Cup, 27, 32, 54, 61
Feherty, David, 133–134, 261–264, 272
Ferguson, Doug, 150
fifteenth major quest, 121
Finau, Tony, 154, 159–160, 171, 172
  hole in one followed by ankle twist, 159
Fiori, Ed, 128
first-tee jitters, 168

Fitzpatrick, Matt, 258, 260, 272
Fleetwood, Tommy, 126–127
Floyd, Raymond, 17
Foley, Sean, 14–15, 116, 269–271, 281
Foster, Billy, 260
Fowler, Rickie, 127, 149, 164, 216
France, 163
Furyk, Jim, 62, 65, 124

Galea, Anthony, 64
Garcia, Sergio, 53, 290
Gay, Brian, 140
Genesis Invitational, 142–143, 164, 213, 220, 274
golf
  generations in, 136
  retiring from, 257
Golf Digest/GolfTV collaboration, 15
golfers
  engaging with, 117
  greatest ever, 32
  mutual respect of, 271
  number competing, 247
  that TW has surprisingly lost to, 60
  younger generation of, 13, 135–136
GolfTV, 183
Golf Writers Association of America (GWAA), 148–149
Goosen, Retief, 32, 103, 134
Grand Slam, 77, 245, 287
Green, Bob, 249
green jackets, 177–179
Greenspan, Glenn, 148
groupings, 139–140
Gumbel, Bryant, 67
Guyer, Richard, 9, 101–103, 105–107, 113, 149

Haas, Bill, 137
Hagen, Walter, 249–250, 289
Haney, Hank, 33, 39–40, 42, 58, 63, 67–70, 251, 266, 268–269, 281, 291
Hardin, Justin, 170
Harig, Bob, 149
Harmon, Butch, 33, 51, 267–268
Hart, Dudley, 103–105
Hazeltine National, 59
Hellman, Dan, 8, 96–97, 100
Henley, Kip, 140
Herman, Erica, 193, 200, 240, 281
herniated disk in lumbar spine, 4–5

Hero MotoCorp, 85
Hero World Challenge, 8, 54, 85, 113–114, 163, 266–267
Hickok, Kramer, 143, 276
Hicks, Justin, 44
Hochschuler, Stephen, 102–103, 107
Hogan, Ben, 16, 150, 200, 219
Homa, Max, 222–223, 258, 261
Honda Classic, 115
Horschel, Billy, 131
Hughes, Mackenzie, 138–139
Huston, John, 23

Immelman, Trevor, 38, 41, 177, 181–182
injuries, 147, 280–281
  and career, 250
interviews, 183, 270
irons, sound of, 141
Irwin, Hale, 31, 47, 251
Isleworth, Orlando (TW's home course), 19

Japan, golf in, 188–196
Jenkins, Dan, 146
Johnson, Dustin, 5, 149, 170, 227
Johnson, Zach, 55, 57, 177
Jones, Bobby, 91, 126, 145, 153, 162, 249–250, 288
  who quit on top, 1

Karlsson, Robert, 45–46
Kindred, Dave, 151
Kisner, Kevin, 120, 158, 235, 240
Kleven, Keith, 44
knee, 47
  brace, prescribed, 42
  pain in, 1, 42
  surgery, 52, 64, 187, 189–190, 196–197
Koepka, Brooks, 122–123, 148, 154, 167, 169, 170, 178, 185
Kuchar, Matt, 67, 69
Kuehne, Trip, 21

LaCava, Joe, 28, 79–80, 86, 92, 123, 130, 137, 151, 156, 164–166, 185, 188, 206, 230–231, 236, 237, 260
Langer, Bernhard, 177
leg injuries, 214, 221
Lehman, Tom, 18–19, 35
LIV Golf League, 227–228, 259
Lord, Gareth, 46
Los Angeles Open, 275

Love III, Davis, 196, 252–253
Lowry, Shane, 209–210, 235

Mackay, Jim "Bones," 44
Masters
- 1997 Victory, 18, 20–25, 146, 286
- 1998, 252
- 2001 Victory, 288
- 2002 Victory, 289
- 2005 Victory, 176, 290
- 2009, 67–72
- 2017, 6
- 2019 Victory, 2–3, 12, 16–, 144, 154, 163–180, 285
- 2020, 201–210
- 2020 postponed, 201
- 2022, 10, 141, 229–242, 277

Matsuyama, Hideki, 93, 189, 193–198, 225, 235
May, Bob, 60, 254, 262, 288
McIlroy, Rory, 5, 28, 129–132, 158, 164, 167, 189, 227, 271, 274, 280
McLean, Alastair, 48
McNamara, Rob, 43, 165, 240
Medalist Golf Club, 229
media
- engaging with, 117
- relations with and appreciation of, 150

Mediate, Rocco, 45, 47–51
Memorial Tournament in Dublin, Ohio, 74, 87
Mercedes Championship, 18
Mickelson, Phil, 5, 13–14, 32, 44, 54, 56, 58, 61
microdiscectomy procedures, 5, 82, 87, 91, 206–207
Miller, Johnny, 150
Molinari, Francesco, 118–121, 154–159, 169, 170, 171, 174, 175
Monahan, Jay, 131–132, 228
Monday Japan Skins, 188–196
Montgomerie, Colin, 23–24
Morris, Tom Sr., 258
Muirfield Village Golf Club, 74, 77–78
Murray, Andy, 100

Nantz, Jim, 6–7, 24, 95, 213
Napa, California, 83
news conferences, 63–65, 215–216
Nicklaus, Jack, 7, 9, 16–17, 31, 35, 57–59, 74, 81, 121, 136, 145–147, 152–155, 180, 186–187, 196, 203, 243–256, 257, 283
- comparisons with TW, 244–255

scores, 78
statistics, 246–247
Nicklaus' Memorial Tournament, 58
Niemann, Joaquin, 141, 228, 237
night, golfing at, 55, 262–263
Nike, 10, 86–87, 188
Noah's Ark, 264
non-white players, 24
Norman, Greg, 17, 19, 32, 53

Obama, Barack, 180
Official World Golf Rankings, 89
Ogilvy, Geoff, 41, 47–48, 151
O'Hair, Sean, 54–57
Old Course, 11, 257–260
O'Meara, Mark, 19–20, 66, 78, 253
Oosthuizen, Louis, 169, 170, 235–236
Open
2000 Victory, 287
2005 Victory, 289
2006 Victory, 289
See also The Open
Owen, Greg, 105–108

pain pills, 108–109
Palmer, Arnold, 16, 17, 41, 56–57, 243, 257
Payne, William Porter "Billy", 65–67
PGA Championship, 10, 128–132, 184, 241, 278–279
1999 Victory, 290
2000 Victory, 288
2006 Victory, 291
2007 Victory, 29, 291
PGA Championship at Hazeltine, 59–61
PGA Championship at Oakland Hills, 53
PGA Championship at Southern Hills Country Club, Tulsa, 27–30
PGA Championship at St. Louis (2018), 121–124
PGA Tour, 53, 61, 84, 198
criticism of, 227
cut streak record, 26–30
80th victory, 162
PGA Tour Champions, 282
PGA Tours, 2018, 126–128
Phoenix Open, 75
photographs, 175
physical therapy, 8
pitching, 267
plane, watching golf on TV from, 51
platelet-rich plasma (PRP) therapy, 64

Player, Gary, 7, 16, 203, 243
Player of the Year awards, 148
Players Championship, 164
playoff, 50–51
PNC Championship, 210, 231
Poulter, Ian, 69, 154
practice-round viewing, 230
practicing, 85–86, 110, 165–166
Presidential Medal of Freedom, 184
Presidents Cup
  2011, 114
  2017, 113
pressure, feeling, 173
Price, Nick, 171
punch out, 264

Quicken Loans National, 118, 135, 138, 158

Rae's Creek, 154, 174, 205–206
Rahm, Jon, 142, 162, 163
rainstorms, 192–193
Reed, Patrick, 117, 163, 178–179
retiring from competitive golf, 91–92
Ridley, Fred, 179, 200, 201
Riviera Country Club, 20, 115, 275
Roberts, Clifford, 154
Rodgers, Phil, 247
Rose, Justin, 5, 80, 127, 129–130
Rosenberg, Thomas, 39–40, 188
rough fescue, 119
Royal & Ancient Clubhouse (R&A), 260, 273
rules violations, 265
Ryder Cup, 54, 124, 159

Safeway Open, 89
Sanders, Doug, 249
Sands, Steve, 266
Sarazen, Gene, 136
Saudi Arabia, money in sports, 227
scandals, 146
Schauffele, Xander, 120, 158, 170, 178, 285
Scheffler, Scottie, 208–209
scorecard
  assessment of, 74, 76–81, 191
  turning in, 240
scores
  highest (85), 87
  worst, 205–206
Scott, Adam, 12, 31, 32, 44, 169, 170, 235
Scott, Steve, 21
seeing breaks, 236–237

senior golf, 282
Shipnuck, Alan, 227
Simpson, Webb, 174–176
Singh, Vijay, 32, 134
Smith, Cam, 235
Smith, Jada Pinkett, 15
Snead, Sam, 9, 10, 190, 196
Snedeker, Brandt, 115–116
Sorenstam, Annika, 91
Southern California, 87
Southern Hills, 241
spectators, 126, 193
  raucous or dangerous, 131
Spieth, Jordan, 5, 115, 120, 157
spinal fusion, 9, 101–104, 110, 217
Stanford friends, 23
St Andrews, Scotland, 255–256, 272
  Old Course, 256–260
statements by TW, of apology, 62
statistics
  of great golfers, 16
  on TW, 9, 12, 16–17, 34
Steinberg, Mark, 5, 109, 148
Stenson, Henrik, 115
Streelman, Kevin, 44
stress fractures in the tibia of left leg, 1–2, 46, 52
Stricker, Steve, 31–32, 111
Summerall, Pat, 249
surgeries, 3, 8–9, 30, 38, 87–88, 100–108, 147, 149, 279
Swilcan Bridge, 257–260, 283
swings
  painful, 28–29
  variety of, 281

tabloids, 62
Target World Challenge, 54
Tesori, Paul, 176
TGR Foundation, 220
Thailand, 186
The 1997 Masters: My Story (TW book), 21
The Open at Carnoustie, 118–121, 158
The Open at Muirfield, 77–78
The Open at Royal Birkdale, 53
The Open at Royal Lytham, 18
The Open at St. Andrews, 11, 220, 225, 273
The Open at Turnberry, 58
Thomas, Justin, 11, 14, 149, 166, 193, 216–217, 220–221, 230, 260–261
tibia, pain from, 1–2, 42
Tiger Slam, 10, 41, 250
Tiger Woods Ventures (TGR), 43
Torrey Pines course, 98

Tour Championship, 61, 162–165, 187
Tournament of Champions, 18
Townsend, Ron, 146
TPC Los Colinas, 33
Trahan, D. J., 47
Trevino, Lee, 180–181, 257
Trump, Donald, 180, 184

U.S. Amateur, 245
U.S. Open, 40–41
  2000 Victory, 286
  2002 Victory, 290
  2006, 185
  2008 Victory, 287
U.S. Open, Torrey Pines, San Diego, 2008, 1, 38–39, 41, 43–52
U.S. Open at Bethpage, 58
U.S. Presidents Cup, 190, 199–286
U.S. Ryder Cup, 147, 259

Valspar Championship, 2018, 114–117
video lessons given by TW, 213
videos of TW, 212–213
  showing feelings after the accident, 217–220
Villanueva, Alex, 215, 222

Walker, Jimmy, 5
walking
  TW and, 224, 231
  walking legs, 92–93
Wanamaker Trophy, 59
Watson, Bubba, 5, 29, 177, 240
Watson, Tom, 16, 243, 257
weather, bad, 192, 277–279
wedge shot, 49
Wells Fargo Championship, 58, 138, 183
Westwood, Lee, 47, 49
WGC-Accenture Match Play Championship, 54
WGC Match Play, 41, 53, 164
WGC-Mexico, 164
Willett, Danny, 5
Williams, Serena, 120
Williams, Steve, 1–2, 41, 63
Wind, Herbert Warren, 155
Woodland, Gary, 122, 178, 191, 193, 199
Woods, Charlie (son), 82, 158, 166, 174, 200, 217, 224, 230, 240, 274
Woods, Earl (father), 39, 43, 85, 177, 254
Woods, Sam (daughter), 43, 47, 82, 158, 174, 200, 217, 240
Woods, Tida (mother), 97, 186, 240

Woods, Tiger
admirers of, 133–135, 143
attention-seeking, 21
business dealing by, 188
called greatest athlete ever, 268
child prodigy, 9, 112
comeback of 2022, 225–226
considerateness toward other players, 140
consistency, 32
despair about career, 6–7
determination of, 207
disappointment at losing, 69–72
drive of, 2, 11
earnings, 61
effort to be more human, 151
fighting spirit, 34
future plans, 276, 282
health issues, 64, 73, 183–184, 185–186
how he thinks on the course, 156
intimidating manner of, 133
love for, 13–14
major championships, 16–20
marriage and divorce (2010), 280
mental toughness of, 28
non-white player status, 24
perserverance of, 277
quoted, 79, 81, 92, 112, 117, 233
ranking of major victories, 285–291
rebuked by Payne, 66–67
respect for, 13–14
scandals, 62–67, 280
statistics, 34, 246–247, 280
stubbornness of, 3–4
upbringing in golf, 254
what-ifs, 280–282
worst scores, 30
worth, 9
year 2018, 127, 147
year 2022, 27
Woods foundation, 142
Wright, Mickey, 90, 92

Yang, Y. E., 59–61, 128, 134

Zoeller, Fuzzy, 17
ZOZO Championship, 188–199